PRAISE FOR *CELEBRACIONES MEXICANAS*

"Hablar de nuestra cocina implica mostrar no solo comida, sino un sistema de vida; mostrar en un plato la cadena de procesos culturales no es tarea fácil y más cuando las prácticas culturales y saberes que constituyen el tronco común de la gastronomía Mexicana, son amplios y diversos, transmitidos de generación a generación sin recetas, solo a través de la práctica. *Celebraciones Mexicanas* contribuye, como gran legado, a difundir tradiciones de una gran nación: México."

—**Enrique Farjeat**, Conservatorio de la
Cultura Gastronómica Mexicana

"Adriana and Andrea have done a masterful job sharing the celebrations of Mexico with their words and recipes. They delve deeply into the rich history, customs, and culture that will make you not only want to take this book to bed as bedtime reading but also keep it in your kitchen library and cook up some of the fantastic recipes they share. Books like this one are rare today! This is a must for anyone who loves food, culture, history, cooking, and Mexico!"

—**Joanne Weir**, James Beard Award–winning
cookbook author; television food personality;
restaurateur and executive chef, Copita Tequileria y Comida

"Every society has special dishes to celebrate important occasions, but festival foods are particularly important to Mexican identity. This splendid cookbook guides readers through the highlights of Mexican history and includes recipes for recreating banquets from the past."

—**Jeffrey M. Pilcher**, author of *Planet Taco:*
A Global History of Mexican Food

"I like to think I have an educated impression of Mexico but reading *Celebraciones Mexicanas* makes it clear how much I didn't know before I read the book. You can use it as a reference piece, but if you're like me, you'll want to read every word from the beginning and not miss one delicious detail. Both the fiesta and the food are put into context, and I get the feeling this will become a treasured family heirloom for those who remember and for those who want to start celebrating à la Mexicana."

—**Steve Sando**, founder, Rancho Gordo New World Specialty Food;
coauthor of *Heirloom Beans: Great for Dips and Spreads,*
Soups and Stews, Salads and Salsas, and Much More

CELEBRACIONES MEXICANAS

Studies in Food and Gastronomy

General Editor: Ken Albala, Professor of History, University of the Pacific (kalbala@pacific.edu)

Food Studies is a vibrant and thriving field encompassing not only cooking and eating habits but issues such as health, sustainability, food safety, and animal rights. Scholars in disciplines as diverse as history, anthropology, sociology, literature, and the arts focus on food. The mission of **Studies in Food and Gastronomy** is to publish the best in food scholarship, harnessing the energy, ideas, and creativity of a wide array of food writers today. This broad line of food-related titles will range from food history, interdisciplinary food studies monographs, general interest series, and popular trade titles to textbooks for students and budding chefs, scholarly cookbooks, and reference works.

Appetites and Aspirations in Vietnam: Food and Drink in the Long Nineteenth Century, by Erica J. Peters

Three World Cuisines: Italian, Mexican, Chinese, by Ken Albala

Food and Social Media: You Are What You Tweet, by Signe Rousseau

Food and the Novel in Nineteenth-Century America, by Mark McWilliams

Man Bites Dog: Hot Dog Culture in America, by Bruce Kraig and Patty Carroll

New Orleans: A Food Biography, by Elizabeth M. Williams (Big City Food Biographies series)

A Year in Food and Beer: Recipes and Beer Pairings for Every Season, by Emily Baime and Darin Michaels

Breakfast: A History, by Heather Arndt Anderson (The Meals series)

Celebraciones Mexicanas: History, Traditions, and Recipes, by Andrea Lawson Gray and Adriana Almazán Lahl

CELEBRACIONES MEXICANAS

HISTORY, TRADITIONS, AND RECIPES

Andrea Lawson Gray and Adriana Almazán Lahl

ALTAMIRA
PRESS

A division of
ROWMAN & LITTLEFIELD
Lanham • New York • Toronto • Plymouth, UK

Published by AltaMira Press
A division of Rowman & Littlefield
4501 Forbes Boulevard, Suite 200, Lanham, Maryland 20706
www.rowman.com

10 Thornbury Road, Plymouth PL6 7PP, United Kingdom

British Library Cataloguing in Publication Information Available

Library of Congress Cataloging-in-Publication Data

Gray, Andrea Lawson, 1954–
  Celebraciones mexicanas : history, traditions, and recipes / Andrea Lawson Gray and Adriana Almazán Lahl.
      pages cm.—(Studies in food and gastronomy)
    Includes bibliographical references and index.
    ISBN 978-0-7591-2281-9 (cloth : alk. paper)—ISBN 978-0-7591-2283-3 (electronic)
    1. Cooking, Mexican. I. Almazán Lahl, Adriana, 1967– II. Title.
  TX716.M4G73 2013
  641.5972—dc23   2013015978

Printed in the United States of America

To my mother, whose encouragement started me on the path to food writing, and to my amazing children, Cienna, Armand, and Andre, for their endless patience and support while I wrote this book. Thanks to Marc Bruckel for his assistance with research.

—ANDREA LAWSON GRAY

To the loves of my life, Audrey, Lawrence, Helen, and Elias. Thank you for your love and support, for always believing in me. To my aunts Carmela, Coni, and Melquia for a lifetime of love and to *mi Mexico lindo y querido*.

—ADRIANA ALMAZÁN LAHL

CONTENTS

PART I: HOLIDAYS AND FESTIVALS 27

CHAPTER 14: DAY OF THE HOLY CROSS / DÍA DE LA SANTA CRUZ (MAY 3)

CHAPTER 15: CINCO DE MAYO (MAY 5)

PART II: RITES OF PASSAGE, FAMILY CELEBRATIONS, AND EVENTS 287

MENUS

MENU 1.1: DAY OF THE VIRGIN OF GUADALUPE, P. 33

Small Plates / *Antojitos*

Corn Tamales / *Tamales de Elote*

Oaxacan Tamales in Banana Leaf / *Tamales Oaxaqueños*

Dessert / *Postre*

Strawberry-Pineapple Tamales / *Tamales de Piña y Fresa*

Beverage / *Bebida*

Guava Atole / *Atole de Guayaba*

MENU 2.1: LAS POSADAS, P. 46

Small Plates / *Antojitos*

Traditional Fried Quesadillas (Mexico City–Style) / *Quesadillas Fritas*

with Cheese and Jalapeño Strips / *Queso y Rajas de Jalapeño*

with Squash Blossom / *Flor de Calabaza*

with Potato and Cheese / *Papas con Queso*

Tlacoyos

Sopes

Dessert / *Postre*

Mexican Sweet Fritters / *Buñuelos*

Beverage / *Bebida*

Warm Holiday Punch / *Ponche Navideño*

MENU 3.1: CHRISTMAS EVE, P. 64

Entrées / *Platos Fuertes*
Turkey with Meat and Apple Stuffing / *Pavo con Relleno de Carne y Manzanas*
Mexican Greens with Cactus Paddles and Shrimp Patties / *Romeritos con Nopales y Tortitas de Camarón*
Bacalao a la Vizcaina
Salad / *Ensalada*
Christmas Eve Salad / *Ensalada de Noche Buena*
Dessert / *Postre*
Christmas Log / *Tronco de Navidad*

MENU 3.2: CHRISTMAS EVE, P. 72

Entrée / *Plato Fuerte*
Leg of Pork Adobado / *Pierna Adobada* or
Pork Leg with Bacon Lardons and Adobo Sauce / *Puerco Adobado Mechado*
Salad / *Ensalada*
Christmas Apple Salad / *Ensalada Navideña de Manzana*
Side / *Guarnición*
Tamale Casserole / *Tamal de Cazuela*
Dessert / *Postre*
Mexican Fruit Punch Gelatin Dessert / *Gelatina de Ponche de Frutas*
Beverage / *Bebida*
"Clay Pot" Coffee / *Café de Olla*

MENU 4.1: CHRISTMAS, P. 80

Entrée / *Plato Fuerte*
White Pozole / *Pozole Blanco*
Side / *Guarnición*
Toasted Tortillas / *Tostadas*
Dessert / *Postre*
Torrejas

MENU 5.1: NEW YEAR'S EVE, P. 85

Soup / *Sopa*
Lentil Soup with Fruit and Bacon / *Sopa de Lentejas con Fruta y Tocino*
Entrée / *Plato Fuerte*
Roasted Suckling Pig with Fruit or Vegetable Stuffing /
Lechon Asado con Relleno de Frutas o Vegetales
Pistachio Sauce / *Pipián de Pistache*

Sides / *Guarniciones*
Spinach Mushroom Pie / *Pie de Espinacas y Hongos*
Mexican Angel Hair Pasta / *Fideos con Crema y Queso*
Dessert / *Postre*
Rompope with Floating Islands / *Islas Flotantes con Rompope*
Santa Clara Sweet Potato "Cigars" / *Camotes de Santa Clara*

MENU 6.1: THREE KINGS' DAY, P. 100

Three Kings' Bread Ring / *Rosca de Reyes*
Churros with Thick Chocolate Dipping Sauce
Mexican Hot Chocolate

MENU 7.1: FEAST OF SAN ANTONIO ABAD, P. 109

Small Plates / *Antojitos*
Mexican Sausage with Potatoes Tacos / *Tacos de Chorizo con Papas*
Fried Pork Rind in Roasted Green Sauce Tacos / *Tacos de Chicharrón en Salsa Verde*
Beans with Pork Tacos / *Tacos de Chilorio con Frijoles*
Shredded Beef Tacos / *Tacos de Carne Deshebrada*
Sides and Garnishes / *Guarniciones*
Pickled Chiles or Chiles Chipotles and Vegetables / *Chiles o Chiles Chipotles en Escabeche*
Mexican-Style Corn on the Cob / *Elotes*
Dessert / *Postre*
Prickly Pear Popsicles / *Paletas de Tuna*
Beverage / *Bebida*
Watermelon or Strawberry Water / *Agua de Sandía o Fresa*

MENU 8.1: CANDLEMAS, P. 123

Small Plates / *Antojitos*
Tamales with Chicken Fricassée / *Tamales de Picadillo de Pollo*
Tamales with Mole Filling with Chicken or Pork / *Tamales de Mole con Pollo o Puerco*
Tamales with Cheese and Chile / *Tamales de Rajas con Queso*
Tamales with Salsa Verde (Green Sauce) with Chicken or Pork / *Tamales Verdes*
Beverage / *Bebida*
Chocolate Atole / *Champurrado*

MENU 9.1: BENITO JUAREZ DAY, P. 129

Cazuelas
Poblano Chile with Corn in Cream Sauce / *Rajas con Elote y Crema*
Pork Rinds in Green Sauce / *Chicharrón en Salsa Verde*
Green or Traditional Mexican Sausage with Potatoes / *Chorizo Tradicional o Verde con Papas*
Mexican Chicken Fricassée / *Tinga de Pollo*
Sides / *Guarniciones*
Mexican Rice / *Arroz a la Mexicana*
"Clay Pot" Beans / *Frijoles de Olla*
Dessert / *Postre*
"Scribble" Cookies / *Garabatos*
Beverage / *Bebida*
Sweet Rice Water / *Agua de Horchata*

MENU 10.1: CARNIVAL, P. 141

Appetizer / *Botana*
"Return to Life" Seafood Cocktail / *Vuelve a la Vida*
Entrée / *Plato Fuerte*
Pork in Pibil Sauce with Pickled Onions and Habaneros / *Cochinita Pibil con Habanero y Cebolla*
Sides / *Guarniciones*
Mexican "Red" Rice / *Arroz a la Mexicana*
"Clay Pot" Beans / *Frijoles de Olla*
Dessert / *Postre*
Corn Custard with Mexican Eggnog Sauce / *Flan de Elote con Rompope*

MENU 11.1: WEEK 1, P. 151

Entrée / *Plato Fuerte*
Mexican Greens with Shrimp Patties / *Romeritos con Tortitas de Camarón*
Sides / *Guarniciones*
White Rice Mexican-Style with Peas / *Arroz Blanco a la Mexicana con Chicharos*
Refried Beans / *Frijoles Refritos*
Dessert / *Postre*
Quince Paste with Cheese / *Ate de Membrillo con Queso*

MENU 11.2: WEEK 2, P. 153

Appetizer / *Botana*
Tuna-Stuffed Cuaresmeño Chiles / *Chiles Cuaresmeños Rellenos de Atún*
Entrée / *Plato Fuerte*
Seven Seas Soup / *Sopa Siete Mares*
Sides / *Guarnición*
Toasted Tortillas / *Tostadas*
Beverage / *Bebida*
Hibiscus Water / *Agua de Jamaica*
Dessert / *Postre*
Plantains or Bannas with Sour Cream / *Plátanos o Plátanos Machos con Crema*

MENU 11.3: WEEK 3, P. 158

Soup / *Sopa*
Fava Bean Soup / *Sopa de Habas*
Entrée / *Plato Fuerte*
Hard-Boiled Eggs with Poblano Chiles and Creamed Tomato Sauce / *Rabo de Mestiza*
Sides / *Guarniciones*
White Rice Mexican-Style with Peas / *Arroz Blanco a la Mexicana con Chicharos*
Refried Beans / *Frijoles Refritos*
Dessert / *Postre*
Mexican Shaved Ice with Fruit Syrup / *Raspados de Frutas*

MENU 11.4: WEEK 4, P. 161

Entrée / *Plato Fuerte*
Fish Rolls in Banana Leaf with Achiote Sauce / *Rollos de Pescado Pibil*
Sides and Garnishes / *Guarniciones*
Pickled Habaneros and Onions
Habanero Salsa
"Green" Rice / *Arroz Verde*
Fried Sweet Plantains / *Plátanos Machos*
Dessert / *Postre*
Mexican Chocolate Cake / *Pastel de Chocolate Mexicano*

MENU 11.5: WEEK 5, P. 167

Entrée / *Plato Fuerte*
Seafood Bundles / *Mixiotes de Mariscos*
Salad / *Ensalada*
Cactus Paddle Salad / *Ensalada de Nopalitos*
Sides / *Guarnición*
Cauliflower Fritters / *Tortitas de Coliflor*
Dessert / *Postre*
Vanilla Flan / *Flan de Vainilla*

MENU 11.6: WEEK 6, P. 170

Entrée / *Plato Fuerte*
Veracruz-Style Fish / *Pescado a la Veracruzana*
or
Fish Zarandeado / *Pescado Zarandeado*
Side / *Guarnición*
Chayotes con Crema
Salad / *Ensalada*
Green Salad / *Ensalada Verde*
Dessert / *Postre*
Pound Cake Cupcakes with Lime-Apricot Glaze and Nonpareils / *Garibaldis*

MENU 12.1: HOLY WEEK, P. 179

Entrée / *Plato Fuerte*
Lamb Bundles / *Mixiotes de Cordero*
Side / *Guarnición*
Chiles Stuffed with Beans, Plantain, and Cheese / *Chiles Rellenos de Frijoles,*
Plátano Macho y Queso
Salad / *Ensalada*
Beet Salad with Oranges and Peanuts / *Ensalada de Betabel con Naranja y Cacahuates*
Dessert / *Postre*
Mexican Bread Pudding / *Capirotada*

MENU 13.1: CHILDREN'S DAY, P. 186

Soup / *Sopa*
Mexican Meatball Soup / *Sopa de Albóndigas*
Side / *Guarnición*
Warm Corn Salad / *Esquites*
Entrée / *Plato Fuerte*
Open-Faced Refried Beans and Melted Cheese Sandwiches / *Molletes*
Dessert / *Postre*
Choice of sweets and treats

MENU 14.1: DAY OF THE HOLY CROSS, P. 201

Soup / *Caldo*
Slow-Cooked Lamb (or Goat) Soup / *Caldo de Borrego*
Entrée / *Plato Fuerte*
Slow-Cooked Lamb (or Goat) with Drunken Sauce / *Barbacoa con Salsa Borracha*
Side / *Guarnición*
Grilled Cactus Paddles with Beans au Gratin / *Nopalitos Asados con Frijoles*
y Queso Gratinado (Volcanes)
Dessert / *Postre*
Corn Cake / *Pastel de Elote*

MENU 15.1: CINCO DE MAYO PARTY, P. 210

Appetizer / *Botana*
Cheese Fondue with Mushrooms / *Queso Fundido con Hongos*
Entrée / *Plato Fuerte*
Chilaquiles with Chicken / *Chilaquiles con Pollo*
Dessert / *Postre*
Horchata Gelatin / *Gelatina de Horchata*
Beverage / *Bebida*
Brain Freeze Margarita / *Margarita Congela Cerebros*

MENU 15.2: CLASSIC MEXICAN BBQ PARTY, P. 214

Entrée
Grilled Steaks / *Carne Asada*
Sides / *Guarniciones*
Guacamole
Cowboy Beans / *Frijoles Charros*
Salsa of choice
Salad / *Ensalada*
Classic Baja Caesar Salad / *Ensalada Cesar Clásica*
Beverage / *Bebida*
Tamarind Water / *Agua de Tamarindo*
Dessert / *Postre*
Peanut Marzipan / *Mazapanes de Cacahuate*

MENU 15.3: FRENCH-MEX / COMIDA AFRANCESADA, P. 221

Entrées / *Platos Fuertes*
Shrimp Vol-au–Vents / *Volovanes de Camarón*
Chicken Mole Vol-au-Vents / *Volovanes de Pollo con Mole*
Side / *Guarnición*
Poblano, Corn, and Zucchini Quiche / *Quiche de Calabaza con Chiles Poblanos y Elote*
Dessert / *Postre*
Dulce de Leche Crepes / *Crepas de Cajeta*

MENU 16.1: MOTHER'S DAY, P. 228

Appetizer / *Antojitos*
Stuffed Squash Blossoms / *Flores de Calabaza Rellenas*
Soup / *Caldo*
Squash Blossom Soup / *Sopa de Flor de Calabaza*
Entrée / *Plato Fuerte*
Chicken Breast Rolls in Rose and Hibiscus Sauce / *Rollos de Pollo
con Salsa de Rosas y Jamaica*
Side / *Guarnición*
Tortillas with Pressed Flowers / *Tortillas con Flores Prensadas*
Dessert / *Postre*
Lavender Almond Custard / *Flan de Lavanda y Almendras*
Beverage / *Bebida*
Hibiscus Flower Water / *Agua de Jamaica*

MENU 17.1: CORPUS CHRISTI DAY, P. 243

Salad / *Ensalada*
Corpus Christi Salad / *Ensalada de Corpus Christi*
Entrées / *Platos Fuertes*
Stuffed Zucchini / *Calabacitas Rellenas*
Green Beans Scramble in Tomato Sauce / *Ejotes con Huevo en Salsa de Tomate*
Side / *Guarnición*
Chayote au Gratin / *Chayotes con Queso y Crema*
Dessert / *Postre*
Peaches and Guava in Syrup / *Duraznos y Guayaba en Almibar*
Beverage / *Bebida*
Strawberry Shake / *Licuado de Fresa*

MENU 18.1: ORIGINAL MENU AS SERVED BY PORFÍRIO DÍAZ IN 1910, P. 252

Chilled Cantaloupe Drizzled with Pink Champagne / *Melon Glacé au Clicquot Rosé*
Christopher Columbus Cream Soup / *Potage Christophe Colomb*
Rhine River Grilled Salmon in St. Malo Sauce / *Saumon du Rhin sautée à la St. Malo*
Scarlett Chicken / *Poularde a L'écarlate*

MENU 18.2: MEXICAN INDEPENDENCE DAY, P. 256

Soup / *Sopa*
Tortilla Soup / *Sopa de Tortilla*
Entrée / *Plato Fuerte*
Stuffed Peppers in Walnut Sauce / *Chiles en Nogada*
Side / *Guarnición*
Mexican Rice with Peas and Carrots / *Arroz a la Mexicana con Chicharos y Zanahorias*
Dessert / *Postre*
Chongos Zamoranos

MENU 18.3: INDEPENDENCE DAY, P. 261

Soup / *Sopa*
Zucchini Corn Soup / *Sopa de Calabacitas con Elote*
Entrée / *Plato Fuerte*
Cold Beef Salad / *Salpicón de Res*
Side / *Sopa Seca*
Mexican-Style Pasta with Chorizo / *Fideo Seco con Chorizo*
Dessert / *Postre*
Three-Color Gelatin Dessert / *Gelatina de Tres Colores*

MENU 19.1: DAY OF THE DEAD, P. 271

Entrée / *Plato Fuerte*
Pumpkin Mole / *Mole de Calabaza*
Sides / *Guarniciones*
Mexican "Red" Rice / *Arroz a la Mexicana*
Refried Beans / *Frijoles Refritos*
Dessert / *Postre*
Day of the Dead Cookies / *Galletas de Día de Muertos*

MENU 19.2: DAY OF THE DEAD, P. 275

Entrée / *Plato Fuerte*
Marigold Patties in Tomato Stew / *Tortitas de Cempazúchitl en Caldillo*
Sides / *Guarniciones*
White Rice Mexican-Style with Peas / *Arroz Blanco a la Mexicana con Chicharos*
"Clay Pot" Beans / *Frijoles de Olla*
Dessert / *Postre*
Candied Pumpkin / *Calabaza en Tacha*

MENU 20.1: DAY OF THE MEXICAN REVOLUTION, P. 282

Entrée / *Plato Fuerte*
Rabbit or Pork al Pastor / *Conejo o Puerco al Pastor*
Casserole / *Cazuela*
Potato-Stuffed Taquitos in Green Sauce / *Taquitos de Papas en Salsa Verde*
Side / *Guarnición*
Guacamole
Beverage / *Bebida*
Pineapple Atole / *Atole de Piña*

MENU 21.1: QUINCEAÑERAS, P. 296

Soup / *Sopa*
Mushroom Walnut Soup / *Sopa de Nuez con Champiñones*
Entrée / *Plato Fuerte*
Pork Pipian Almazán Reyes / *Puerco en Pipián Casa Almazán Reyes*
Side / *Guarnicíon*
Fiesta Rice Casserole / *Cazuela de Arroz Fiesta*
Dessert / *Postre*
Layered Fruit Gelatin Dessert / *Gelatina de Frutas*
Dulce de Leche Crepes / *Crepas de Cajeta*

MENU 22.1: WEDDING, P. 306

Entrée / *Plato Fuerte*
Casa Almazán's Mole / *Mole Casa Almazán*
Sides / *Guarniciónes*
Bean Tamales / *Tamales de Frijol*
Mexican "Red" Rice / *Arroz a la Mexicana*
Fried Sweet Plantains / *Plátanos Fritos*

MENU 22.2: WEDDING, P. 309

Entrée / *Plato Fuerte*
Bride's Mole / *Mole de Novia*
Sides / *Guarniciónes*
"Green" Rice / *Arroz Verde*
Fried Sweet Plantains / *Plátanos Fritos*

MENU 22.3: WEDDING, P. 311

Entrée / *Plato Fuerte*
Chicken in Almond Sauce / *Pollo Almendrado de Josefina*
Sides / *Guarniciónes*
Cilantro Spaghetti / *Espagueti Gratinado al Cilantro*
Chayotes au Gratin / *Chayotes con Crema y Queso*

MENU 23.1: BAPTISM, P. 319

Entrée / *Plato Fuerte*
Motul-Style Eggs (Yucatan) / *Huevos Motuleños*
Dessert / *Postre*
Royal Eggs / *Huevos Reales*
Beverages / *Bebidas*
Watermelon or Strawberry Water / *Agua de Sandia o Fresa*
"Clay Pot" Coffee / *Café de Olla*

MENU 24.1: FIRST COMMUNION OR CONFIRMATION, P. 324

Entrée / *Plato Fuerte*
My Mother's Carnitas / *Carnitas de Mi Mama*
Sides / *Guarniciones*
Guacamole
Cowboy Beans / *Frijoles Charros*
Dessert / *Postre*
Mexican Rice Pudding / *Arroz con Leche*

MENU 25.1: FUNERAL, P. 330

Entrée / *Plato Fuerte*
Adobo de Jocoque
Sides / *Guarniciones*
"Clay Pot" Beans / *Frijoles de Olla*
White Rice Mexican-Style with Peas / *Arroz Blanco a la Mexicana con Chicharos*
Dessert / *Postre*
"Scribble Cookies" / *Garibaldis*
Beverage / *Bebida*
"Clay Pot" Coffee / *Café de Olla*

MENU 25.2: FUNERAL, P. 331

Entrée / *Plato Fuerte*
Salsa Verde Chicken Enchiladas / *Enchiladas de Pollo con Salsa Verde*
Sides / *Guarniciones*
Refried Beans / *Frijoles Refritos*
Mexican "Red" Rice / *Arroz a la Mexicana*
Dessert / *Postre*
Horchata Gelatin Dessert / *Gelatina de Horchata*
Beverage / *Bebida*
Guava Atole / *Atole de Guayaba*

PREFACE

THIS IS AN exciting time for Mexican cuisine—in the United States, in Mexico, and internationally. Many think that Mexican culinary arts are well on the way to taking a legitimate place next to those of Italian and French cooking as an integral part of an accomplished chef's culinary toolbox, no longer relegated to the "ethnic cuisine" compartment. Cooking techniques, ingredients, and complex flavor profiles that have been refined and preserved, some for over five hundred years, merit this elevation.

In fact, in 2010 UNESCO awarded Mexico the organization's first-ever recognition of a gastronomic tradition as a world cultural treasure, inscribed on the list of Intangible Cultural Heritages of Humanity alongside such marvels as the Taj Majal and the Summer Palace in Beijing. In doing so, the UNESCO committee noted on its website that Mexico takes great care to safeguard its culinary arts, acknowledging that they are "central to the cultural identity of the communities that practice and transmit [them] from generation to generation":

> Traditional Mexican cuisine is a comprehensive cultural model comprising farming, ritual practices, age-old skills, culinary techniques and ancestral community customs and manners. It is made possible by collective participation in the entire traditional food chain: from planting and harvesting to cooking and eating . . . and singular utensils including grinding stones and stone mortars. . . . Mexican cuisine is elaborate and symbol-laden, with everyday tortillas and tamales, both made of corn, forming an integral part of Day of the Dead offerings. Collectives of female cooks and other practitioners devoted to raising crops and traditional cuisine are found . . . across Mexico. Their knowledge and techniques express community identity, reinforce social bonds, and build stronger local, regional and national identities.[1]

This truly speaks to the ancient and modern marvel that is Mexican gastronomy. Rather than being lost and rediscovered, like so many ancient treasures, it has been and is a living, evolving cultural legacy, one that has been passed from generation to generation, for centuries. Many cooking techniques and recipes have been preserved since the pre-Columbian era and are still in use.

Fiestas and the Rhythm of Mexican Life

Life in Mexico is marked by its fiestas more than anything else, living remembrances of past and sometimes even ancient events. Octavio Paz, the Nobel laureate Mexican poet, interprets the place of these celebrations in Mexican culture this way:

> The fiesta is by nature sacred, literally or figuratively, and above all is the advent of the unusual. . . . It all occurs in an enchanted world: time is transformed to a mythical past or total present; space, the scene of the fiesta, is turned into a gaily decorated world of its own; and the persons taking part cast off all human or social rank and become, for the moment, living images. And everything takes place as if it were not so, as if it were a dream. . . . Fiestas are our only luxury.[2]

When the fiesta ends, Paz maintains, there is a kind of rebirth, a reinvigoration, which leaves the participants ready to get back to work, to conform to the normal predictable pace of daily life.

If the fiesta is the heart of the Mexican community, food is the heart of the fiesta. Food has played an important role in the fiesta system since the pre-Hispanic era. The Aztecs, for example, followed religious dictates around which foods could be eaten and by whom (some foods, like chocolate, were reserved for rulers and the elite) and which were to be offered to the gods.

This focus on food and cooking continues to permeate the Mexican culture, especially around festivals. When asked recently about the importance of cooking, the women of Octepec in central Mexico "clearly [thought] this a strange question and respond[ed] categorically, 'If no one cooks there is no fiesta.'"[3]

Preparing to Celebrate

In pueblos throughout Mexico, fiestas are preceded by special market days, at which the requisite ingredients appear up to a week before the holiday. Often, and not just in Mexico's most remote and rural areas, the food prep begins with a trip to the local molino (mill).

Adriana Almazán Lahl remembers picking up ingredients early in the morning as a child at the local market and taking them to the mill. Her aunts believed the earlier you got to the mill, the less chance your ingredients would be mixed with those of other customers and become polluted with other flavors. She recalls that the ingredients were as important as the recipe itself, which had to be followed with precise care as it had been passed down from her great-grandmother to her grandmother, and down to her aunts. She still has her grandmother's *molcajete* as a reminder of the love and devotion she passed through generations of cooks in her family.

About *Celebraciones Mexicanas: History, Traditions, and Recipes*

In our book, the reader/cook will travel through a year of life in Mexico with all of its major festivals and fiestas that include special food. Our hope is that this journey will broaden your understanding of Mexican cuisine and culture by delving into the history behind the special events that occasion fiesta menus.

Mexico is almost 90 percent Catholic,[4] and many of the holidays described in this book have religious roots or overtones. The liturgical calendar begins with Advent and the first holiday of the year is Día de la Virgen de Guadalupe on December 12. That is where we begin our book as well, with the story of the Virgin of Guadalupe and that most quintessential of Mexican foods, tamales. Chapter by chapter, the celebrations in this book reveal a culture rich with folklore.

While we have included many, even most, of the recipes that are traditionally prepared for these special days and events, we have omitted those that require ingredients that cannot be found in the United States, such as *pambazos*, served up for Semana Santa but made with a bread roll that is essential to the dish and not available outside of Mexico, or recipes that call for huitlacloche or fruits such as mamey, zapote, or guanabanas.

This is just a glimpse into the festivities: with some historians counting over five thousand festivals, fiestas, fairs (*ferias*), and saint's days, there is a celebration somewhere in Mexico every day of the year.[5] In the pueblos, it may be a feria or the feast day of the patron saint that occasions a *kermesse* (street fair with food and games). Other celebration days are regional, usually highlighting an event or tradition important to the local culture or indigenous group, like *el Noche de los Rábanos* (Radish Night), celebrated December 23 in Oaxaca, when the central plaza is filled with stalls offering radishes carved into flowers, animals, saints, and even entire nativity scenes.

Authentic Family Recipes

To immerse oneself in Mexican cuisine is to immerse oneself in history and create a bond with an ancient culture and generations of Mexican women—not in some

Almazán family cookbook.
Photo by Adriana Almazán Lahl.

esoteric sense but in a very real way. Tamales are made the same way today as they were by Aztec women, with some minor modifications. The molcajete, a utensil used to ground seasoning and create salsas, is today made of the same volcanic rock of which it has been fashioned for centuries. Much of what we know about Mexican cuisine had, for years, been passed down through an oral tradition, and to this day, recipes are faithfully handwritten in the personal notebooks of Mexico's daughters, as dictated by their mothers and grandmothers.

Every family has its own unique menus, and every family has its own special and secret recipes. Adriana Almazán Lahl, whose family recipes we share in this book, learned from her great-aunts and aunts, who, in turn, learned from previous generations of Almazán women: Consuelo Almazán Reyes (Tía or "Aunt" Coni); Melquiades Almazán Reyes (Tía Melquia, who mostly baked breads and made *sopas*); her mother, Elena Romano de Almazán; and the family matriarch, Carmen Almazán Reyes. The food prepared by these women, their celebrations, menus, techniques, and culinary traditions have barely changed over time. That is part and parcel of what makes them so special. Newer, more convenient cooking implements are rarely substituted for old ones and ingredients are not swapped out;

the cuisine is truly a testament to slow food. Adriana's exuberance for the project comes through: "In this book I want to release my family recipes. They have been a tradition for many generations and I am proud to share them, since they are too good to be kept secret."

We have provided complete menus, sometimes several, for each festive occasion, so as to allow the reader to plan a meal very much like what would be prepared in Mexico for the holiday. In most cases, the dishes suggested are the same as those that come out of Mexico's kitchens for the fiesta or celebration covered in a particular chapter. There are days that do not have requisite menus, and for these, we have made thematic selections—for example, traditional Mexican street foods for Benito Juarez Day and edible flowers incorporated into the dishes for Mother's Day. The recipes are designed for a broad audience, from those seeking basic knowledge of Mexican cooking to the Mexican food aficionado. Our hope is that your culinary discoveries will leave you as enchanted by Mexican cuisine as we are!

ABOUT THE PHOTOS

WE HAVE CHOSEN photography of Mexico's fiestas as diverse as the people themselves. Some celebrations have clear Catholic influences, others are secular, and many give a rare glimpse into a world that has almost stood still over time—festivals as they are celebrated by Mexico's indigenous people. Through these pictures and their captions, we hope you will, for a moment, enter a world apart, just as our photographer has. In the photographer Jorge Ontiveros's words,

As Mexicans, so much of who we are today is connected to our love of the Earth and the wisdom passed to us by our elders—this despite denying for many generations the flavors, textures, traditions, principles and ways of understanding the world of our own legacy. All has survived and is still present after more than five hundred years.

In Mexico there are over 63 distinct indigenous peoples, speaking more than 653 languages and dialects: about 12 million indigenous Mexicans, representing 10 percent of the total Mexican population, scattered throughout the country from small villages to enclaves of four or five houses in municipalities or urban centers. Mexico's great strength lies in the word . . . in the language; through it, her culture and values, even the way Mexico is seen by the world, all this comes alive and can be understood. There is power and nobility in our everyday rituals as we interact with and take care of our environment and all living things around us.

Facing discrimination, much of the indigenous population no longer looks to teach the language of their grandparents to their children. The United Nations says that when a language is lost, a culture is lost and that this loss is a crime against humanity. To this very point, in Mexico there are studies indicating that within as little as two generations, the number of indigenous speakers of these languages may decrease to less than half the current level, and that these ancient cultures face a very real and present threat of extinction.

My photos seek to shine a light on a distinguished presence and nobility in the everyday of the native peoples of Mexico. This, in spite of the blood shed throughout history and the threat of demise, continues shining through—a passionate love for what they are: their colors, their features, their bodies, their sounds, their traditions. These images make a loud and poignant statement: that these people are vibrant, possessing great life force and continue to face a tough fight for visibility and their rightful place in the world. The aim is to bring to others their richly textured differences and subtle nuances—to win hearts and minds and share a rare, intimate look at the first settlers of this land.

Special thanks to John Weir, who has been Jorge's teacher, mentor, and inspiration for many years. We are as amazed by Jorge Ontiveros's photos as we are by his talent and generosity. He has donated his fees for the photos to Juan Carlos Lopez, who runs an organization supporting some of the Raramuris communities from the State of Chihuahua in Mexico.

Adriana Almazán Lahl developed a passion for photography while at Universidad Iberoamericana in Mexico City. Adriana's food styling and photography skills became handy while writing and developing this book.

TIMELINE

AD 100–650: The most important and largest city of pre-Colombian central Mexico, Teotihuacan (Nahuatl translation: "Where Men Become Gods" or "The City of Gods"), is planned at about the beginning of the Christian era and sacked and burned by invading Toltecs in AD 650.

AD 200–300: Campeche (Mexico), from the third century, is the principal town of the Maya kingdom of Ah Kin Pech ("Place of Serpents and Ticks").

1325: The Aztecs found Tenochtitlan, later known as Mexico City.

1507: Last Aztec New Fire Ceremony (*nemontemi*) is celebrated.

AUGUST 31, 1521: Spanish conqueror Cortés (1485–1547) captures and burns the city of Tenochtitlan. Nearly one hundred thousand people die in the siege. The Spanish bring European ingredients that would forever change what was to become known as Mexican food.

1526: First Corpus Christi celebrations in Mexico.

DECEMBER 9, 1531: Appearance of Virgin of Guadalupe. Today, her appearance is celebrated on December 12.

CHRISTMAS, 1538: First *Misa de Gallo* (Mass at the Crow of the Rooster) is celebrated in Mexico.

1586: Christmas Mass officially is established in Mexico as a *novena* (nine-day prayer period), today celebrated as Las Posadas. The tradition of posadas begins with the publication of a papal bull in 1586 ordering a "Misa de Aguinaldo," literally a "Christmas Gift Mass."

1618: The Corpus Christi celebration in Mexico City has grown to become the largest annual festival in the country.

1692 AND 1701: Revolts by the Mexicas give the Spanish Crown cause to begin to repress Mexico's indigenous peoples and their participation in large festivals, like Carnaval and Corpus Christi.

1731 AND 1780: Carnaval is abolished.

MARCH 21, 1806: Birth of Benito Pablo Juarez García, Mexico's first and only indigenous president.

SEPTEMBER 15, 1810: *El Grito* begins Mexico's War for Independence.

SEPTEMBER 17, 1821: Independence from Spain.

1858–1872: Benito Juarez presidency, during which he ends the French occupation of Mexico, overthrowing the Second Mexican Empire and restoring the Republic.

1862–1867: French Intervention, roots of *Comida Afrancesada*.

MAY 5, 1862: Battle of Puebla.

MAY 25, 1862: First Cinco de Mayo celebration in the town of Los Angeles, California.

1864: Carnaval is revived in Mazatlan.

1866: Last Corpus Christi celebration of the colonial period.

1877–1911: Porfírio Díaz presidency.

SEPTEMBER 15–16, 1910: 100th anniversary of independence from Spain is celebrated by Porfírio Díaz with a huge banquet with a French menu.

NOVEMBER 20, 1910: Mexican Revolution begins.

1910: The revolutionary period in Mexico marks the beginning of the *Mexicanidad* movement, led by artists like Frida Kahlo and Diego Rivera, embracing Mexico's indigenous heritage over that imposed by European conquerors, including indigenous art and cuisine.

1920: Generally considered the end of the revolutionary period, although there are subsequent uprisings in 1923 and 1926.

1924: Children's Day is established.

1958: The first recorded *telenovela* is Mexico's *Senda Prohibida*. Eventually, these televised dramas lead to the popularization of wedding and *quinceañera* traditions that have previously been embraced only by Mexico's elite.

HOW TO USE THIS BOOK

THE RECIPES in this book are organized by menu by fiesta. While some may choose to produce an entire menu for a specific occasion, we realize that others may want to use the book in a more traditional manner. Therefore, all recipes are also listed in the "Index of Recipes by Course" beginning on p. 355 (appetizer, salad, entrée, etc.).

At the end of the book, there is a list of "Common Mexican Cooking Tools and Techniques" (p. 333), which are referred to in some of the recipes, for example, how to dry-roast and sweat chiles to remove their skins. This is designed as a reference but is also a good place to start to immerse yourself in cooking *à la Mexicana*. In the same list, you'll find some Mexican kitchen tools that are in every Mexican kitchen. Most are easily accessible (see "Ingredient and Cooking Ware Sources Online," p. 341, if you cannot find them locally) and inexpensive. While there are modern substitutes for most, if not all of these implements, there is a certain joy in cooking with the same tools that have been in use in Mexico for over five hundred years.

We have also provided a list of "Basic Recipes for Mexican Cooking" (p. 9), such as chicken stock, tomato purée, and tortilla and tamale dough (*masa*). Some will be familiar to the experienced cook and others perhaps less so. Generally, these are recipes for stocks and sauces that you can prepare in advance and freeze so as to have them on hand as needed. While we realize that time does not always allow for home preparation of every ingredient, as traditional cooking in Mexico precludes ready-made soup stocks or tomato purée in a can, we have written the book with this approach, providing recipes for many items that can also be store bought. In many cases, the quantity called for in a given recipe is half of what comes out of the "Basic Recipes for Mexican Cooking" ingredients and instructions, so as to allow for future use. You'll want to bookmark this page, as these are referred to in many of the recipes in the book.

We have also provided a "Guide to Mexican Chiles" (p. 339) and a "Salsa Recipes" (p. 17) section, with recommended "Salsa Pairings" (p. 25). For so many Mexican dishes, the salsa is the finishing touch. We invite you to experiment, using different salsas when preparing a dish for the second or third time, or offering a selection of salsas to your guests. The change in flavor profiles will surprise and delight you.

INTRODUCTION
MEXICAN FOOD
HISTORY

FOOD AND food preparation are central to life in Mexico and reaffirm *"Mexicani-dad,"* a term used to describe Mexico's connection to its pre-Hispanic roots. The ingredients are a tie that binds, especially as many have been used for centuries. Poet Victor Valle expresses this beautifully in his 1995 poem "Comida" (Food):

> Food
> one eats
> the moon in the tortilla
> one eats beans
> and eats the earth
> one eats chile
> and eats sun and fire
> one drinks water
> and drinks the sky.[1]

To understand Mexican cuisine is, in a way, to come to know the very core and *espíritu* of what it means to be Mexican. A living mirror of the history of a people emerges in the food stories, the fiesta menus especially, and even in the recipes themselves. There is a certain dignity in Mexico's foodways, in ancient ingredients and techniques that have survived to become one of the important threads that bind Mexico's richly textured culture.

Modern Mexico is very much a nation that was born out of another, the result of European culture and religion superimposed on that of the Aztecs, Mayans, and the many other indigenous peoples of the area that is now Mexico. Try to imagine the United States not as a new nation of pilgrims and immigrants bringing their religions, cuisine, and customs very much unchanged from Europe; instead imagine all of these fusing with those of the Native Americans. In Mexico, this fusion is described by the word *metizaje* (mixture), set into motion when the Spanish explorer Hernan Cortés landed in Mexico in 1519. What we know today as Mexican food is a metizaje primarily of pre-Columbian foodways fused with those of the invading Europeans of the Colonial period.

The Evolution and Politics of Mexico's Festivals

Upon its arrival in Mesoamerica and throughout the colonial period, the Catholic Church was intent upon and quite successful in its conversion of the Aztecs. Religious festival days, which were quickly embraced by the indigenous population because of their similarities to rites already practiced by the Mexicas, played a major role in this prosthelytization. The Crown and the Church, looking to control the indigenous population, realized the need to erase

> memories of conquest . . . [achieved] by representing [Spain's] domination as social progress. Representing conquest as progress required that the conquerors symbolically include the pre-colonial elite in their power structures. Pageants and fiestas often provided the opportunity for bestowing ceremonial positions of authority upon the defeated [Aztec leaders].[2]

Thus, ironically, the very rites and rituals that were core to the Aztec cultural identity became the key to the unraveling of that identity, as, quickly, most of the customs associated with indigenous festivals were absorbed into Catholic religious ceremonies or left behind completely.

Still, the influx of Aztecs into the capital of New Spain for important fiesta days often resulted in civil unrest and revolt, which became a source of great concern for the ruling viceroys. Exacerbating the situation, in some instances, separate rituals were celebrated in the same city for the same festival day: one in Mexico's *barrios* among the lower classes, often irreverent and even making fun of the authorities and their highbrow festivities (this tone of sarcasm and "gallows humor" has survived and permeates many holiday celebrations in Mexico today), and another among Mexico's elite. In fact, the most important popular revolt of this era took place during the Festival of Corpus Christi in Mexico City in 1692. Subsequently, the Spanish Crown, seeking firm control over Mexico's indigenous people, banned any vestiges of Indian rituals that had not previously been rooted out by the Church.

With the seat of power residing in Mexico City, the result of these efforts to wipe out native rites had the effect of relegating them to Mexico's more rural areas, far from the scrutinizing eyes of the authorities. The resulting belief system and festivals had dual overtones, as noted in the writing of Brantz Mayer, secretary of the United States Legation to Mexico in 1841–1842: "In Mexico, even after three centuries of the dominion of a foreign Priesthood, the Indian worship . . . still tinges the rites of the Catholic."[3]

Even today, a hybrid folk Catholicism can be found in Mexico's pueblos and among her indigenous people, and is at the heart of many of the festivals described in this book. Sadly, few, if any indigenous rites have survived intact on a wide scale. The Aztecs had a celebration monthly, each dedicated to a specific deity, and their year was eighteen months long. Of these, the festival marking the Day of the Dead (*Día de los Muertos*) is the only one celebrated nationally that is a true carry-over from pre-Hispanic times.

Before Mexico's independence in 1821, and to a lesser degree afterward as well, major festival days, like Día de Corpus Christi, were used to solidify the power of Mexico's elite, as political guilds controlled participation and expenditures. When Benito Juarez, Mexico's first and only president with 100 percent indigenous lineage, instituted separation of Church and State in Mexico in 1859, the religious festivals that had been used as way to wield political power were no longer celebrated with huge processions through the streets of Mexico City, in which participants were assigned a place in the parade based on their rank in society.

Ancient Ingredients, Modern Politics

The survival and celebration of indigenous techniques, tools, ingredients, and recipes are victories in and unto themselves. At the turn of the twentieth century, Encarnación Pineda was already able to see the importance of writing her cookbook, *El Cocinero Español*, as an "act of creating a culinary legacy for succeeding generations thus express[ing] self-love in the face of denigration, and faith in the possibility of some day reestablishing a lost cultural continuity."[4] Her vision of the role that cuisine had played, and would continue to play in the struggle for respect for Mexicanidad, could not have proved truer. Some ingredients that proved to be testing grounds for the strength of ancient foodways are corn and chiles.

Corn is a staple of the Mesoamerican diet; there is evidence of cultivated *maiz* (Spanish for corn) as early as 5000 BC in the valleys of southern central Mexico. Mayan creation myth holds that the first humans were formed by the gods from corn dough, and the Aztecs or Mexicas journey through the history of the role of corn (the base of such quintessential Mexican dishes as tamales and tortillas) in

Mexico is examined in detail by Jeffrey Pilcher in his book *¡Que Vivan Los Tamales! Food and the Making of Mexican Identity* in which he notes that

> part of the ongoing effort . . . to Europeanize Mexico was an attempt to replace corn with wheat [which was introduced to Mexico by the Europeans of the Spanish Conquest]. But [corn], native foods and flavors persisted and became an essential part of . . . what it means to be authentically Mexican.[5]

As for chiles, Mexicans tend to be especially proud of how spicy a dish is that they have prepared or are about to eat. The term *picoso* specifically refers to the level of chile, as in mild, medium, or hot. If there seems to be a certain kind of machismo Mexicano that borders on the competitive at the Mexican table around one's ability eat truly spicy, steam-coming-out-of-your-ears food, maybe it comes from this: chiles, a distinctly native ingredient, were distasteful to the Europeans arriving with the French Intervention,[6] who viewed them as a stimulant, making the "love of chiles a significant distinction between Mexicans and foreigners . . . thus form[ing] part of the national identity."[7]

The culinary traditions of the Aztecs and Mayans continued to flourish. This despite efforts to replace corn with wheat, to eradicate chiles from the kitchen (there were public cooking classes during the colonial era, the focus of which was to wean the Mexican lower class off chiles and corn), and even despite a very deliberate and ongoing attempt by the Church, throughout the colonial era, to eradicate foods that were central to indigenous festivals.

The Fusion That Is Mexican Cuisine

Acknowledging both the significance of pre-Columbian ingredients (corn, beans, and squash were the most important of these) and the then newly introduced European dairy and meats, the prominent Mexican writer Justo Sierra (1848–1912) captured the place of food in the development of modern Mexico in a single, succinct sentence: "The grocer, not the conquistador, is the real Spanish father of Mexican society."[8]

With the conquest of Mexico by Spain came an influx of ingredients that would forever alter what would become known as Mexican cuisine. Prior to the arrival of the Europeans, there was no meat from domesticated animals (beef, pork, chicken, goat, and sheep) and therefore no lard or fried foods. Tamales became fluffier with the introduction of lard. Neither were there dairy products: no butter, milk, or cheese. Sugar was not known either; subsequently blended with cacao, chocolate as we know it was born in Mexico. *Atole*, a signature Mexican beverage, blends new ingredients with old: dairy and sugar with corn. Food pathways of the Spanish told their own historic tale as well, as various herbs and spices introduced to Mexico by the Spanish had their origins with the Moors. The candied fruit of the *Rosca de Reyes*, an integral part of Día de los Reyes Magos on January 6, and spices used in *Calabaza en Tacha* and *ponche* are just some examples of this meeting of foodways.

And so, Mexican cuisine is one of true fusion over time: an indigenous culinary base heavily influenced by the various cultures that have found either a temporary (in the case of the invading French and Spanish) or permanent (as with the Mennonites who brought their famous cheese or the Lebanese who introduced the famous al pastor flavors) home there. The recipes in this book are the living legacy of that amazing melding of cultures.

Without a doubt, the most enduring symbol of Aztec cuisine is the tortilla, which occupies an almost sacred place on the Mexican table. We have this description of tortillas served to Motecuhzoma (better known as Moctezuma) from Bernal Díaz del Castillo's 1568 text, *The Truthful History of the Conquest of New Spain*: "The tortillas were very white, and they were brought to him in plates covered with clean cloths."[9]

Even today, tortillas are presented this way, in baskets covered with embroidered towels. Other things remain unchanged as well. Though cornfields may have given way to housing tracts, and markets, more so than farms, become the principal source of food, corn and beans remain staples of the Mexican diet, and firewood still burns in the outdoor kitchens called *tlecuiles* that are used to prepare tortillas and fiesta foods.

The Economy of the Festival and the Role of Women

Extraordinary events in Mexico are celebrated with menus and recipes that call on extended families to congregate in kitchens to make tamales, roast chiles, and work together on the often complex, labor-intensive dishes that benefit from collective preparation. It has been observed that

> food is the heart of ritual celebrations marking life-cycle and seasonal transitions in Mexico. Women prepare special dishes for community fiestas . . . [and] depend on women's reciprocity networks for the various meals at their center. . . . [As] hosting a fiesta is a serious commitment requiring extensive social networks for support, preparing for the fiesta means a party of sorts before the party, with women gathering in the kitchen, planning, cooking and chismeando (sharing stories or gossiping). The group will typically include the extended family as well as comadres, or godmothers."[10]

Interestingly enough, rather than demeaning women or relegating them to the kitchen, "women's work in preparing food for fiestas gives women status in their communities and creates social networks of reciprocal obligation . . . a source of power and a place in which to transmit the traditions and beliefs of older genera-tions through quasi-sacramental food rites."[11] When there are community fiestas, such as those commemorating the patron saint of the town, even the poorest of households is expected to contribute financially as well, based on the number of occupants, even counting the children; and there is great social pressure to cooper-ate. Often, the planning, roles, responsibilities, and costs of such fiestas are formal-ized in community forums.

Hosting a religious festival, which is often the result of a religious promise or vow taken by the host with the prayer that a particular saint or the Virgin of Guadalupe or God might intercede on the family's behalf in time of crisis, is a serious undertak-ing. The family will be expected to arrange for everything through their network of cooperation—and be judged by the event's success. While the women come together to prepare the food, the men are expected to clean the streets; hang the lights, *papel picado* (cut-out paper banners), and/or floral arcs; and sometimes even paint the exteriors of some of the houses in the neighborhood. All of this contributes to and preserves what has been identified by social scientists as community space.

Age-Old Wisdom, Modern Diets

No doubt, the Aztecs were on to something. Just look at the parallels between their dietary staples and the health-conscious movements of our times. First, pre-Colum-bian (and much of modern Mexican) cuisine is naturally gluten free, with corn rather than wheat as the predominant grain. More than a dietary fad, there is evidence sup-porting the fact that our intestines do not completely break down gluten, triggering inflammation and blocking nutrient absorption,[12] making a gluten-free diet a good option for more than just those with celiac disease. Then there are beans, one of the big three of the Mesoamerican diet, and a component of the slow-carb diet, a popular weight-control method based around eating foods that are naturally nutrient dense and low in calories while high in protein and fiber. And many of the grains eaten by the Aztecs, including amaranth and chia seeds, are on the list of what are being called "super foods," rich in vital amino acids, omega-3s, and other nutrients. Con-trary to the bad reputation that Mexican fast food, sadly, has garnered for the real thing, Mexican cuisine is based around many whole foods that are rooted in what can only be seen as a health-wise, pre-Columbian dietary tradition.

Buen Provecho: Customs around Eating in Mexico

In Mexico, where 45 percent of the population live below the poverty level, social norms around eating are very much in effect. As in many parts of the world, being invited to "share a taco," this most humble of invitations to dine with your Mexican friends, is a real honor. (This does not literally mean you will be having tacos, but is rather a reflection of a humility that is truly a Mexican trait and would apply even if one were invited to a feast.)

So what should you expect if you are invited to share a meal à la Mexicana? First, the hour that was announced as the time the meal would be served is not accurate. In fact, it is expected that you will arrive at least a half hour late, and arriving on time is frowned upon. Second, it is customary to say "*buen provecho*" or simply "*provecho*" (the Spanish equivalent of "bon appétit!") before starting a meal or when you enter a room where Mexicans are eating, or even if you pass a group taking their lunch break in front of a construction site (expect to win wide smiles with this one in the United States!). The table conversation will revolve only around pleasantries; topics like war, politics, or issues that came up at work are considered poor accompaniments to something as treasured as eating a good meal. Finally, leaving the table for any reason before everyone has finished eating is considered poor form.

Mealtimes in Mexico

Aztec "commoners only ate two meals—one in the mid-morning after working for a few hours and one in the mid-afternoon, when the sun was hottest. . . . One might also partake of a nighttime snack of amaranth gruel."[13] In modern Mexico there are traditionally five meals or food-related breaks in the rhythm of the day.

Early Breakfast

Sold in the streets of Mexico everywhere at food stands (*puestos*), early breakfast (*desayuno*) typically includes two items that have corn as their main ingredient, not surprising as corn is the staple of the Mexican diet: a *torta de tamal* (a tamale on a roll) and atole, a thick, porridge-like beverage, served warm. Street food in Mexico has its own rhythm: atole and tamales are abundant in the mornings but usually gone by noon.

If you are eating breakfast at home in Mexico, it will very likely include reheating (*recalentado*) whatever the family ate for dinner the previous night, plus coffee and *pan dulce* (Mexican pastries). The coffee may be prepared as *café de olla*, that is, made in a traditional clay pot and usually with a cinnamon stick (*canela*). As for the pan dulce, at typical Mexican bakeries (*panaderias*), one simply grabs a tray, a pair of tongs, and walks around the shop picking from a wide assortment of trays of freshly baked pastries, some of which may resemble turtles or snails or, during the Day of the Dead, skulls or bones.

Almuerzo

This is more a substantial morning meal that should not be confused with our brunch (even though it is similarly eaten later than breakfast and earlier than lunch). While "brunch" is a combination of breakfast and lunch and usually something of which Americans partake on weekends, almuerzo is eaten in addition to a light breakfast, especially if that desayuno was eaten early, say at 7 a.m. before the workday begins. *Almuerzo* is a substantial meal, typically eaten sometime between 9 a.m. and noon, and may consist of an egg or meat dish often made with tortillas and a salsa, such as chilaquiles, chiles rellenos, or enchiladas, served with beans and coffee and/or Mexican hot chocolate and fresh fruit.

Comida

The term *comida* as a midday meal is the same word used to mean "food"; context is what differentiates. It is generally eaten between 2 and 4 p.m., and is the main meal of the day. Most fiestas are centered on this meal. Often translated to mean "lunch," this is misleading. Comida is served later, and is more substantial than most American lunches. If anything, it is comparable to the midday dinners that people ate in rural America in the last century, when breakfast, dinner, and supper were the three daily meals. *Comida* may consist of several courses, including soup (*sopa aguada*) or *sopa seca* (these include rice and pasta dishes) or salad and a main dish (*plato fuerte*), dessert (*postre*), and beverage (*agua fresca*). Most of the festival menus in this book are eaten as comida.

Merienda

Merienda is taken around 5 or 6 p.m. This is a cup of café de olla, freshly brewed tea made with fresh herbs, or Mexican hot chocolate and pan dulce. As Mexico becomes more urbanized and the pace of life changes, these traditions are changing as well. In some places, merienda is less common nowadays.

Cena

The final meal of the day, *cena* is typically served between 8 and 9 p.m. and may be just a few tacos filled with whatever was eaten at comida, or soup, or even just a hot drink and some bread.

The attention to ritual, food rhythms, and roles around preparation are all part of how Mexico's foodways preserve its cultural continuity. As you prepare a fiesta meal or just experiment with a new recipe, respecting the ingredients and techniques of the rich diversity that is Mexican cuisine, we invite you to walk along Mexico's food pathways with us.

BASIC RECIPES FOR MEXICAN COOKING

ANNATTO PASTE / PASTA DE ACHIOTE CASERA

(MAKES 1 CUP)

½ cup annatto seeds (lightly toasted using a comal)
10 garlic cloves, first peeled and then dry-roasted (see "Common Mexican Cooking Tools and Techniques," p. 335)
½ teaspoon Mexican oregano
½ teaspoon cumin
Dash of nutmeg
4 ground cloves
4 red peppercorns (*Schinus molle*)
1 tablespoon black pepper
½ teaspoon coriander seeds
1 cup bitter orange juice with 1 tablespoon of white vinegar or use Bitter Orange Marinade (see below)
1 teaspoon salt

USING a molcajete or a mortar and pestle, mix all ingredients, grinding the dry spices and annatto seeds first until they are quite fine, then adding garlic and sour orange/vinegar mixture to form a paste. Alternatively, in a coffee or spice grinder, grind all dry ingredients. Once well ground, pour the ingredients into a small bowl and add garlic cloves, mixing well. Add the orange juice with vinegar mix or marinade to form a thick soft paste (add slowly as you might find you need to use less of the Bitter Orange Marinade or the orange juice/vinegar mix). When your paste is the consistency of playdough it is ready to be used. It keeps well in refrigerator for 1 month or frozen for 6 months. 🐦

BASIC ADOBO

(MAKES 1–1½ CUPS)

6 chiles anchos secos, medium size
3 dry chiles guajillos or New Mexico chiles
2 dry chiles cascabel
1 chile chipotle, dry or in adobo sauce
1 tablespoon whole allspice
1 teaspoon coriander
½ teaspoon cumin sedes
1 teaspoon Mexican oregano
4 fresh epazote sprigs or 2 dry teaspoons dry epazote
½ cup apple cider vinegar
2 tablespoons brown sugar, piloncillo, or honey
½ white onion
6 garlic cloves
1 cup water

PLACE all chiles in hot water to rehydrate. Once hydrated and soft, mix them with all ingredients and the garlic cloves. Mix ingredients well in blender until a thick paste forms (this is the adobo); add water if needed to keep the blender moving. The texture should be that of a thick tomato paste. This keeps well in the refrigerator for 2 weeks or frozen for 6 months. 🐦

BITTER ORANGE MARINADE / NARANJA AGRIA

½ cup sweet orange juice
Juice of 1 lime
½ cup white vinegar

MIX all ingredients. 🐦

CHICKEN, BEEF, OR PORK STOCK PLUS SHREDDED OR PULLED CHICKEN, BEEF, OR PORK / CALDO DE POLLO, CARNE O PUERCO Y CARNE DESHEBRADA DE POLLO, CARNE O PUERCO*

(MAKES ABOUT 1 GALLON OF STOCK, 5 POUNDS SHREDDED CHICKEN)

1½ gallons water
6 chicken legs and 6 chicken thighs, with skin and bones (about 4–6 pounds)
1 head garlic, dry-roasted (see "Common Mexican Cooking Tools and Techniques," p. 335)
½ onion
½ teaspoon whole black peppercorns (or ⅓ teaspoon ground black pepper)
2 carrots, peeled
1 celery stalk
1 sprig fresh cilantro
1 bay leaf
1–2 tablespoons salt

IF time allows, first roast chicken or meat of choice in a pan in the oven at 350° for 30–45 minutes to get a stronger flavor. Bring the water to a boil and add the chicken, beef, or pork (meat). As it returns to a boil, skim the foam and particles that rise to the top with a slotted spoon and discard. Add the garlic, onion, peppercorns, carrots, celery, cilantro, bay leaf, and salt. Lower heat to medium and simmer for 30–45 minutes or until the chicken or meat is tender. (If chicken has been previously roasted, remove after 30 minutes.) Remove the chicken or meat and cool. Strain the stock and reserve. It will keep for 2–3 days in the refrigerator, up to 3 months in the freezer. For convenience, you may want to reduce stock and freeze.

When cool enough to handle, shred the chicken or meat by hand—not with a knife. The meat should not be too finely shredded.

*Note: Pork shoulder or butt can be used for this recipe. You can also use skirt steak or tritip for shredded beef. Beef or pork will take about 1 hour to 1½ hours, depending upon the quantity and cut of meat.

FISH *FUMÉE* OR FISH STOCK / CALDO DE PESCADO

(MAKES 4 QUARTS)

4 pounds fish heads and bones
1½ gallons water
1 white onion
3 celery stalks
2 bay leaves
Small bunch cilantro
Small bunch mint
1 tablespoon salt

WASH fish heads and bone and place them in a large pot with water. Roughly cut onion and celery, add to pot, and bring to a boil. Lower heat and let it simmer for 20 minutes, then add bay leaves, cilantro, mint, and salt, and simmer 20 more minutes.

Allow to cool and pass through a sieve; discard all solid material. Your stock is ready to be used in any recipe. Use it within 48 hours or freeze for up to 3 months.

LARD, HOW TO RENDER / COMO DERRETIR MANTECA

THERE are three types of fat:

- Back fat or fatback rendered—back fat is great for sautéing and frying.
- Belly—the pork belly. We use it to cure bacon.
- Leaf lard—this is the fat from around the pig's kidneys. This is the cleanest fat. This is the fat that you want to render appropriately in order to have a pure white, odorless fat.

HOW TO RENDER LARD:

Place 1 pound leaf lard or back fat ground lard (ask your butcher to grind the fat for you) in a pot over medium-low heat. The lard will start to melt. Stir occasionally. After about 20 minutes you will start seeing and hearing cracklings and lard will start to sputter; at this point you can cover with a mesh screen. Once the sputtering is over and cracklings are floating (about 1 hour), remove cracklings with a sieve. (Cracklings make a great topping for salads, or use them in tacos; if you decide to use the cracklings, they are at their best when freshly cooked.) Line a fine sieve with a coffee filter and strain lard through into a heat-resistant jar, taking extra care as you work with the hot liquid fat.

MOLE SAUCE, HOW TO RECONSTITUTE AND STORE / MOLE, COMO RECONSTITUIR

To reconstitute mole paste as a sauce, add 1½ cups of chicken stock for every ½ cup of thick paste, taking care to keep stirring as you combine over a medium-low heat for 10 minutes or until heated well throughout. Stir constantly; mole tends to stick to the bottom of the pan and can burn very easily. (Recipes for various mole pastes appear throughout the book.) Mole paste keeps well in the refrigerator for 2 weeks or frozen for 6 months. 🐝

ONION PURÉE / PURE DE CEBOLLA

(MAKES ½ CUP)

1 small onion, coarsely chopped
1 garlic clove
¼ cup water
Generous pinch of salt

BLEND all ingredients until smooth; strain and reserve liquid. Use immediately or within a day. 🐝

TAMALE DOUGH / MASA PARA TAMALES

(MAKES 40 TAMALES)

12 ounces lard (*manteca* or shortening)
2 pounds Maseca brand tamal flour (do not use tortilla flour)
½ cup chicken stock
1 cup boiling water with tomatillo husks
1 teaspoon baking powder
Salt to taste

IN a mixer, cream lard or shortening. Add previously sifted Maseca flour, chicken stock, water, baking powder, and salt to make a medium-thick consistency. Refrigerate in a plastic container with a tight lid and use within 24 hours. 🐝

TORTILLA MASA, PREPARED / MASA PARA TORTILLAS, PREPARADA

(ENOUGH FOR 30 TORTILLAS)

2 cups *masa harina* (Maseca brand tortilla mix)
½ teaspoon salt
1 tablespoon baking powder
1⅓ cups ice-cold water
Juice of ⅛ Mexican lime

MIX all ingredients thoroughly with your hands until you get a playdough-like consistency. Put in a plastic container with a tight lid and refrigerate for 1 hour before using. We recommend preparing just the amount to be used for the recipe at hand, rather than preparing extra ahead of time.

TOMATO STOCK / CALDILLO DE TOMATE

(MAKES 4 CUPS)

¼ cup minced onion
1 garlic clove, puréed
2 tablespoons olive oil
1 cup tomato purée (see below)
3 cups chicken stock (see above)
1 large sprig of cilantro
1 large bay leaf
Salt to taste

SAUTÉ onion and garlic in olive oil, add tomato purée, and cook for 12–15 minutes on medium-high until it changes color and volume is reduced by half. Add chicken stock, cilantro, bay leaf, and salt. Allow to boil for at least 10 more minutes to season well. Your stock is ready to be used in any recipe. Refrigerate when cooled for use within 48 hours or freeze for up to 3 months. 🐦

TOMATO PURÉE, COOKED / PURE TOMATE COCIDO

(MAKES 3 CUPS)

1½ pounds tomatoes
1 clove garlic
1 tablespoon olive oil
½ cup medium white onion, coarsely chopped
¾ teaspoon salt
¼ teaspoon ground black pepper

IN a blender, purée tomatoes, onion, and garlic; pass mixture through a strainer and add to a medium saucepan in which olive oil has been heated. Cook over medium-high heat for 10 minutes. Season with salt and pepper and use immediately or within a day or two; you can also freeze for up to 3 months. 🐦

TOMATO PURÉE, FRESH / PURE DE TOMATE

(MAKES ½ CUP)

3 small tomatoes
2 garlic cloves
½ onion

BLEND all ingredients until smooth; strain and reserve. Use immediately, keep refrigerated for up to 2 days, or freeze for up to 1 month. 🐦

SALSA RECIPES

ALL SALSAS RECIPES will yield enough for 4–6 people.
Roasting the ingredients for salsas gives a distinctly different flavor from boiling them, and using raw ingredients gives your salsa yet another flavor profile, as in the next several recipes. Experiment! There is no wrong way to make salsa! Salsas are best served at room temperature, except where noted.

BASIC GREEN SALSA I, COOKED /
SALSA VERDE DE TOMATILLO, FRITA I

1 medium onion
1 pound tomatillos
2 serrano chiles
2 garlic cloves
4 sprigs cilantro, finely chopped
Salt to taste
2 tablespoons vegetable oil

WASH tomatillos, removing husks. Dry-roast onion, tomatillos, chiles, and garlic on comal or griddle until dark spots appear on all sides. Combine all ingredients except oil, salt, and pepper in food processor and purée. Heat oil in a saucepan. Add salsa and cook over medium heat for 10 minutes, add ½ cup of water and season with salt to taste.

BASIC GREEN SALSA II, COOKED /
SALSA VERDE DE TOMATILLO, FRITA II

1 pound tomatillos
2 serrano chiles
¼ onion
1 garlic clove
½ cup cilantro
2 teaspoons corn oil
Salt to taste

WASH tomatillos, removing husks. Boil tomatillos and chiles for 8–10 minutes. Blend tomatillos and chiles with onion, garlic, and cilantro. Heat oil in a saucepan and add blended mix; cook for about 12–15 minutes. Season with salt to taste and set aside; the sauce should be runny (add water if necessary). 🐝

BASIC TOMATO SALSA, COOKED /
SALSA ROJA (DE JITOMATE), FRITA

½ white onion
2 serrano chiles
2 garlic cloves
3 medium tomatoes
½ tablespoon of salt
4 sprigs of cilantro, chopped finely
Salt to taste

DRY-roast onion, chiles, garlic, and tomatoes, until dark spots appear on all sides; remove skin and seeds from tomatoes. Place garlic with ½ tablespoon of salt (coarse salt works best) and purée with pestle (see "Common Mexican Cooking Tools and Techniques," p. 336). Add chiles, onion, and tomatoes and purée again, still using the molcajete and pestle. Mix well and add chopped cilantro; season with salt to taste. Prepare a pan with a small amount of oil; add blended salsa, being careful of splatter. Cook for about 10 minutes or until the liquid is seasoned and reduced by half. 🐝

BLACKENED TOMATO SALSA / SALSA DE TOMATE ASADO

10 guajillo chiles
1 pound tomatoes
1 large white Spanish onion
2 garlic cloves
¾ cup hot water
Salt to taste

SOAK guajillo chiles in hot water; once hydrated, add them to a blender. Dry roast tomatoes, onions, garlic, and chiles on the comal until blackened, making sure to turn tomatoes frequently. (For dry-roasting, see "Common Mexican Cooking Tools and Techniques," p. 335.) Add charred ingredients to the blender, tomato skins may stick to the comal, so scrape off with a rubber spatula and put these into the blender as well, for a smoky flavor, or omit if you wish. Mix well in the blender to make a smooth salsa, salt to taste, let cool, and set aside. 🐝

FRESH GREEN SALSA / SALSA VERDE FRESCA

1 pound tomatillos
¼ white onion
2 serrano chiles
3 garlic cloves
¼ cup fresh cilantro, chopped
½ cup water
Salt to taste

ROUGHLY chop vegetables and add to blender with other ingredients and mix until smooth. Taste for salt and add if needed. 🐝

FRESH RED SALSA / SALSA ROJA (DE JITOMATE)

½ white onion
2 serrano chiles
2 garlic cloves
3 medium tomatoes
4 sprigs of cilantro, chopped finely
Salt to taste

DRY-roast onion, chiles, garlic, and tomatoes until dark spots appear on all sides; remove skin and seeds from tomatoes. Place garlic with salt (coarse salt works best) and purée with pestle in a molcajete (see "Common Mexican Cooking Tools and Techniques," p. 336). Add chiles, onion, and tomatoes and purée again, still using the molcajete. Mix well and add chopped cilantro; season with salt to taste. ꘏

GREEN SALSA WITH AVOCADO I / SALSA VERDE CON AGUACATE I

1 pound tomatillos
1 garlic clove
5 serrano chiles
1 avocado
1 cup of cilantro, chopped finely
¼ onion
Salt to taste

WASH tomatillos, removing husks. In a saucepan, bring 1 cup of water to a boil; cook tomatillos, covered, for 10 minutes over medium heat. Drain and place in blender with all ingredients except avocado (remove seeds and veins from chiles beforehand if you don't want salsa to be too spicy). Place in a large bowl. Cut avocado in small cubes and add avocado and chopped cilantro to salsa. Mix well, and salt to taste. 🦗

GREEN SALSA WİTH AVOCADO II / SALSA VERDE CON AGUACATE II

1 pound tomatillos
1 garlic clove
5 serrano chiles
1 avocado
1 cup of cilantro, chopped finely
½ cup water
¼ onion
Salt to taste

WASH tomatillos, removing husks, and coarsely chop. Place in blender with garlic, onion, cilantro, chiles (remove seeds and veins from chiles beforehand if you don't want salsa to be too spicy), and water. Pulse until well combined. Add avocado and pulse 3 or 4 times until well blended. Salt to taste. 🦗

GRİLLED PİNEAPPLE SALSA / SALSA DE PİÑA ASADA

½ pineapple, peeled, cored, and sliced ¼ inch thick
1 large red tomato, seeded and finely chopped
½ red onion, diced
1 jalapeño chili pepper, finely diced
1 Mexican lime, juice and zest
1 chipotle (canned), seeded
¼ cup cilantro, chopped
Salt to taste

HEAT your grill or skillet to medium-high. Lightly brush pineapple with oil and grill for 2–3 minutes on each side. Dice the pineapple finely and mix all of the ingredients, serve cold. 🦗

GUAJILLO SALSA / SALSA DE CHILE GUAJILLO

3 fresh guajillo chiles, seeded and finely chopped
1 garlic clove
1 medium white onion
½ cup chicken or beef stock (see "Basic Recipes for Mexican Cooking," p. 11)
Salt to taste

MIX all ingredients in a blender until you get a smooth salsa. Cook covered over medium heat for 10 minutes. Salt to taste, remove from heat, and allow to cool. 🐟

HABANERO SALSA / SALSA DE CHILE HABANERO

1 white Spanish onion, quartered
1 garlic clove, peeled
2 medium tomatoes
1 habanero chile, seeded, deveined, and chopped
2 sprigs cilantro
½ tablespoon fresh oregano or ¼ tablespoon dry oregano
Salt to taste
2 tablespoons olive oil

ROAST onion, garlic, and tomatoes in a dry pan or comal until blackened. Place chiles, tomatoes, onion, garlic, oregano, and chopped cilantro in a blender and mix all ingredients well. Salt to taste, add 2 tablespoons of olive oil, and mix well. 🐟

MANGO SALSA / SALSA DE MANGO

1 large ripe mango, diced
1 red bell pepper, finely diced
2 chipotle chiles, seeded and finely chopped
1 small red onion, finely diced
½ teaspoon dried Mexican oregano, crumbled

1 large Mexican lime, juiced
3 tablespoons chopped cilantro
3 tablespoons orange juice
Sea salt to taste
Freshly ground black pepper

COMBINE all ingredients and allow to rest in refrigerator for 1 hour before serving. 🐟

PAPAYA SALSA / SALSA DE PAPAYA

1 small Mexican papaya, peeled, seeded, and finely chopped
½ cup red onion, finely chopped
2 serrano chiles, finely chopped
1 tablespoon chopped cilantro
1 tablespoon tequila (optional)
1 large lemon, juice and rind
Salt to taste

MIX all ingredients and serve cold. 🐟

PEACH SALSA / SALSA DE DURAZNO

4 peaches, peeled, pitted, and finely chopped
¼ cup finely chopped red onion
1 chipotle chile, seeded and finely chopped
1 jalapeño, finely chopped
1 tablespoon white vinegar
1 tablespoon cilantro, chopped
Salt to taste

COMBINE all ingredients and allow to rest in refrigerator for an hour before serving. 🐟

PICO DE GALLO / SALSA MEXICANA

½ onion, chopped
2 tomatoes, chopped
2 tablespoons fresh chopped cilantro
1 or 2 serrano chiles, chopped
Juice of 2 Mexican limes
Salt to taste

MIX all ingredients well in small mixing bowl. Refrigerate immediately.

SALSA PAIRINGS

Basic Green Salsa, Cooked I or II	Chilaquiles, enchiladas, tacos, quesadillas, sopes, tlacoyos
Blackened Tomato / *Salsa de Tomate Asado*	Eggs, stews, tacos
Fresh Green Salsa / *Salsa Verde (de Tomatillo)*	Tacos, chips
Fresh Red Salsa / *Salsa Roja (de Jitomate)*	Chips, tacos, quesadillas, sopes, tlacoyos
Drunken Salsa / *Salsa Borracha*	Barbacoa
Green Salsa with Avocado, I or II	Tacos, tostadas, tortas
Grilled Pineapple Salsa	Tacos al pastor, fish, chicken, steak, pork
Habanero Salsa	Cochinita Pibil, tacos, fish, seafood
Guajillo Salsa	Eggs, chicken, fish, tacos
Mango Salsa	Pork, chicken, fish, tacos, chips
Papaya Salsa	Chips, fish, pork
Basic Tomato Salsa, Cooked / *Salsa Roja (de Jitomate), Frita*	Soups, stews
Peach Salsa	Pork, chicken, rabbit, tacos, chips
Pico de Gallo	Tacos, chips, molletes, salads

PART I

HOLIDAYS AND FESTIVALS

MEXICAN CELEBRATIONS are abundant events, typically with a large guest list and even larger food spread as well as drinking, music, and dancing. Many of Mexico's festivals are rooted in holy days introduced to Mexico by the Catholic Church. There is a festival, fiesta, fair (*feria*), or saint's day somewhere in Mexico every day of the year. These events mark the rhythm of Mexican life, and so, we begin as the liturgical calendar begins: with Advent and the first holiday of the year, the Día de la Virgen de Guadalupe on December 12.

In fact, there are three major holiday cycles: December 12 begins a period fondly referred to by Mexicans as the Guadalupe-Reyes Marathon, a virtual marathon of holidays (and cooking, and drinking, music, and dancing!) that come one after another, starting with the Día de la Virgen de Guadalupe and ending with Día de los Reyes, or Three King's Day, on January 6. Although there are many festivals in between, the next major, if somewhat less raucous, interval is Semana Santa or Holy Week: the week preceding and including Easter Sunday. It is more common in the United States to attend church on Good Friday and gather with family on Easter Sunday; in Mexico the entire week, beginning with *Domingo de Palmas* (Palm Sunday), is a flurry of activity, much of which is centered around meal preparation. The month of November is also a busy time in Mexico, beginning with that most famous of Mexico's festivals, Día de los Muertos (actually several days: October 30 to November 2), followed by Independence Day, and then Día de la Revolucion.

In all, twenty major holidays and fiestas are covered in this section, all of which are celebrated nationally (although there are more than five thousand fiesta days celebrated throughout the Mexican Republic!). The menus presented are, for the most part, true to those served at these events in Mexico. Some festivals do not have specific dishes, and for those, we have presented thematic menus of authentic dishes: fruits and vegetables for Corpus Christi Day, which coincides with the harvest; a floral theme for Mother's Day; and lots of sweet treats and children's favorites for *Día del Niño* (Day of the Child). While we encourage you to share Mexico's cultural heritage with friends and family and re-create these fiestas in your own kitchen, we hope you will reach for an intriguing recipe when you are planning your everyday meals as well.

DAY OF THE VIRGIN OF GUADALUPE / DÍA DE LA VÍRGEN DE GUADALUPE
(DECEMBER 12)

THE LiTURGiCAL calendar of the Catholic Church beings with Advent, making Día de la Virgen de Guadalupe the first major holiday of the year. It is also one of the more important, celebrated in every corner of Mexico from the biggest cities to the smallest ranchos.

La Virgencita, Protector of All Mexicans

All over Mexico, in every pueblo or neighborhood (*vecindario*) her smiling face appears to look tenderly over her people. Most Mexican American homes display her painting or statue or both. And the myriads of Mexican barrios in any number of U.S. cities typically have murals with her image. Far more than a religious figure, the Virgin of Guadalupe is the cement that binds all Mexico. Devotion to Guadalupe is a source of profound pride in being Mexican, and has become a symbol of nationalism and patriotism.

In a country with the second-largest Catholic population in the world (Brazil is first), most Mexicans consider themselves Guadalupanos first and Catholics second. Nobel prize recipient Octavio Paz is widely quoted as saying, "When Mexicans no longer believe in anything, they will still hold fast to their belief in two things: the National Lottery and the Virgin of Guadalupe. In this I think they will do well. For both have been known to work, even for those of us who believe in nothing."

It was in her name that "El Grito," the call to arms that began Mexico's War of Independence on September 16, 1810, went out. Her image graced the banners of Padre Miguel Hidalgo y Costilla's insurgents as they fought the war for liberty from Spain, during which they were required to wear the emblem of Guadalupe. Thus identified by their devotion, soldiers belonging to the insurgent rebel force were summarily executed. Royalists desecrated her image by wearing it on the soles of their shoes. Later, during Mexico's revolution, followers of revolutionary leader Emiliano Zapata—Zapatistas—wore her likeness in the band of their famous wide-brimmed hats. Nearly every major Mexican city has a basilica bearing her name.

Appearance on the Hill and the Story of the Tilma

The Virgin de Guadalupe first appeared on December 9, 1531, on the hill of Tepeya-cac (now Tepeyac), north of Mexico City, revealing herself to Juan Diego Cuauht-latoatzin, an Aztec who had recently converted to Christianity (which explains his Christian first name; interestingly, his Aztec surname means "the eagle who speaks"). Juan Diego was attracted to the spot by a chorus of birds more beautiful than anything he had ever heard. Suddenly, the story goes, the singing stopped and a voice called out, using the diminutive form of his name, "Juantzin, Juan Diegotzin." Before him stood a "beautiful woman adorned in clothing that shone like the sun wrapped in a cloak bearing an array of stars."[1] Speaking to Juan Diego in his native Aztec language of Nahuatl,[2] the vision introduced herself as the "ever-perfect holy Mary"[3] and asked that a church be built in her honor. Juan Diego went to Archbishop Juan de Zumárraga with Guadalupe's request and tried three times to convince the cleric that he had seen her apparition. Each time, his plea was denied and each time La Virgencita reappeared on the same spot to encourage Diego. He succeeded only on the last visit to Zumárraga, when roses suddenly tumbled out of his opened *tilma* (an Aztec article of clothing worn by men, similar to a cloak) and a life-size image of the Virgin miraculously appeared imprinted on its cactus-fiber cloth. On Juan Diego's cloak was the same painted effigy that is central to all Mexican Catholics, the Virgin of Guadalupe.

Miracle or Manipulation?

The miracle of the tilma convinced Archbishop Zumárraga and construction of the original basilica began in 1531. It is little wonder that the Archbishop agreed to the project; at the time, thirty-five years after Spain's conquest of Mexico, the evangelical efforts of the Catholic Church had not been successful in removing all or even most vestiges of the Aztec's pagan beliefs. Here was a story, an image, and an icon that would become invaluable in this effort. There are historians who credit the Virgin of Guadalupe with being the force behind the conversion of six million Aztecs over the next nine years.

While some view the vision as myth and nothing more than a tool in the collective chest of Spanish colonization, most Mexicans and many here in the United States and around the world believe in the beautiful story of the miracle (*milagro*), including several popes. In a papal brief on May 25, 1754, Pope Benedict XIV proclaimed Our Lady of Guadalupe patron of New Spain. Pope Pius X declared her patron of Latin America in 1910. On July 31, 2002, following exhaustive research and more than 250 years after the vision on the hill, Pope John Paul II canonized Juan Diego Cuauhtlatoatzin as the first indigenous Mexican saint. In preparation for the canonization, over four thousand documents related to the Virgin of Guadalupe were reviewed.

Examining La Tilma

The painted cloak that finally convinced Archbishop Zumárraga to build a church dedicated to La Virgencita has been the focus of intensive scientific scrutiny, especially as the Catholic Church was preparing to canonize Juan Diego. Upon its completion in 1709, the cloak was housed in the old basilica, until a bomb placed near the altar in 1974 damaged that structure.[4] Although the interior of the church sustained substantial damage, the tilma survived the incident largely unharmed and was moved to the new Basilica de Guadalupe in Mexico City in 1976, where it has remained perfectly preserved since.

As with the Shroud of Turin, many studies have been conducted over the four centuries since the cloth was presented to the Church, examining the fabric, the tint that produced the image, the eyes of the Virgin, even the positions of the stars on the cloak. One study determined that the stars on the tilma are positioned exactly as they would have appeared in Mexico during the winter solstice of 1531.[5]

The Eyes of Guadalupe

A discovery made by Alfonso Marcuéz Gonzalez, official photographer of the old Basilica of Guadalupe, while he was inspecting black-and-white photos he had taken of the tilma revealed what appeared to be the silhouette of a bearded man reflected in the eyes of the image of Guadalupe. Although the photographer immediately reported his findings to the Church, it was decided not to make the discovery public at that time.

Two decades later, on May 29, 1951, Jose Carlos Salinas Chavez was examining a good photograph of the tilma that detailed the face, when he also discovered the image of what clearly appeared to be a bearded man reflected in the eyes of the Virgin.

Subsequently, ophthalmologists confirmed the presence of a reflection[6] characteristic of all live human eyes.[7] It was officially recognized that the image was that of Juan Diego, a reflection of the Indian in the Virgin's eyes. Over the years,

Zapotec man dancing in front of the basilica in Mexico City on Día de la Virgen de Guadalupe. The Zapotecs are an indigenous people residing primarily in the southern Mexican state of Oaxaca, with communities in neighboring states as well. Zapotec languages and dialects are spoken by approximately 410,905 persons, many of whom are monolingual. The Zapotec civilization was one of the more highly developed cultures of Mesoamerica prior to the Spanish Conquest and used a system of writing similar to hieroglyphics. Benito Juarez, president of Mexico (see chapter 9), was a full-blooded Zapotec.
Photo by Jorge Ontiveros.

more than twenty ophthalmologists have studied these photos and the eyes of the image on the tilma.

An Epidemic Gives Birth to a Patron

The Virgin of Guadalupe came to garner widespread devotion. One reason may lie in the 1737 epidemic, during which Guadalupe was said to have intervened collectively for "her people" to protect them from a virulent plague that had already taken the lives of forty thousand in Mexico City and fifty thousand in Puebla over a period of eight months. It has been noted that several of other images of the Virgin had been invoked before that of the Virgin of Guadalupe, to no avail. Her efficacy was proclaimed when there appeared to be a cessation of deaths after her aid was sought, and she was converted into an official emblem, embraced even by the reticent upper class.

Día de la Virgencita Today

Every year, on December 12, between eighteen and twenty million people make the pilgrimage to the Basílica de la Virgen de Guadalupe, making it Christianity's most visited sanctuary. Thousands of Mexicans come from their pueblos to Mexico City, many on bicycle, riding through the night for long, dark, cold hours. Indigenous people, young and old, make up a significant number of those visiting the hilltop. Many walk or run from their villages, some barefoot, carrying torches and banners to show their devotion and even ascend the stairs on their knees.

For those who do not make a pilgrimage to Mexico City, the celebration is observed traditionally by getting up around 4 or 5 a.m., going to church, bringing flowers, singing songs, and praying. Pilgrims join the observance at the basilica or main cathedral in almost every city and town in Mexico, and La Virgencita is honored with *"Las Mañanitas,"* a song for birthdays and saints' days sung before the rosary at dawn (although this practice is more recent). At the end of the celebration, tamales, chocolate, and cookies are served. In Oaxaca, La Virgencita is honored with a novena (a nine-day prayer series) that ends on this day.

Throughout Mexico on December 12, small Mexican boys are dressed in peasant clothes and are called Juan Diegitos, with mustaches painted on their faces. On their tilmas, the image of Guadalupe appears as she did on the cloth of Juan Diego, centuries ago. The girls are called *las Malinches* (see below). The traditional costume for the girls is an embroidered blouse and a gathered flowered skirt, with a brightly colored *rebozo* (a woman's garment, similar to a shawl, worn as an accessory but also used to carry children or products to markets, common to Spain and Mexico) draped over their shoulders, their hair in long braids (*trenzas*) with colored yarn ingeniously braided into to their shorter hair. The girls carry baskets of flowers, usually roses like the ones that spilled out of Juan Diego's tilma. Often, the costume includes pilgrimage essentials, even though these children are too young to make the trip. They may be equipped with a *costalito* (a bag made from sacks from rice or flour) filled with all the necessary items, like water, a *petate* (a sort of rug made of palm leaves for sleeping), and easy-to-carry food like tamales—everything they might have needed were they actually making a long pilgrimage.

La Malinche is one of the most important and controversial figures in Mexican history, at once Eve and Judas, progenitor and traitor. Widely considered the mother of the "First Mexican" (i.e., a mixture of Spanish and Indian blood), she was an Aztec woman who bore Spanish explorer Hernán Cortés a son, whom he acknowledged. And yet, today, in Mexico, her name is synonymous with betrayal, and the term *malinchismo* signifies something injurious to Mexican pride.

> **MENU 1.1: DAY OF THE VIRGIN OF GUADALUPE**
>
> **Small Plates / *Antojitos***
> Corn Tamales / *Tamales de Elote*
> Oaxacan Tamales
> in Banana Leaf /
> *Tamales Oaxaqueños*
> **Dessert / *Postre***
> Strawberry-Pineapple Tamales /
> *Tamales de Piña y Fresa*
> **Beverage / *Bebida***
> Guava Atole /
> *Atole de Guayaba*

Noble-born with the given name Malintzin, her father, a *cacique*, or tribal leader, took the unusual step of providing an education for his daughter, a decision that was to change the course of Mexico's history. Widely acclaimed for her beauty and her unique language abilities (she was fluent in Nahuatl as well as Mayan), Malintzin came to the attention of Cortés by way of becoming his property along with nineteen other unlucky girls, as reparations paid by a Mayan cacique who had been defeated by the Spaniard. She quickly learned Spanish and was one of the first of her people to convert to Christianity, taking the name Marina. Soon after, she became Cortés's beloved and was known as Doña Marina, a title of respect.

Malintzin's role was much more than that of a translator and linguist. As the indigenous tribes of what is now Mexico fought among themselves, her ability as a translator and linguist was almost overshadowed by her negotiating skills. Historians credit her with amassing greater numbers of Indians to assist in Cortés's fight against the marauding Aztecs, who had made many enemies due to their harsh treatment of other tribes. Regardless of how much of a role she played in the final defeat of Montezuma, her language skills, at the very least, facilitated the conversion of the Aztecs to Christianity, which contributed heavily to the ultimate disappearance of much of their culture, except for the cuisine.

TAMALES: A HISTORICAL LOOK

TAMALES are an essential part of many Mexican festivals. Preparation is complex, time consuming, and an excellent example of Mexican communal cooking, where this task usually falls to the women. Preparing tamales is a ritual that has been part of Mexican life since pre-Hispanic times, with special fillings and forms designated for each specific festival or life event. Franciscan monk Bernardino de Sahagún, considered one of the father's of culinary history, wrote in an amazing 1590 text based on personal observations, detailing that the first thing Aztec women did when preparing a festival was to make lots of *tamalli* (in Nahuatl):

> Salted wide tamales, pointed tamales, white tamales . . . rolled-shaped tamales, tamales with beans forming a seashell on top [with] grains of maize thrown in; crumbled, pounded tamales; spotted tamales, white fruit tamales, red fruit tamales, turkey egg tamales; turkey eggs with grains of maize; tamales of tender maize, tamales of green maize, abode-shaped tamales, braised ones; unleavened tamales, honey tamales, beeswax tamales, tamales with grains of maize, gourd tamales, crumbled tamales, maize flower tamales. These were passed around in a basket at banquets, [and custom mandated that they] were held in the left hand.[8]

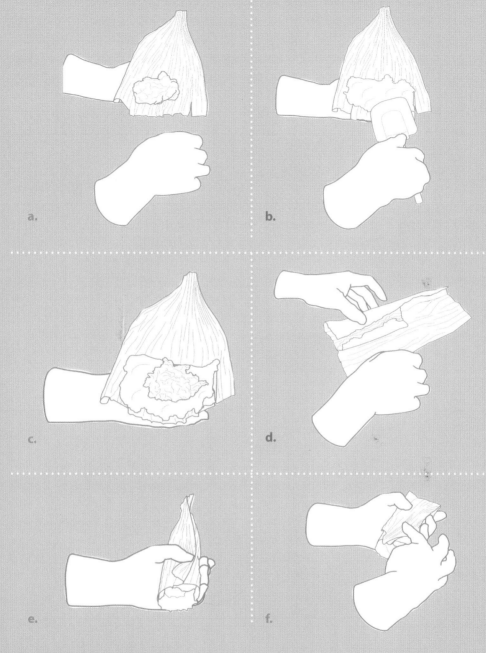

a.

b.

c.

d.

e.

f.

Making tamales.
Figure by Verticalarray, Inc.

A Step-by-Step Guide to the
Ancient Art of Making Tamales

First, to prepare the cornhusks: Rinse and soak them in a sink full of warm water for about 2 hours. You will need to carefully separate them when they get soft. Try to not tear the cornhusks. It is easier to make the tamales if the husks are in one piece. After the husks are soft, shake to remove excess water and pat them dry with a paper towel.

To fill the tamales:

A. Pick up one husk and lay it across your hand; the wide part of the husk should be facing your body and the thin part outside (think of a triangle, the thin part should be away from your body and the thick part toward you).

B. Scoop up about 2 tablespoons of masa dough with a spatula, and then smear the husk creating a ⅛-inch-thick layer. Cover about ⅔ of the husk with masa; leave ⅓ uncovered on one side.

C. Add the meat or stuffing of your choice. Take about 1 tablespoon of meat, or the desired stuffing, then lay it on the masa dough about one inch from the left edge, do not over stuff the tamale, as you will need to have room to close it.

To fold:

D. Starting on the left side, roll the tamale.

E. Roll the tamale all the way to the right edge.

F. Now, fold the top of the husk over (think of an envelope) and lay the tamale on the counter, fold facing down.

To Cook:

In a steamer pot, add about 2 cups of water, place a stainless steel vegetable steamer in it and then start piling the tamales so they stand upright. The folded end of the tamale should be on the bottom. Try to fill the steamer so the tamales do not fall over and begin to unfold. Cover the pot, and bring the water to a boil, then reduce to medium-low heat and cook, covered, for 2 hours. Check water several times as you will need to add water frequently, so as to not let your pot run out of water.

To create an assembly line, after you master steps 1 and 2 you can lay several husks out on the counter as you put the masa on them, between 5 and 10 husks.

Corn Tamales with flowers embedded / *Tamales de Elote con flores.*
Photo by Adriana Almazán Lahl.

CORN TAMALES / TAMALES DE ELOTE

(MAKES APPROXIMATELY 35 TAMALES)

3½ quarts (14 cups) fresh corn kernels
1 cup corn meal
1 cup butter
½ cup lard or shortening
1 cup sugar
2 eggs
1 tablespoon salt
1 tablespoon baking powder
70 cornhusks, washed and patted dry
Fresh salsa of your choice (see "Salsa Pairings," p. 25)
Mexican sour cream
Queso Cotija

USE a blender or food processor to create a purée from the corn kernels (uncooked). Transfer corn mixture to a large mixing bowl with the corn meal; beat by hand, adding butter and lard slowly. Keep beating for 5 minutes, adding sugar, eggs, salt, and baking powder. Beat for an additional 20 minutes using an electric mixer on slow or by hand until smooth. Set aside and let it rest for 15 minutes.

Prepare tamales by adding a couple of spoonfuls of the mix in a double corn husk (using 2 overlapping husks) and fold the tamale according to instructions (above). Serve these with your favorite fresh salsa, Mexican sour cream, and Cotija cheese.

CORN TAMALES / *TAMALES DE ELOTE*

A N *abuelita* (meaning "grandmother" but also a term used to refer to the old-est generation of women in the village) describes how the women gather to carry on a tradition that has been passed through the generations, making sweet tamales de elote. You can make them yourself, following the recipe in the text below:

> Three pair of hands, work together, seamlessly . . . in a process [that] includes husking the corn, cutting it off the cob, grinding the kernels in the *molino* [mill] with pieces of cinnamon, breaking fifteen eggs and separating out the yolks, opening cans of sweetened condensed milk . . . [and beating] all the ingredients together in the *masa* for a long time. . . . Next we fill the husks with the *masa* [dough] . . . sprinkle raisins on top. Finally we fold the husks to enclose the dough.[9]

Wixáritari man preparing corn. The Huichol, or Wixáritari, are an indigenous people living in the Sierra Madre Occidental Range in the Mexican states of Nayarit, Jalisco, Zacatecas, and Durango, known as the Huichol, they refer to themselves as Wixáritari ("the people"). Almost 36,000 persons spoke the Huichol language in 2005. Extended Huichol families live together in small communities consisting of individual houses that belong to a nuclear family, each with a communal kitchen and a family shrine, dedicated to the ancestors of the rancho, known as a *xiriki*. Wixaritari have a long tradition of rejecting Catholic influences and have sought to maintain their religious and cultural freedom since the era of the Conquest. Photo by Jorge Ontiveros.

OAXACAN TAMALES IN BANANA LEAF / TAMALES OAXAQUEÑOS

(MAKES 24)

4 large plantain leaves
1 onion
4 garlic cloves
½ pound pork shoulder, chopped in 1-inch chunks (or substitute chicken or turkey)
3 cups water
½ onion
2 garlic cloves
1 bay leaf
3½ cups pork or chicken stock
½ tablespoon salt
½ pound or 1 cup lard or shortening
2 pounds masa harina
2 tablespoons *tequesquite*
2 cups Mole Casa Almazán (see recipe, p. 306)
Cooking twine

BOIL plantain leaves for 20 minutes, until they become dark. Rinse and pat dry and cut into 8-inch squares using kitchen shears. In a separate pot, add 3 cups of water and cook pork with onion, garlic, and bay leaf for 15 minutes. Add chicken stock and salt. Cook for 20 additional minutes. Set aside, reserve stock, and let the meat cool before shredding.

In a large electric mixer (KitchenAid or similar), mix lard or shortening until creamed; add masa harina, dissolve tequesquite into stock, and alternate adding masa harina and stock to the creamed shortening. Add salt to taste. Mix well.

NOTES FROM THE ALMAZÁN KITCHEN

TO test the consistency of masa, form into a small ball and drop it in a glass of water; if it floats, it is ready.

To make sure there is sufficient water in the bottom of your steamer pot when cooking the tamales, put a penny in with the water. If you hear the penny rattling, your water is getting low and you need to add more.

Lay out a single banana leaf and add a thin layer of prepared masa, 1 tablespoon of mole sauce, and 2 tablespoons of meat. Place another leaf on top and fold carefully; fold forming a square pocket and tie with twine. Cook over a Baño Maria (see "Common Mexican Cooking Tools and Techniques," p. 333) for 1½ hours, checking the water every half hour, adding 2 cups of boiling water every half hour as necessary. 🕷

ATOLE

It's traditional to drink atole with tamales. From the Nahuatl *atl* for water and *tlaoli* meaning ground corn, atole is a maize-based beverage originating in the pre-Columbian era.

STRAWBERRY-PİNEAPPLE TAMALES / TAMALES DE PİÑA Y FRESA

(MAKES 70 TAMALES)

70 cornhusks, cleaned and submerged in warm water
2 pounds butter
Pinch of salt
2 tablespoons baking powder
4 pounds corn masa harina
1 pound fresh strawberries, puréed in the blender
¾ cup sugar
1 cup small diced pineapple, fresh or canned
¼ tablespoon ground cinnamon
⅛ tablespoon ground cloves

IN a large electric mixer (KitchenAid or similar), blend butter with salt and baking powder until well creamed. Add masa harina slowly and keep mixing uniformly. Add strawberry purée and keep mixing. It is important to taste the mix, adding sugar to your taste; it should have a pleasant sweetness but not be overly sweet. Incorporate cinnamon and cloves and mix well. Add pineapple pieces to the center of the tamal on top of the masa. Proceed to assemble the tamales the same way as you do on page 36. Cook for an hour over a Baño Maria (see "Common Mexican Cooking Tools and Techniques," p. 333). 🕷

GUAVA ATOLE / ATOLE DE GUAYABA

(SERVES 8)

4 pounds guavas (better fresh, substitute canned if unavailable)
2 cups water
1 cinnamon stick
6 ounces fresh tortilla masa, can be Maseca (be sure it is the tortilla masa and not
    tamale masa)
4 ounces sugar or piloncillo to taste (for working with piloncillo, see "Common Cooking
    Techniques and Tools for Mexican Cooking," p. 336)

WASH and cut guavas into small cubes. In a blender, purée guava until smooth. Pass blended guava through a sieve, straining it into a large bowl. Reserve and set aside. Boil water with the cinnamon stick.

Place the masa in a separate bowl and pour a little water to make a soft masa paste with your hands, adding more water if necessary. Make as smooth a paste as possible—or it won't dissolve in your atole.

Once the cinnamon water boils, add masa paste and stir vigorously until well combined and dissolved, about 3 to 4 minutes. Wait for this mixture to boil again, add the guava purée, and stir again. Let boil once more. Taste for sweetness and add more sugar or piloncillo if necessary. Lower heat to medium-low and simmer; it will become thick and bubbles will start to form. Cook, stirring constantly, until the atole thickens and tastes cooked, about 30 minutes. To serve, remove cinnamon stick and pour into mugs.

You can make your atole with strawberries or any fruit you want; just substitute the fruit or flavor of your choice for the guava. The options are endless. Here are some suggestions: vanilla, prunes, chocolate, mango, berries, coconut, cinnamon peaches, or pecans.

LAS POSADAS
(DECEMBER 16–24)

DECEMBER 16 marks the beginning of Las Posadas (a *novenario*, nine days of religious observance), during which Mexican families participate in nightly Christmas processions that re-create the holy pilgrimage of Mary, Joseph, and the baby Jesus on their way to Bethlehem.

Early History and the Aztec Festival of Winter Solstice

Many Mexican holidays include dramatizations of original events, a tradition that has its roots in the ritual of Bible plays used to teach religious doctrine to a largely illiterate population in Europe as early as the tenth and eleventh centuries. These plays lost favor with the Church as they became popularized with the addition of folk music and other nonreligious elements. The plays were eventually banned, only to be reintroduced in the sixteenth century by two Spanish saints as the Christmas pageant, a new kind of religious ceremony to accompany the Christmas holiday.[1]

In Mexico, the Aztec winter solstice festival had traditionally been observed from December 7 to December 26. According to the Aztec calendar, their most important deity, the sun god Huitzilopochtli, was born during the month of December (*panquetzaliztli*). The parallel in time between this native celebration and the birth of the Christ lent itself to an almost seamless merging of the two holy days. Seeing the opportunity to proselytize, Spanish missionaries brought the custom of the reinvented religious pageant to Mexico, where they used it to teach the story of Jesus's birth to Mexico's indigenous people. In 1586, Friar Diego de Soria obtained a papal bull from Pope Sixtus V, stating that a Christmas Mass (*Misa de Aguinaldo*) be observed as novenas on the nine days preceding Christmas Day throughout Mexico.

Festivities in Modern Mexico

The nine days of celebration mark the nine months that Mary carried Jesus in her womb, leading up to Christmas Eve (*Noche Buena*). Originally organized by the Church, at first these were celebrated as formal masses. With time they became what they are today: festivities which include singing, food, and a simulation of the holy pilgrimage from Nazareth to Bethlehem, as Mexicans everywhere recreate the journey of the Holy Pilgrims (*los Santos Peregrinos*) seeking shelter.

One of Mexico's most charming traditions, Las Posadas, occurs between 8 and 10 p.m. each night beginning on December 16 and is truly a community affair. A reenactment in song, families in a neighborhood each host the Posada at their home on one of the nine nights, playing the role of the innkeepers (*los hosteleros*). Costumed children and adults are *los peregrinos*, who have to request lodging by going from house to house (*casa a casa*); this usually involves three to four homes. As they go, they sing "Searching for an Inn" carols ("*Villancicos para Pedir Posadas*"), carrying small candles in their hands. Participants either carry statuettes of or may be costumed as Joseph, leading a donkey on which Mary is riding, followed by an assortment of shepherds, angels, and animals, with a star either at the beginning or the end of the procession.

As the group travels from home to home, they ask for lodging by singing the appropriate lines of the carol. At each participating household, the residents respond by refusing lodging, with the chorus going back and forth between the two groups. When the pilgrims reach the designated site for that night's party, the chorus changes to "Enter Holy Pilgrims" ("*Entren Santos Peregrinos*") as "Mary" and "Joseph" are finally recognized and allowed to enter. Once the "innkeepers" let them in their home, the group of traveling guests kneels around the Nativity scene and the festivities begin, marked, as in all things Mexican, by song, dance, and an opportunity for each household to outdo that of its neighbors. It has been noted that

> the cultural genius of the Posadas is to successfully combine the affirmation of ideals like reciprocity, hospitality and cooperation with the living reality of competition and conspicuous consumption. Competition is expressed above all in an unmistakable rivalry between participating streets and barrios, whose residents derive a sense of pride if they are able to put on a lavish show.[2]

Special customs include the breaking of piñatas and partaking of Christmas punch (*ponche Navideño*), tamales (see chapters 1 and 6), and *buñuelos* (sweet fritters).

"Searching for an Inn" Carol (*Villancico para Pedir Posadas*)

(The Pilgrims)
In the name of the heavens
I request lodging from you,
Because she cannot walk,
My beloved wife.
(The Innkeepers)
This is not an inn,
Go on ahead
I can't open up for you
In case you're a crook.
(The Pilgrims)
Don't be cruel,
Give us charity
That the gods of the heavens
Will bless you.
(The Inkeepers)
Enter holy pilgrims
Receive this haven
That although it's a poor dwelling
The dwelling
I offer to you from the heart.

Piñata.
Photo by Jorge Aranda.

The Piñata

The tradition of the piñata comes from Italy. When they first made an appearance in Mexico, piñatas were clay pots decorated to give a horrific appearance resembling the devil and were placed outside the church by the missionaries to attract Mexico's indigenous people to attend their services.

With time, the piñata took the form of a sphere with seven cones, a star symbolizing the seven deadly sins (lust, gluttony, greed, sloth, wrath, envy, pride).

The candy and fruits inside the piñata symbolized the temptation of wealth and earthly pleasures.

Whoever struck the piñata was blinded with a cloth over his eyes, representing that faith is blind. His effort to break the piñata represented the fight against the devil's forces and the stick used to hit the piñata symbolized virtue (loyalty and faith). When the piñata broke, spilling its contents of prizes, it was the Church's way of rewarding all participants for being loyal and for keeping their faith in God. While much of this faith-related history has been forgotten, piñatas remain common at most family celebrations in Mexico today.

MENU 2.1: LAS POSADAS

Small Plates / *Antojitos*
Traditional Fried Quesadillas (Mexico City–Style) /
Quesadillas Fritas
with Cheese and Jalapeño Strips /
Queso y Rajas de Jalapeño
with Squash Blossom /
Flor de Calabaza
with Potato and Cheese /
Papas con Queso
Tlacoyos
Sopes
Dessert / *Postre*
Mexican Sweet Fritters / *Buñuelos*
Beverage / *Bebida*
Warm Holiday Punch /
Ponche Navideño

Quesadillas.
Photo by Adriana Almazán Lahl.

TRADITIONAL FRIED QUESADILLAS [MEXICO CITY–STYLE] / QUESADILLAS FRITAS

(MAKES 12)

3 cups vegetable oil
Tortillas (see step-by-step instructions for handmade tortillas, p. 236,
Filling of choice (see A, B, and C below; or you can opt for no additional filling to make cheese quesadillas)
Salsa of your choice (see "Salsa Recipes" and "Salsa Pairings," pp. 17–25)
Shredded iceberg lettuce

THE process starts with making your own tortillas. Remove top square of plastic from your tortillas (step 3 of instructions on p. 236) and add 1 teaspoon of filling of choice and ½ teaspoon of cheese (see below) in center of round.

Fold tortilla (the bottom sheet of plastic will still be in place under the tortilla) over filling, folding it to form a half-moon, and pinch edges together to seal. Gently peel off plastic, then place quesadilla into hot oil (375°) and fry for about 4–6 minutes or until light golden color. Remove and drain oil on a paper towel or brown paper bag. Serve with sour cream and salsa of your choice on a bed of shredded lettuce. 🐦

A. Cheese and Jalapeño Strips Filling / Queso y Rajas de Jalapeño

(MAKES 12)

1 cup shredded Oaxaca cheese
3 jalapeño chiles, seeded and quartered to form thin strips or *rajas*
½ cup cooked corn kernels

ADD about a quarter of a jalapeño (so one raja), 1 tablespoon cheese, and 1 tablespoon of corn kernels to center of quesadilla. Then follow instructions (above) for Traditional Fried Quesadillas. 🐦

B. Squash Blossom Filling / Flor de Calabaza

(MAKES 12)

5 ounces shredded Oaxaca or Mozzarella
2 tablespoons unsalted butter or olive oil
1 cup white onion, minced
¼ pound squash blossoms, petals only, chopped
2 teaspoons chopped fresh epazote leaves or ¼ teaspoon dry epazote
¼ teaspoon salt, or to taste

HEAT oil and add onions. Cook for 3 minutes and add squash blossoms. Add epazote and cook 3 more minutes. Turn off and set aside to cool to room temperature. Add 1 tablespoon of stuffing in center of quesadilla and then follow instructions (above) for Traditional Fried Quesadillas. 🐟

C. Potato and Cheese Filling / Papas con Queso

(MAKES 12)

1 cup mashed potatoes
2 teaspoons fresh epazote leaves or ½ teaspoon dry epazote
8 ounces queso fresco or shredded Oaxaca cheese

ADD 1 tablespoon of mashed potatoes, 1 epazote leaf, and 1 teaspoon shredded Oaxaca or mozzarella in the center of the quesadilla. Then follow instructions (above) for Traditional Fried Quesadillas. 🐟

TLACOYOS

(MAKES 6)

½ pound prepared masa (see "Basic Recipes for Mexican Cooking," p. 14)
1 cup refried beans (see p. 152) or mashed potatoes
1 cup of salsa verde of choice (see "Salsas Recipes," pp. 17–24)
½ cup Cotija or queso fresco
Mexican sour cream for garnish

FORM a 2-inch ball of masa, about the size of a golf ball. **A.** Stretch and shape the masa to form a 3-inch rectangle. **B.** Flatten using a tortilla press, first pressing gently on one side, then flipping the rectangle of masa and pressing gently on the other side. This way, the dough should be of an even thickness. If you do not have a tortillas press, you may use a rolling pin, being careful to control the shape so you have a nice rectangle.

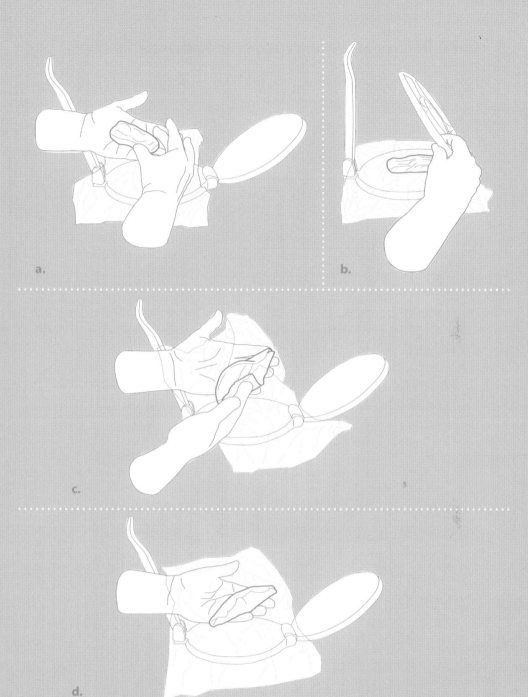

a.

b.

c.

d.

Making tlacoyos.
Figure by Verticalarray, Inc.

Add 1 tablespoon of refried black beans or mashed potatoes in the center; spread filling carefully along the masa.

C. Proceed to wrap the masa around the filling. **D.** As you close the tlacoyo, fold each corner toward the center to form a diamond shape, taking care that the tlacoyo is flat.

Cook on a comal or in a sauté pan without oil for 3–4 minutes on each side. Serve with Mexican sour cream, salsa, and Cotija cheese or queso fresco.

SOPES

(MAKES 10 MEDIUM, 2½-INCH-DIAMETER SOPES)

11 pounds prepared masa (see "Basic Recipes for Mexican Cooking," p. 14)

¾ cup refried beans (see p. 152)

1 cup shredded carnitas (see p. 324) or shredded chicken or beef (see "Basic Recipes for Mexican Cooking," p. 11), sautéed with onions and tomatoes and well seasoned with salt and pepper

1 cup Mexican sour cream

3½ ounces Cotija cheese

1 cup salsa of choice (see "Salsas Recipes" and "Salsa Pairings," pp. 17–25)

1 cup shredded lettuce

½ Spanish white onion, finely chopped

Salt to taste

Sopes.
Photo by Adriana Almazán Lahl.

FORM a 2½-inch ball of prepared masa. Flatten it to a ¼-inch round.

Cook on a comal or a sauté pan without oil for 2 minutes on each side. While still hot, pinch the edges so as to create a small wall all around the edge to retain filling.

Add refried beans first, then meat, next sour cream and cheese, and cook for 2 more minutes. Serve with fresh salsa, shredded lettuce, and chopped onions. ❧

MEXICAN SWEET FRITTERS / *BUÑUELOS*

THERE is an interesting holiday tradition in the Oaxaca region of Mexico. Street vendors sell buñuelos in the town plazas on pottery dishes that are cracked or have other flaws. After eating their buñuelos, people throw the plates on the ground, breaking them, in a custom that has its roots in Aztec New Year's ceremonies (see chapter 6).

MEXICAN SWEET FRITTERS WITH ORANGE-CINNAMON SUGAR / BUÑUELOS CON AZUCAR DE CANELA Y NARANJA

THIS RECIPE IS MADE USING A ROSETTE MOLD.
(MAKES ABOUT 5 DOZEN)

3 cups shortening or frying oil, heated in a pot to 365°
1 cup all-purpose flour
1 cup milk
2 tablespoons sugar
1 cup Orange-Cinnamon Sugar Mix (A)
1 egg unbeaten
½ teaspoon salt

MIX ingredients in a blender until they form a smooth batter, without lumps. Let rest overnight, refrigerated or for at least 3–4 hours.

Preheat oil to 375°. Assemble the mold and heat it for about 2–3 minutes in the hot shortening or oil. Remove mold and drain excess oil.

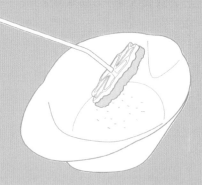

a.

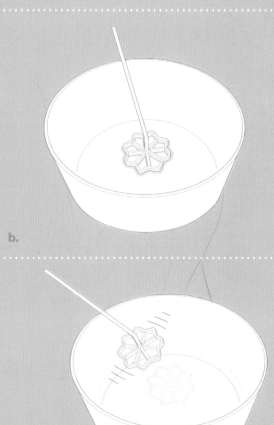

b.

c.

Making buñuelos with rosette mold.
Figure by Verticalarray, Inc.

Mexican Sweet Fritters with Atole / *Buñuelos con Atole*.
Photo by Adriana Almazán Lahl.

A. Dip mold into batter, only allowing the batter to come to the halfway point of the mold so that when frying the shell will slide off. *Do not submerge completely into batter.*

B. Dip battered mold into the heated oil and fry for about 45 seconds or until shell is lightly brown. To avoid greasy or soggy shells, do not overfry. **C.** Remove. Shells should easily drop off the mold. Drain excess oil off on paper towels.

Dip in the orange-cinnamon sugar. This must be done while the buñuelos are still warm. Store at room temperature in an uncovered container in a dry place. 🐝

A. Orange-Cinnamon Sugar Mix

6 tablespoons sugar
1 teaspoon freshly ground cinnamon
1 teaspoon orange zest

MIX sugar with cinnamon and orange zest. 🐝

TRADITIONAL STREET FRITTERS WITH PILONCILLO SYRUP / BUÑUELOS CON MIEL DE PILONCILLO

THIS RECIPE IS MADE WITHOUT A ROSETTE MOLD.
(MAKES 10–12)

3 cups all-purpose flour plus 3 spoonfuls
1 teaspoon baking powder
Pinch of salt
1 tablespoon sugar
1 egg
½ cup freshly squeezed orange juice
1 teaspoon ground anise seeds
4 tablespoons unsalted butter, vegetable shortening, or lard, plus more for buttering the bowl
1 cup water
5 tomatillo husks
¼ cup boiling water
4 cups vegetable oil, for frying
Piloncillo Syrup (A)
Orange-Cinnamon Sugar Mix (see above, p. 53)

BRING ¼ cup of water to a boil and add tomatillo husk, using a wooden spoon to push husk into the water, remove from heat and let rest for 10 minutes, reserve and let it cool to room temperature.

In the bowl of a mixer set (KitchenAid or similar) with the hook attachment, add flour, baking powder, salt, and sugar. Make room in the middle and add egg, orange juice, reserved tomatillo water, and ground anise seeds. Begin beating, at low speed, for 2 minutes. Add the butter and continue beating for another 10 to 12 minutes. The dough should be very smooth and elastic.

Place dough in a large greased bowl and let it rest for 30 minutes covered with a towel. Divide the dough into twelve ½-inch balls. Place these on a baking sheet and let them rest another 10 minutes, covered with a towel.

Sprinkle a large flat surface with flour and flour a rolling pin. Roll each ball into rounds about 6 inches wide and as thin as you can without tearing them. Stretch them as if they were pizza rounds. Place each circle on a table or countertop. Dust the surface with flour each time you roll out a new disc, being sure to keep the rolling pin well floured as well.

Place all the rounds on a countertop and let them rest for 30 minutes. In a large, deep skillet heat 2 cups of oil to 375°. Fry one buñuelo at a time. Fry for about 20 seconds per side, until you see bubbles forming and buñuelo turns a golden brown. Turn with tongs and cook the other side until it is brown and crisp. Place on a plate with paper towels to drain oil; cover with cinnamon sugar while still warm or drizzle with piloncillo syrup. 🐦

A. Piloncillo Syrup

1 pound piloncillo, chopped (or substitute 2 cups dark brown sugar)
1 cup boiling water
½ tablespoon fresh orange rind
1 cinnamon stick

IN a medium saucepan add the piloncillo, pouring the boiling water over it, and add cinnamon and orange rind. If the piloncillo is not broken up into small pieces or grated, let it melt just a few minutes in the hot water. Bring to a simmer and cook over medium heat until it achieves a syrupy consistency, about 15 minutes. Remove from the heat. Remove the cinnamon, or, if it is broken into pieces, strain. 🐦

PILONCILLO VERSUS BROWN SUGAR

Called *piloncillo* (little loaf) because of the traditional shape in which this smoky, caramel-like, earthy sugar is produced, it has far more flavor than brown sugar, which is generally just white sugar with a small amount of molasses added back to it. Just like brown sugar, there are two varieties of piloncillo: one is lighter (*blanco*) and one darker (*oscuro*). It is unrefined and commonly used in Mexico, where it has been around for almost five hundred years. Made from crushed sugar cane (which was introduced to Mexico by the Spaniards), the juice is collected, boiled, and poured into molds, where it hardens into blocks. To use it, pound with a meat hammer while it is still in its plastic baggie, or it can be grated using a cheese grater. In Mexico, it is common to throw the plastic bag of piloncillo on the floor to break it up into usable pieces.

SOME ingredients used to make *ponche* are more seasonal and even exotic. Depending upon where you live, you may be able to locate fresh *tejocotes*, known to the Aztecs as *texocotli* (stone fruit). The fruit of the hawthorn tree, these resemble crab apples, have a sweet-sour flavor and an orange-to-golden-yellow color. Although abundant in the Mexican highlands, tejocote could not be imported to this country because of its potential to harbor exotic insects. Mexicans are all about authentic ingredients for their special family recipes, so devotees had to resort to illegal enterprise to obtain the tejocotes. In 2009, the *Los Angeles Times* reported that "nationwide, tejocote was the fruit most seized by the U.S. Department of Agriculture's Smuggling, Interdiction and Trade Compliance program from 2002 to 2006."[4]

Demand and seizures gave birth to a lucrative new industry, the report continued, after "a market vendor named Doña Maria asked [a USDA smuggling control officer] how to obtain legal supplies, and he suggested that farmers grow tejocotes domestically."[5] And so, a successful exotic fruit farmer in Pauma Valley in San Diego County added tejocotes to his crop. In 1999, Jaime Serrato, who was familiar with tejocotes from his childhood in Michoacán, started grafting trees from bud wood in his orchard and today has thirty-five acres of trees. Today, tejocotes can be widely found jarred or canned and fresh during the holidays in regional Latino markets.

WARM HOLIDAY PUNCH / PONCHE NAVIDEÑO

(SERVES 10–12)

25 tejocotes, cut in half
2 small pears, cut bite-sized
1 cup raisins
2 cups prunes
4 small yellow apples, chopped bite sized
2 gallons boiling water
1⅓ cups tamarind pods, peeled
3½ ounces dry hibiscus
1 star anise
6 cinnamon sticks
2 whole cloves

2 cups of fresh orange juice
6 pieces sugar cane, cut in quarters lengthwise
1 orange, sliced and cut in half

WASH all fruits and cut as required. In a large pot, boil water and add tamarind, hibiscus, star anise, cinnamon sticks, and cloves. Boil on high for 10–15 minutes; strain mixture to remove any remains of flowers, spices, or tamarind. Once strained, add all cut fruits and cook 5 minutes. Add dry fruits, orange juice, and sugar cane. Cook for additional 20 minutes. Serve in a mug or a clay cup garnished with a sugar cane stick intended to be used as a spoon and for eating the fruits.

Decorate with half a slice of orange. Optional: add a splash of rum, cane spirit (*aguardiente*), or brandy. 🦋

PONCHE

According to historians, ponche comes from Persia, where they used to consume a very similar drink they called *"panch,"* made with water, lemon, herbs, sugar, and rum. This tradition migrated to Europe and acquired the name "punch," known in Spain as *"ponche."*

The First Midnight Mass

Pedro de Gante, the first Franciscan missionary to make contact with the Mexicas (the indigenous people we know as the Aztecs) began the custom of celebrating Christmas with a Misa de Gallo, or "Mass at the First Crow of the Rooster," in 1538. The Aztec festival commemorating the birth of the sun god Huitzilopochtli, which occurred in December, began at midnight, so the transition to a Midnight Mass, celebrating the birth of Jesus with the recently converted Indians, was not difficult. Father de Gante "invited all the Indians for twenty leagues around Mexico City to attend, and they came in droves, some by land and others by water. . . . [They] loved the new feast day and adopted it wholeheartedly."[1] By 1587 skyrockets (*cohetes*), torches, and sparklers (*luces de bengala*) had been added to the Aztecs' contributions to the festivities of flowers and feathers. All this made the Mass so popular that in that same year the Pope had to grant permission for it to be held outdoors.

Christmas Celebrations in Modern Mexico

Christmas in Mexico is a religious as well as a national holiday and midnight on Noche Buena (Holy Night) is when the real fiesta begins, even today. Catholic families get together to celebrate the last day of posadas (see chapter 2) at the home of the host for the evening. The posada carol is sung when the door is opened and guests are welcomed with luces de bengala and a baby Jesus figurine, called *El Niño Dios*, which is carried all the way to the altar and inserted into the nativity.

A special lullaby is sung before the baby is laid on the manger (*pesebre*). In just about every household, Christmas Eve in Mexico is a dress-up occasion.

Mexico's Famous Nativities

Nacimientos

While every Mexican home may not have a Christmas tree (a European tradition that came late to Mexico, in the 1950s), nearly everyone does have a nativity scene (*nacimiento*) that is set in place December 16 and stays up until February 2. Nacimientos originated in Italy (St. Francis of Assisi is credited with creating the first one in 1223), but there is nothing quite like those found in Mexico.

These nativity scenes are absolutely the centerpieces of Mexican Christmas home décor. Entire villages appear on tabletops, and in some homes, a room is devoted to the display—that's how expansive it can be! Appearing among the traditional figures of Joseph, Mary, the Three Wise Men, and the manger may be the rooster who crowed to announce the birth of baby Jesus, fish in the river (*los peces en el rio*) from a Mexican carol, a multitude of animals, even pork roasting on spits and women making tortillas. In a rather literal interpretation of events, notably

Nacimiento.
Photo by Adriana Almazán Lahl.

El Niño Dios
figures.
Photo by Victoria
Tarpin.

missing from the nacimiento until Christmas Eve is the baby Jesus, since his birth has not yet occurred. Still, there is often a charming disconnection between fact and fantasy in these scenes, which may have snow alongside tropical palms or cactus. Some even include an evil serpent or grotesque Lucifer lurking in the shadows.

El Niño Dios

The figure of the baby Jesus is of particular importance in Mexico, and he may be dressed in elaborate, handmade outfits for presentation at the altar, especially on Noche Buena. Adoration of the infant figure began in the late 1500s, and interestingly, it was Mexico's indigenous people, rather than the Church leaders, who promulgated this devotion and tradition. In some areas, the Holy Infant is venerated with his own festival day. In Xochimilco in Central Mexico, February 6 is *Día de Niñopa*, when meal is prepared for over five thousand followers, attracting visitors from all over Mexico.

Pastorelas

Pastoral plays (*pastorelas*) start at the beginning of December and continue through January 6, Día de los Reyes (see chapter 6). They are a dramatization of the fight between good and evil, between temptation and faith, populated with a mix of the real and the divine. Characters often include angels and demons with human characteristics. They have a long and fascinating history.

When the Franciscans arrived in Tenochtitlan, the capital of the ancient Mexica, they found the Aztecs entertaining themselves with performances in the plazas that combined song, theater, and dance. Dramatic reenactments were more than a form of entertainment for the indigenous; they saw them as a way to communicate with their gods. It was not uncommon for their priests to act out battles or dramatize a victory or defeat. In a culture with no written language, these plays also served to pass down the Aztecs' verbal history.

When the Spanish conquered Tenochtitlan in 1521, the monks quickly took advantage of the native people's artistic ability, using it to bridge two cultures that had nothing in common, and the pastorela as a rite of the Christmas holiday in Mexico was born. The first formal record of these plays dates back to 1536 and is called *"El Auto de Adoración de los Reyes Magos"* (The Adoration of the Three Kings). Written in Nahuatl, it included dancing and music and had thirteen actors: the baby Jesus, Mary, Joseph, the Three Kings, their messenger, an angel, King Herod, his chief steward, and three Jewish priests.

The indigenous people were enthralled with the story of the shepherds who followed a shining star, similar to their own legend in which a great comet would appear to announce the end of one empire and the birth of a new one. They soon assumed control of the entire production of the pastorelas. Not only were they the actors, musicians, costume and set designers, and dancers, adding their own pre-Hispanic dances (*mitote*), it is believed that it was also the Aztecs who translated the texts into Nahuatl, ironically facilitating the evangelizing mission of the plays.

With time, the mischievous Mexicans added funny and irreverent touches to the pastorelas, causing them to be banned from the churches and relegated to the streets. Freed of restraints, they acquired a certain spontaneity and thus were subsequently declared irreligious and prohibited altogether. They survived primarily in Mexico's pueblos and ranchos, far from the capitals of political and Church influence.

Revived in 1821 thanks to a play by famed Mexican writer and political thinker José Joaquín Fernández de Lizardi, the pastorela reappeared in Mexico City and never again lost its place among Mexico's Christmas traditions. Today, pastorelas are distinct from those of the past and vary widely in their characters and presentation; some even contain mild sexual innuendo. While the basic theme continues to be the struggle between good and evil, the message is more one of good news and renewal than religious doctrine. Famous for their double entendres, political irony, and mockery of public personages figure strongly in today's pastorelas.

Poinsettias: La Flor de Noche Buena

La flor de Noche Buena (the flower of the Holy Night) is the poinsettia, in and of itself an almost miraculous plant: the flower's red petals are really not petals at all, rather, they are petal-like leaves, red in response to the longer nights of November and December. The starry yellow center is the actual flower. The Aztecs called the poinsettia *cuetlaxochitl*. They used it to make a reddish-purple dye and to reduce fever.

The beautiful legend of la flor de Noche Buena began in the sixteenth century, and by the seventeenth century, Franciscan monks in Mexico had begun to include the plants in their Christmas celebrations. Much like the Little Drummer Boy, the legend recounts a poor child with no gift to leave at the altar for Mary and the baby Jesus. In some versions it is a boy named Pablo; in others it is a girl named Maria; in still others, they are brother and sister. In some, an angel appears and points out a gift right there beside the path where the child or children are walking, while in others, the children think of this themselves. They gather some weeds growing along the roadside and place the sorry-looking plants on the altar. The children are ridiculed for this gift, but then, all of a sudden, the weeds burst into beautiful red blossoms with yellow stars in their centers.

Widely considered "Mexico's Christmas Present to the World," today, $220 million worth of poinsettias are sold globally during the holiday season every year. This all began in 1825, when Joel Roberts Poinsett was appointed the first American ambassador to Mexico. While there, he noticed the beautiful flor de Noche Buena, brought some cuttings back to the United States and began cultivating what were to become known outside of Mexico as poinsettias in his greenhouse. His cultivation techniques are still in use today.

A Midnight Dinner

Christmas dinners in Mexico vary depending on one's family background, with some following traditions fused with those of Europe, a remnant of the Spanish occupation and French Intervention. Among families in Central Mexico, where the European impact was strongest, the menu will likely include turkey with meat stuffing, cod stew (*bacalao*) and *romeritos* (Mexican greens typically served with shrimp cakes), beet salad, dessert, followed by hot holiday punch (*ponche*) or café de olla (coffee prepared in a clay pot, which imparts a subtle but detectable flavor, which on Noche Buena is served with *piquete*, or spiked), and Spanish hard almond nougat (*turrones*).

A Noche Buena dinner that might be more common to Mexico's pueblos and ranchos, where there is typically less regard for traces of European traditions, might include pozole, tostadas, or pork shoulder with adobo sauce, and a fruit salad.

TURKEY

TURKEY was part of the Aztec diet and is native to America. The Aztec word for turkey, *huexoloti*, has evolved to become *guajolote* in Mexico today. It is still usual to serve a fresh-killed guajolote for a special occasion. The Spanish Jesuits were the first ones to bring turkey to Europe, and they referred to it as *gallina de las Indias* (hen from the Indians). As appreciation of turkey grew among European royalty and nobles, it became as a symbol of good taste, and the custom of serving turkey for Christmas gained popularity as it was considered a feast suitable for kings and even popes. The first recipes for turkey appeared in a cookbook published in 1570, written by Bartolomeo Scappi, private chef to Pope Pius V.

TURKEY WITH MEAT AND APPLE STUFFING / PAVO RELLENO DE CARNE Y MANZANAS

(SERVES 8–10)

8–12 pound turkey, cavities washed and cleaned
Juice of 1 lemon
½ onion
1 garlic clove
1 glass white wine
2 tablespoons sweet paprika (*pimentón dulce*)
Salt to taste
Stuffing (A)

MENU 3.1: CHRISTMAS EVE

Entrées / *Platos Fuertes*
Turkey with Meat and Apple Stuffing / *Pavo con Relleno de Carne y Manzanas*
Mexican Greens with Cactus Paddles and Shrimp Patties / *Romeritos con Nopales y Tortitas de Camarón*
Bacalao a la Vizcaina
Salad / *Ensalada*
Christmas Eve Salad / *Ensalada de Noche Buena*
Dessert / *Postre*
Christmas Log / *Tronco de Navidad*

P LACE turkey on cooking rack and rub with lemon juice inside the cavities and out; check that it is completely clean, with no feathers. (If you decide to brine your turkey: purée onion and garlic with wine in a blender. Strain mix and inject turkey with a large brine syringe all over with the liquid, following instructions of syringe manufacturer. Allow to rest for at least half a day [or a day if possible] in refrigerator during this process, covered well with foil.)

Prepare stuffing according to directions, below. Once the stuffing is cold, place turkey, breast side up, on a flat wire rack in a shallow roasting pan 2–2½ inches deep. Tuck wings tips under shoulders of bird, stuff carefully, and truss with legs crossed. It may be necessary to use pins or skewers to close turkey's cavity to pre-vent stuffing from spilling (you should be able to find a turkey set at your local store that includes everything you'll need to close the turkey well). Add chicken stock to bottom of the roasting pan.

Melt butter and mix with sweet paprika; brush the turkey with this mix to cover the outside completely. Cover with foil and place in oven at 350° for 3 hours (35 minutes per pound). Remove and bake an additional 40 minutes, basting every 25 minutes, until breast reaches 170° (check with meat thermometer) and turkey is golden brown. Let bird stand on carving board covered with foil for at least 30 minutes before serving. 🐦

A. Stuffing / Relleno

¼ cup olive oil
1 Spanish white onion, minced
1 large carrot, finely chopped
2 celery stalks, finely chopped
½ pound ground pork
½ pound ground beef
2 cloves garlic
4 tablespoons tomato purée (see "Basic Recipes for Mexican Cooking," p. 15)
4 apples, peeled and small chopped
2 bay leaves (or ground ½ teaspoon)
¼ teaspoon ground cumin powder
¼ cup fresh parsley, finely chopped
¼ tablespoon ground cinnamon
¼ teaspoon ground cloves
4 ounces bread crumbs
3½ ounces almonds, peeled and chopped
6 ounces raisins
1 teaspoon ground pepper
Salt to taste
½ cup dry white wine or sherry
4 ounces bread crumbs, croutons, or unflavored prepared stuffing mix
½ teaspoon ground nutmeg

IN a large saucepan, heat olive oil and add onions, carrots, and celery. Cook on high temperature until lightly browned (5 minutes). Add ground meat, bay leaves, and garlic and continue cooking until browned (25 minutes). Add parsley and cumin with tomato purée, herbs, apples, and spices (cinnamon and clove) and continue cooking for an additional 10 minutes. Add wine and cook for 5 more minutes. Add bread crumbs, almonds, raisins, pepper, nutmeg, and salt to taste. Cook covered for 10 minutes more and set aside to allow stuffing to completely cool down. The stuffing should be completely dry with no drippings (if needed, add more bread crumbs, or croutons if you prefer). 🐟

CHRISTMAS EVE SALAD / ENSALADA DE NOCHE BUENA

(SERVES 8–10)

4 beets, cooked, peeled, and small-chopped
6 carrots, peeled and shredded
1 cup celery, finely chopped
1 cup pineapple, fresh or canned, small-chopped
1 cup apple, peeled and small-chopped
1 cup almonds, peeled and chopped, or pine nuts (do not use both)
½ cup raisins
1 cup mayonnaise
2 tablespoons vinegar
2 tablespoons Worcestershire sauce
½ cup Mexican sour cream
½ tablespoon tarragon
Salt and pepper

Mix all ingredients and place in refrigerator for at least 1 hour. Serve inside half of a carved pineapple or a serving platter on top of fresh lettuce leaves. 🐟

SEAFOOD AND CHRISTMAS EVE

THE introduction to Mexico of the Spanish diet was an imposition of the Church. Therefore, some of Mexico's traditional Christmas dinner dishes have their roots in the Catholic customs. One such custom is fasting. As this type of fast often included abstinence from meat (as with Lent and Fridays, for example), seafood became and still is frequently eaten for special holy days. While the 1983 Code of Canon Law eliminated the fast on Christmas Eve (before the Vigil Mass) the seafood-centric menus still abound.

Christmas Eve Salad / *Ensalada de Noche Buena.*
Photo by Adriana Almazán Lahl.

BACALAO A LA VIZCAÍNA

VIZCAYA IS THE SPANISH WORD FOR "BISCAY," A BASQUE PROVINCE IN SPAIN. THIS RECIPE LIKELY ORIGINATED THERE, AS DRIED COD, POTATOES, OLIVE OIL, OLIVES, AND CAPERS WERE COMPLETELY UNKNOWN IN MEXICO BEFORE THE SPANISH CONQUEST. THE GÜERO CHILES ARE DEFINITELY A MEXICAN UPDATE OF THE DISH, THOUGH, AND DO NOT APPEAR IN SOME OTHER VERSIONS OF THIS RECIPE. (SERVES 8–10)

2 pounds dry salted cod
1 cup red bell pepper, roasted, peeled, and cut in long strips
2 pounds tomatoes
1 cup good-quality olive oil for frying
4 garlic cloves, finely chopped
2 small white onions, finely chopped
2 cups parsley, finely chopped
1 cup stuffed green olives
2 cups capers

Bacalao a la Vizcaina.
Photo by Adriana Almazán Lahl.

2 pounds small potatoes, cooked and peeled
1 cup water
6 güero chiles or banana wax peppers (canned or jarred)
½ cup slivered almonds, peeled and toasted
Salt and pepper to taste (salt is most likely unnecessary)

RINSE cod with hot water for at least 12 hours (even overnight), changing water three or four times. The next morning, cover with fresh water and boil until cooked (20 minutes). Rinse again and shred fish finely, being careful to remove fish bones.

On a comal, dry-roast (see "Common Mexican Cooking Tools and Techniques," p. 335) the bell peppers and tomatoes (they will then be easy to peel). Remove seeds and stem from bell peppers, cut in strips, and set aside. Peel and chop tomatoes very fine or, using a molcajete, crush to purée (see "Common Mexican Cooking Tools and Techniques," p. 336), but do not allow to liquefy. Heat olive oil and add garlic and onions, and cook until lightly browned. Add tomatoes and parsley and cook covered at low heat until well done and seasoned, around ½ hour. Add olives, capers, potatoes, and shredded cod; cook for 25 minutes, adding up to 1 cup of water if mixtures becomes too dry. Add güero chiles (do not add liquid from the jar or can) and cook for another ten minutes for flavors to marry. Serve garnished with the red bell pepper and almonds; season to taste.

It is very unlikely that you will need to add salt, as the cod continues to release salt. If it is too salty, add two more cubed potatoes and ½ cup of water. The potatoes will absorb the extra salt. Cook for an additional 20 minutes stirring constantly to be sure the cod is not sticking to the bottom of the pan. Add more water if needed. 🐟

ROMERITOS

ROMERITOS are from Mexico City and are considered a sacred herb, named for their resemblance to rosemary. They grow wild and are succulent, stringy-looking greens that taste like spinach—and may be prepared the same way. Find romeritos at your local Latino market. Note: when asking for romeritos, don't get them confused with *romeros* (rosemary). They are typically only stocked seasonally (romeritos are traditionally eaten during Lent and at Christmas) and for a few days. Feel free to substitute spinach.

MEXICAN GREENS WITH CACTUS PADDLES AND SHRIMP PATTIES / ROMERITOS CON NOPALES Y TORTITAS DE CAMARÓN

(SERVES 10–14)

2 pounds romeritos or fresh spinach, cleaned and well rinsed (be sure to discard any thick stalks), or 2 packages of frozen spinach, thawed and drained
6 cups water, divided
1 pound nopales (cactus paddles), thorns removed, and cut into strips
1 small onion
Pinch of baking soda
1 pound small potatoes, peeled and cut in half
3½ ounces dried shrimp
1 cup mole paste (see p. 306)
Shrimp Patties (A)
Salt to taste

PLACE romeritos or spinach in a saucepan with 3 cups of water. Cook on low heat for 15 minutes; rinse and set aside. In the same saucepan, bring 2 cups of water

Mexican Greens with Cactus Paddles and Shrimp Cakes / *Romeritos con Nopales y Tortitas de Camarón.*
Photo by Adriana Almazán Lahl.

to a boil. Add nopales, onion, baking soda, and salt to taste. Cook on high heat for 15–20 minutes till tender. Remove slime from nopales by rinsing a couple of times; place in colander and set aside.

Cook potatoes until tender but firm (15 minutes in boiling water).

Soak shrimp in 1 cup of very hot water for 10 minutes.

In a large saucepan, reconstitute mole paste according to instructions (see "Basic Recipes for Mexican Cooking," p. 13), dissolving mole sauce with shrimp water in place of chicken stock. Add romeritos, nopales, potatoes, and dry shrimp. Cook on medium-low heat and season with salt to taste for 10 minutes, stirring constantly to avoid burning and sticking to the pan. Add shrimp patties. Drench patties in mole sauce before serving. 🦐

A. Shrimp Patties / Tortitas de Camarón

2 egg whites
2 yolks, lightly beaten
1 cup dried, ground shrimp
1 cup vegetable oil

BEAT the egg whites until stiff. Add beaten yolks and shrimp. Mix well but gently with a spoon. Form small pancakes or patties, approximately 2½ inches in diameter, and drop into preheated oil (350°). Deep fry in small batches. The fritters should be golden brown on both sides. Drain oil by letting the fritters rest on a paper towel. 🐟

CHRISTMAS LOG / TRONCO NAVIDEÑO

THIS IS AN ORIGINAL RECIPE OF THE ARELLANO-ANGELES FAMILY.
(SERVES 6–8)

7 eggs
5 tablespoons sugar
4 tablespoons flour
Rind of 1 orange
1 cup fruit jam of your choice.
Cocoa Frosting (A)

SEPARATE egg whites from yolks and whisk whites until they form stiff peaks. Gently whisk in sugar, slightly beaten yolks, flour, and orange rind. Fold all ingredients together. Spread this batter evenly into a 9-inch pregreased baking pan lined with parchment paper. Bake for 7–10 minutes in the preheated (350°) oven.

Christmas Log / *Tronco de Navidad*.
Photo by Adriana Almazán Lahl.

Meanwhile, dust a clean dish towel with confectioner's sugar. Remove cake and run a knife around the edge of the pan, turning the warm cake out onto the towel. Remove parchment paper. Roll the cake up with the towel. Cool for 30 minutes.

Unroll the cake, and spread jam or desired filling within 1 inch of the edge. Roll the cake up with the filling inside. Place cake side down onto a serving plate. Cut 2 inches off the cake and place on the side of the cake simulating a tree trunk. Add Cocoa Frosting and refrigerate until serving. Dust with confectioner's sugar before serving. 🦗

A. Cocoa Frosting

5 ounces cocoa butter
7 ounces powdered sugar
3½ ounces powdered milk
1 teaspoon lecithin

MELT butter to 160° (check with candy thermometer). Add powdered sugar, milk, and lecithin, in order. Mix well and let rest. 🦗

LEG OF PORK ADOBADO / PIERNA ADOBADA

WE OFFER TWO DELICIOUS RECIPES FOR LEG OF PORK. THIS ONE IS FOR A SUCCULENT AND GARLICKY ADOBO SAUCE. THE NEXT ONE IS FOR A PORK LEG THAT IS LARDED WITH BACON SLICES, ALMONDS, GARLIC, AND PRUNES: FLAVOR IS RELEASED AS THE BACON LARD MELTS AND THE PRUNES AND GARLIC CARAMELIZE INSIDE THE MEAT AS IT SLOWLY ROASTS.

(SERVES 10–12)

3 dry guajillo chiles or New Mexico chiles
2 dry cascabel chiles
6 medium anchos chiles
1 chipotle chile, dry or in adobo sauce
1 tablespoon whole allspice
1 teaspoon coriander
½ teaspoon cumin seeds

MENU 3.2: CHRISTMAS EVE

Entrée / *Plato Fuerte*
Leg of Pork Adobado / *Pierna Adobada* or
Pork Leg with Bacon Lardons and Adobo Sauce / *Puerco Adobado Mechado*

Salad / *Ensalada*
Christmas Eve Salad / *Ensalada de Noche Buena*

Side / *Guarnición*
Tamale Casserole / *Tamal de Cazuela*

Dessert / *Postre*
Mexican Fruit Punch Gelatin Dessert / *Gelatina de Ponche de Frutas*

Beverage / *Bebida*
"Clay Pot" Coffee / *Café de Olla*

1 teaspoon Mexican oregano

10 fresh epazote or 2 teaspoons dry epazote

½ cup apple cider vinegar

2 tablespoons brown sugar, piloncillo, or honey

½ Spanish white onion

1 cup water

8 pounds pork leg or butt

20–25 pitted prunes

16 garlic cloves

Salt to taste

PLACE all chiles in hot water to rehydrate. Once hydrated and soft, mix them with all ingredients except the pork, the prunes, and the garlic cloves. Mix ingredients well in blender until a thick paste forms (this is the adobo). Add water if needed to keep the blender moving. The texture should be that of a thick tomato paste.

Place pork in a baking pan and insert a long knife or knife-sharpening steel lengthwise all the way through the meat, creating four long "tunnels" in the meat. Alternating between garlic cloves and prunes, insert them into each "tunnel" until all four tunnels are full. Cover the roast with adobo mix and let it rest 3 hours in the refrigerator or overnight covered with plastic wrap.

Preheat oven to 350°. Before placing the pork in the oven, cover with foil and add ½ cup of water to the bottom of the roasting pan. Roast at 350° for 3 hours, basting pork every 30 minutes. After 3 hours, uncover and bake for an additional 45 minutes, basting every 15 minutes, adding water as needed during the basting process. Let roast rest for at least 25 minutes before serving. 🐖

PORK LEG WITH BACON LARDONS AND ADOBO SAUCE / PUERCO ADOBADO MECHADO

(SERVES 10–12)

Juice of 6 oranges

¼ cup white vinegar

6 pounds pork butt or leg, boneless

6 anchos chiles, stems removed

8 dry pasilla chiles, stems removed

2 prunes

½ stick of cinnamon

10 peppercorns

1 tablespoon marjoram

½ tablespoon cumin

6 garlic cloves, quartered

1 tablespoon fresh grated ginger

¼ Spanish white onion

Salt to taste

2 tablespoons vegetable oil

3 slices of bacon, cut in half lengthwise

15 almonds

IN a saucepan add orange juice, vinegar, chiles, 2 prunes, cinnamon, peppercorns, marjoram, cumin, 2 garlic cloves, ¼ onion, ginger, and salt. Simmer for 10 minutes on low heat. Allow to cool for 10 minutes and add to a blender, mixing to make a smooth purée (this is the adobo). In a saucepan add oil and adobo, simmer for 10 minutes, and set aside; allow to cool completely.

To lard meat, with a sharp knife, create six deep "tunnels" lengthwise into the pork butt. Cut the bacon into long, thin strips and with a larding needle push bacon inside the meat, push in the prunes, almonds, and pieces of garlic as far as you can get inside the meat. If you don't have a larding needle, use a long knife or knife-sharpening steel to make deep holes through the meat to help you push the ingredients inside.

Place pork in a baking dish, rub all over with adobo, and cover with plastic wrap. Allow to marinade inside refrigerator for 3 hours or overnight. Bring pork to room temperature and place on a baking rack; with a baking brush, cover with adobo sauce again. Bake at 375° for 90 minutes or until you reach an internal temperature of 145°. You can also barbeque over open fire if desired. 🦟

CHRİSTMAS APPLE SALAD /
ENSALADA NAVİDEÑA DE MANZANA

(SERVES 8–10)

3 yellow apples

2 cups cold water

Juice of 1 lemon

1 celery stalk, finely chopped

1 slice of pineapple, diced (can use canned)

¼ cup raisins

½ cup Mexican sour cream

¼ cup pecans, chopped

¼ cup condensed milk

¼ teaspoon salt

PEEL and dice apples, place in 2 cups of cold water with the juice of one lemon; set aside for 10 minutes. Meanwhile, dice pineapple. Proceed to mix all ingredients, incorporate apples, and refrigerate for at least an hour before serving. 🦟

Tamale Casserole / *Tamal de Cazuela*.
Photo by Adriana Almazán Lahl.

TAMALE CASSEROLE / TAMAL DE CAZUELA

(SERVES 6)

3 chiles (ancho, mulato, and pasilla, one each) roasted, deveined, seeds removed, and
    minced (see "Common Mexican Cooking Tools and Techniques" p. 334)
1 tomato, seeded, roasted, and puréed
½ pound cooked pork or chicken, pulled (see "Basic Recipes for Mexican Cooking," p. 11)
2 tablespoons olive oil
2 pounds corn tamal flour (Maseca brand, must be tamal flour not tortilla flour)
1 cup chicken broth (see "Basic Recipes for Mexican Cooking," p. 11)
¾ pound lard
1 tablespoon chopped epazote leaves or ½ tablespoon dry epazote
Salt to taste
1 tablespoon yeast or baking powder
15 cornhusks
1 avocado
Mexican sour cream

PREPARE a chile sauce by mixing chiles and tomato. Purée in blender until smooth
and set aside. Mix the chile sauce with the meat or chicken. Add sauce and meat

mixture to a sauté pan with 2 tablespoons of hot olive oil and heat until it thickens and is cooked (10 minutes). Salt to taste and set aside.

To make the masa, pour tamal flour in a saucepan with the broth, mixing by hand until you obtain a thick paste. Cook over low heat for 7 minutes. Pour melted lard into the flour and broth mixture; add epazote and salt. Add the baking powder, mix again, and cook for additional 5–10 minutes.

To prepare the tamal, in a deep 9-inch round baking dish place cornhusks (about 6) to cover bottom and spread a layer of masa on top of husks. Pour the meat with chile sauce over the masa layer and cover with another thick layer of masa, carefully placed, working with your bare hands. Cover with cornhusks. Put it in the oven at 350° covered with foil over Baño Maria (see "Common Mexican Cooking Tools and Techniques," p. 333) for 1 hour and 15 minutes.

Allow to rest for 15 minutes before serving. Remove cornhusk and cut the tamal de cazuela, carefully removing from baking dish using a spatula. Serve garnished with avocado slices and a dollop of sour cream or crema Mexicana. ><

MEXICAN FRUIT PUNCH GELATIN DESSERT / GELATINA DE PONCHE DE FRUTAS

(SERVES 8–10)

4 cups water
¼ pound fresh tejocotes or ½ cup frozen or canned, seeded and chopped
1 cinnamon stick
2 gelatin envelopes, lemon flavor
1 (8-ounce) can chopped pineapple, drained
¾ cup apple, chopped
12 prunes, finely chopped
1 (5-ounce) can condensed milk
Rum (optional)

EXCEPT for the prunes, cut all fruit into slices, retaining their natural shape as much as possible. Bring water to a boil, add tejocotes and cinnamon stick, and cook for 10 minutes over high heat. Rinse tejocotes and reserve the liquid; remove cinnamon stick. Add 1⅓ cups of the reserved liquid to 1 envelope of gelatin and mix for 2 minutes, dissolving gelatin completely. Incorporate all fruit and place in a gelatin mold (mold should not be filled to top); refrigerate for an hour or until gelatin dessert sets.

Meanwhile, add 1 envelope of gelatin to the remaining liquid and mix for 2 minutes, until gelatin dissolves completely; add condensed milk and mix well. Once first gelatin layer is set, pour this second, opaque, layer of gelatin over the first while it is still in the mold, refrigerate 2 additional hours or overnight.

To unmold gelatin dessert, place bowl in a larger bowl filled with hot water, for 10–15 seconds. Place a serving plate on top and flip mold in one motion. Gelatin should unmold easily. For a fun adult version, add a generous splash of rum and mix before adding the fruit. 🐟

"CLAY POT" COFFEE / CAFÉ DE OLLA

THE CLAY POT USED FOR THIS RECIPE ADDS A SUBTLE BUT PERCEPTIBLE FLAVOR TO THE COFFEE
(SERVES 8)

4½ ounces piloncillo, roughly chopped
Zest of ½ orange, finely chopped
2 whole cloves
3-inch piece of cinnamon stick
¾ cup freshly ground, dark-roasted Mexican coffee

IN a clay pot (*olla*) or a kettle bring 9 cups of water to boil, combine the ingredients, stirring until the piloncillo is dissolved. Let steep at least 10 minutes.

Pour through a strainer before serving. For special occasions, it is traditional to add a splash of rum or brandy to the individual coffee cups (*piquete*). 🐟

CHRISTMAS / NAVIDAD
(DECEMBER 25)

IN MEXICO, there's always a get-together the afternoon after a big party, as these last until the wee hours. This is when the guests return for *recalentado* (reheated leftovers) and to *chismear* (gossip) about the previous night's adventures. Christmas morning usually starts this way: everyone bring the gifts they have received to show to friends and family, the great feast from Noche Buena is reheated, and all pitch in the get the house back in order. As afternoon gives way to evening, it's time to eat again. The menu is festive, but lighter. Pozole is traditional as a way to stretch the recalentado.

POZOLE

THE name of this cross between a broth and a stew comes from the Nahuatl "*pozolli.*" Corn (*maíz*) was a sacred plant for the Aztecs, and pozole was usually made with whole hominy kernels. When combined with meat, the dish was called *tlacatlaolli*, which was to be consumed on special occasions. The Aztecs used human meat, according to research by the National Institute of Anthropology and History and the Universidad Nacional Autónoma de México. The meal was shared among the whole community as an act of religious communion. After the conquest, pork was substituted.

WHITE POZOLE / POZOLE BLANCO

HOMINY TENDS TO EXPAND, SO KEEP BOILING WATER READY, AS YOU MIGHT NEED TO ADD A COUPLE OF CUPS TO YOUR POZOLE SO IT WILL HAVE ENOUGH STOCK.
(SERVES 6)

MENU 4.1: CHRISTMAS

Entrée / *Plato Fuerte*
White Pozole / *Pozole Blanco*
Side / *Guarnición*
Toasted Tortillas / *Tostadas*
Dessert / *Postre*
Torrejas

4 cups precooked hominy (available
    canned)
6–8 cups boiling water
1 small onion
2 garlic cloves
2 pounds pork shoulder or chicken breast, cut into large chunks
Salt to taste

Garnish:
1 Mexican lime per serving
Ground chile piquín
Mexican oregano
Radishes, finely sliced
Avocado slices
Shredded lettuce
Tostadas (A)

BOIL 6 cups of water and add hominy, onion, and garlic. Add meat and let cook on high heat for 35 minutes until hominy starts to open and break down. Add more hot water if needed, season with salt to taste, and let boil for additional half hour. Serve hot and garnish. Traditional service for pozole is to provide all of the above garnishes and allow guests to add to their taste, accompanied by tostadas. 🐦

A. Toasted Tortillas / Tostadas

THESE oven-baked tortillas are a healthy alternative to the deep-fried version. Just place tortillas in oven rack at 350 degrees for 10 minutes or until crisp. 🐦

Pozole Blanco.
Photo by Adriana Almazán Lahl.

TORREJAS

(MAKES 6–8)

2 eggs
4–5 Mexican *bolillo* rolls (or substitute 1½ large French baguettes or pound cake)
Vegetable oil for frying
Pinch of salt
Cinnamon Syrup (A)

SEPARATE egg yolks and whites. Beat the egg whites with a hand beater until spongy and firm. Add the egg yolks and continue to beat until they are mixed well.

Cut the bolillos, pound cake, or bread into slices about 2 inches thick. Dip each slice in the egg mixture and transfer into a very hot pan to which sufficient oil has been added so that the bottom is covered with about ⅛ inch of oil. Cook completely and turn over. Remove and pat the cooked pieces with a paper towel to drain any excess oil.

A. Cinnamon Syrup

¼ pound piloncillo, chopped (or substitute ½ cup dark brown sugar)
2½ cups boiling water
3 cinnamon sticks

IN a medium saucepan add the piloncillo, pouring the boiling water over it (if the piloncillo is not broken up into small pieces or grated, let it melt in just a few minutes in the hot water). Add cinnamon. Bring to a simmer and cook over medium heat for 15 minutes. Remove from the heat. Remove the cinnamon.

To serve, add ¼ cup cinnamon syrup to a bowl, place two torrejas on top, and add more syrup so they are completely soaked with syrup.

NOTES FROM THE ALMAZÁN KITCHEN

YOU can use a marble pound cake as well with great results. Just be careful when handling, as a pound cake will be more likely †to crumble during this process.

NEW YEAR'S EVE / FIN DE AÑO
(DECEMBER 31)

Mesoamerican Calendars and the New Year

While the Aztec and Maya calendars both recognized the 365-day year, these were divided into eighteen months of twenty days each, plus five nameless days referred to as *nemontemi* and considered an unstable period of the year. This was a period of fasting and abstinence and the only food permitted was tortillas, which were to be prepared in advance and only eaten once a day. These may have been the last five days of the Mesoamerican calendar year. Although there is some evidence to suggest that the New Year may have begun in February, we do not know exactly when these ominous days fell.

The yearly recurrence of these five extra days was a time of great trepidation among the Aztecs. Accounts note that they destroyed their household idols and domestic utensils, tore their clothes, and waited anxiously for New Year's morning. At dawn, there was great rejoicing, and new items were brought out to replace that which they had destroyed the night before. Surviving this custom is one common to Oaxaca on New Year's Eve, where buñuelos (see p. 51) are served on cracked pottery, which is then smashed on the ground.

Both the Aztecs and Mayans also used a 260-day ritual or sacred calendar. Every fifty-two years, the cycle of these two calendars coincided, an event referred to as "Binding of the Years" and celebrated with the New Fire Ceremony. A solemn and sacred rite, all fires were extinguished and, in hope of provoking the return of the morning sun marking the commencement of a new fifty-two-year cycle, a "new fire" was lit. The last ancient ceremony was held in 1507.

New Year's Day in Modern Mexico

Mexicans celebrate with a late-night dinner with their families, the traditional meal being turkey and mole. Some families attend *Misa de Gallo* (an early morning Mass, literally "Mass of the Rooster"; for more on the origins of this custom, see chapter 3) and ask the priest to bless twelve holy candles, which they then light at home on the first day of every month in the year ahead. Mexico's strong folkloric culture dominates on New Year's Eve, with plenty of rites, rituals, and superstitions.

ADRIANA'S MEMORIES

IN my house, we wrote our wishes on tissue paper, which we tied to a balloon and released outside, watching our hopes soar. At dinner, we ate lentils for prosperity. After the "Feliz Año" hugs, we would all grab a suitcase and run outside, making sure to go in and out of the house three times—a way to ensure that we would enjoy a year full of travel adventures. We also threw coins and candies from outside into the house for prosperity and sweetness all year round and burned candles and incense to get rid of any evil spirits, thoughts, and bad karma in general. My mom used to make a garland with rosemary, olives, and assorted herbs to welcome the New Year.

An amusing tradition is that of wearing colored underwear on New Year's Eve, with the color one chooses representing some desire for the coming year: red for love, yellow for good luck, green for improved finances, and white for peace.

Another tradition is that of making a list of all the bad events that occurred over the past twelve months, and just before midnight, throwing the list into a fire to remove negative energy from the New Year. The traditional dinner fare has special significance and usually includes

- pork as a symbol of abundance; it is common to have *pierna adobada* or *lechon*
- lentils, representing coins, hence lentil soup is often on the menu, for prosperity
- pasta or noodles, symbolizing long life
- twelve grapes, which are eaten and twelve wishes are made at midnight with the hope that for every grape you eat comes a great month in the year ahead

LENTİL SOUP WİTH FRUİT AND BACON / SOPA DE LENTEJAS CON FRUTA Y TOCİNO

(SERVES 6 CUPS OR 4 LARGE BOWLS)

1 pound lentils

4 cups chicken stock (see "Basic Recipes for Mexican Cooking," p. 11)

1 tablespoon olive oil

4 slices of chopped bacon

½ onion finely chopped

1 garlic clove, finely chopped

1½ cups tomato purée (see "Basic Recipes for Mexican Cooking," p. 15)

2 bay leaves

1 ripe pineapple, chopped

1 pound sweet plantain, peeled and chopped in ¼-inch pieces

Dash of nutmeg

Salt and pepper to taste

RINSE lentils two or three times, before adding them to 4 cups of chicken stock for 20 minutes. Meanwhile in a separate pot, add olive oil and chopped bacon. Cook until crisp and brown; remove bacon and set aside, retaining some oil/bacon fat.

Drain most of the oil from the pot leaving only 2 tablespoons of the oil/bacon fat. Add chopped onions and garlic to the pot with the oil and stir frequently for 3 to 4 minutes. Add tomato purée and bay leaves and cook 8–10 minutes on medium-high until mixture reduces to a thick paste.

Add tomato mixture to lentils and incorporate pineapple chunks, chopped plantain, and a dash of nutmeg. Continue cooking for another 15 minutes or until lentils become nice and tender, stirring occasionally. Finally, add salt and pepper to taste.

To serve, garnish with crispy bacon.

Roasted Suckling Pig / *Lechón Asado.*
Photo by Adriana Almazán Lahl.

ROASTED SUCKLİNG PİG WİTH FRUİT OR VEGETABLE STUFFİNG / LECHON ASADO CON RELLENO DE FRUTAS O VEGETALES

(SERVES 10)

20-pound piglet (3 to 6 weeks old)
Juice of 5 lemons
2 heads garlic, peeled, plus 6 garlic cloves
2 red onions, cut in slices
5 rosemary sprigs
Fruit or Vegetable Stuffing (A & B) (optional)
Salt and pepper to taste
½ pound lard (store bought or see "Basic Recipes for Mexican Cooking," p. 12)
Pipián de Pistache (see recipe below) (optional)

PAT-dry piglet and rub with lemon juice inside and out. Let it sit in the fridge for 30 minutes, take piglet out of the fridge, and pat-dry again. Stuff with 2 heads of peeled garlic, sliced onions, and 3 whole rosemary sprigs (at this point, you have the option to stuff the pork with prepared Fruit or Vegetable Stuffing, see A and B below). Sew the pig's cavity with butcher's needle and string, like you would with a turkey's cavity (the skin is tougher than turkey, so be careful).

Season generously with salt and pepper, inside and out. Cut leg joints, so you can place the piglet sitting straight in the oven on a tray and cover ears and tail with aluminum foil to avoid burning. Stab pork twelve times all over the body so the skin doesn't burst while cooking.

In a blender, mix 6 garlic cloves, 2 sprigs of rosemary leaves, and lard previously melted (in oven at low temperature, 250°). Cover piglet (now in tray) with garlic mixture and place on the oven rack at 275–300° for 4 hours. Roast until the pig is cooked to an internal temperature of at least 160°F (check with meat thermometer). This should take around 4 hours for a 20-pound pig. By this stage, the skin will be pale and soft. To crisp it up, heat the oven to 500° and broil the piglet for 30 minutes, watching carefully that it doesn't burn. You will see the skin stretching, crackling, and getting roasted.

For entertaining, you can take the piglet out of the oven before the final crisping stage and let it rest at room temperature covered with foil for up to 2 hours before putting it back in an oven preheated to 500° to crisp up. Serve as is or accompanied by *Pipián de Pistache*. 🐖

A. Fruit Stuffing

2 apples, cut, peeled, and sliced
2 apricots, cut and sliced
2 pears, cut, peeled, and sliced
1 onion, sliced
1 rosemary sprig
1 cup bread croutons
¼ pound butter, cold and cut in small pieces

COMBINE all ingredients well. 🐖

B. Vegetable Stuffing

3 large carrots, peeled and roughly cut
2 cups butternut squash
1 parsnip, peeled and julienned
1 rosemary sprig
3 garlic cloves
½ onion
¼ pound butter, cold and cut in small pieces
1 cup bread croutons
Salt and pepper

COMBINE all ingredients well. 🐗

The following recipe for *Pipián* (Pistachio Sauce) is a great option as an accompaniment to your Roast Suckling Pig. If you want to make the Pipián but are not planning to prepare a roast pig, we have provided a recipe using a pork shoulder or butt (just below).

PISTACHIO SAUCE / PIPIÁN DE PISTACHE

(SERVES 10–12)

3 pounds prepared pork (A) or serve with Roasted Suckling Pig (above)
2 ounces ground, peeled pumpkin seeds (purchase ground or use a coffee grinder to grind whole seeds)
7 ounces pistachios, peeled, roasted, and unsalted
½ cup sliced onion
2 chard leaves
4 garlic cloves
1-inch cinnamon stick
5 whole black peppers
3 cloves
2 serrano chiles
2 poblano chiles, charred, peeled, and seeded (see "Common Mexican Cooking Tools and Techniques," p. 334)
5 tomatillos
4 lettuce leaves
4 sprigs epazote or ¼ ounce dry epazote
6 sprigs fresh cilantro
3 sprigs fresh parsley

4 leaves fresh root beer plant (*hoja santa*, also called Mexican pepperleaf)

6 radish leaves

1 cup corn oil or lard, plus ¼ cup

2 cups pork stock (from the meat), if you are serving with Roasted Suckling Pig, you will
    need 4 cups pork stock (see "Basic Recipes for Mexican Cooking," p. 11)

Pinch of cumin

Salt to taste

IN a large pan, sautée each of the following ingredients independently and set aside in a large bowl: pumpkin seeds, pistachios, sliced onion, chard leaves, garlic cloves, cinnamon stick, black pepper, cloves, serrano chiles, and poblano chiles. Prepare tomatillos by removing husks, cleaning the tomatillos well and boiling until they change color. Then combine all the sautéed ingredients in the blender and incorporate the tomatillos, all the greens, and one cup of oil or lard.

Blend everything until smooth. (You may need to do this step in two or three parts to prevent the blender from jamming or overflowing.) In a large pot, heat ¼ cup of oil or lard. Once really hot, add blended mixture, stirring constantly with a wooden spoon until you have a thick paste. You will see the oil separating from the mixture; at this point you can remove extra oil with a spoon. Set aside half the mixture for future use (if you are serving with the Roasted Suckling Pig, use all the paste); keeps well in the fridge for 3 weeks or 6 months in the freezer.

Now, add reserved pork stock to the remaining paste until you get the desired consistency. It should be a thick but runny sauce, add meat and let simmer for 20 minutes more. Add a pinch of cumin and salt and pepper to taste. Serve with warm tortillas, rice, and beans. 🐟

A. Preparing the Pork

(SERVES 6)

3 pounds pork shoulder or pork butt, cut into medium-size pieces

½ white onion

1 garlic clove

2 bay leaves

3 cups boiling water

Salt and pepper to taste

ADD boiling water to roasting pan and add the pork. Roast pork for 1 hour in an oven at 350° with ½ onion, garlic clove, bay leaves, salt, and pepper, basting frequently. Once cooked set aside. Reserve stock for future use if desired. Stock will keep well in the freezer for 3 months. 🐟

SPINACH MUSHROOM PIE / PIE DE ESPINACAS Y HONGOS

(SERVES 8)

2 pounds white mushrooms, cleaned and sliced

1 medium onion, chopped

2 poblano chiles, charred, seeded, and peeled (see "Common Mexican Cooking Tools and
  Techniques," p. 334)

3 tablespoons vegetable oil

2 garlic cloves, chopped

3 pounds fresh baby spinach, cleaned and stems removed (or 2 10-ounce packages frozen
  chopped spinach, thawed and well drained)

⅛ teaspoon nutmeg

½ cup Mexican sour cream

Salt to taste

¼ teaspoon pepper

6 eggs, beaten

4 ounces (¼ stick) butter

1 tablespoon flour

2 pie shells with tequila (A), or thaw if using frozen, packaged shells

1 tablespoon water

IN a skillet or cast-iron pan, add oil and cook mushrooms until liquid is gone and they get a golden color (if mushrooms brown but a bit of liquid remains in the pan, drain before proceeding with next step). Once mushrooms are done, add onion and sauté until it becomes tender and browns a little (5–7 minutes). Add poblano chiles, garlic, and spinach. Mix well, cook for 7 more minutes. Add nutmeg and Mexican sour cream; season with salt and pepper to taste. Let it cool for ½ hour. Then separate one egg and set the yolk aside. In a bowl, beat the remaining egg white and 5 eggs until well scrambled and mix together with the vegetables.

Butter a 10-inch pie pan and cover with flour; place pastry round at bottom of the pie mold and punch holes with a fork. Add filling. Place top of pie crust, sealing the edges with water and pressing together the edges of the pie crust with your fingers; cut some slits on top of crust to let the steam out. Combine 1 tablespoon of water with reserved egg yolk; brush over top crust. Bake at 375° for 50 minutes or until golden brown. Let stand 15 minutes before cutting and serving. 🐟

A. Flaky Pie Crust with Tequila

2½ cups all-purpose flour
1 teaspoon salt
2 tablespoons sugar
6 ounces (1½ sticks) cold unsalted butter, cut into ¼-inch slices
½ cup cold vegetable shortening, cut into 1-inch pieces
¼ cup ice-cold tequila
¼ cup ice-cold water

PROCESS 1½ cups flour, salt, and sugar in food processor and combine with two or three pulses. Add butter and shortening and process until you get a uniform dough (15 seconds or until it resembles cottage cheese and flour is all incorporated). Add remaining cup of flour and pulse until mixture is evenly mixed and separated in large chunks. Empty mixture into medium bowl.

Sprinkle tequila and water over mixture. With your hands, use folding motion to mix, pressing down on dough until it sticks together. Divide dough into two even balls and flatten each into a round disk (4 inches). Cover each in plastic wrap and refrigerate at least 45 minutes or up to 2 days, or freeze for future use, up to 3 months. 🐟

NOTES FROM THE ALMAZÁN KITCHEN

THIS dough is quite sticky, so use plenty of flour to work it. The alcohol makes it moist, so try to work fast and chill it before you attempt to cover your pie pan. When the alcohol evaporates, it will bake into a really flaky crust. It is a little harder to work with this dough, but the results are worth it.

Fideos, which are generally made from wheat or durum wheat (*semolina*) with water, or flour and eggs, were introduced to Mexico from medieval Spain. This Spanish recipe for *Potaje de Fideos* comes from *Libro de guisados*, 1529.[1]

Rinse the fideos to remove any dirt that might be present until they are very clean. Place a large clean pot on the fire, add chicken stock or stock from good fat lamb. Once the stock is boiling, add the pasta with a lump of sugar. Once they are half-way cooked, add goat's milk to the stock or you can add almond milk instead, as this is always good, and cook well. Once noodles are well cooked, remove from the fire and let rest for a few minutes, Serve in shallow soup bowls adding sugar and cinnamon on top. The quality of the dish depends on the quality of the meat stock. Some people say you should not add milk or sugar, but that depends on individual taste. Truly with noodles or rice that has been cooked with meat stock it is best to add good quality cheese on top of each bowl.

MEXICAN ANGEL HAIR PASTA / FIDEOS CON CREMA Y QUESO

(SERVES 4–6)

2 tablespoons olive oil or corn oil

8 ounces dried fideos noodles or angel hair broken into smaller pieces

1 cup tomato purée (see "Basic Recipes for Mexican Cooking," p. 15)

2 cups chicken broth (see "Basic Recipes for Mexican Cooking," p. 11)

2 bay leaves

1–2 tablespoons adobo sauce from chipotle chiles (canned)

1 whole (canned) chipotle chile (optional)

4–6 ounces queso fresco or Cotija

¼ cup crema Mexicana or sour cream

¼ cup of milk

1 ripe avocado, peeled and cut into slices

¼ teaspoon ground black pepper

¾ teaspoon salt

Chopped cilantro for garnish

HEAT olive oil in a large sauté pan. Sautée the fideos or angel hair pasta over medium-high heat for a few minutes, stirring often, until the pasta changes color and starts to brown. Watch carefully as it can easily burn; strain extra oil.

Pour the cooked tomato purée over the pasta. Cook for about 5 minutes over medium heat, stirring often. Add the chicken broth, bay leaves, and adobo sauce from the chipotle chiles. If desired, add the whole chipotle chile; this will add additional heat.

Add salt and pepper, mix well, and cook uncovered for 8 minutes, stirring gently occasionally to prevent pasta from sticking. The pasta should be dry at this point. Serve hot, topped with crumbled queso fresco, grated Cotija, fresh Mexican sour cream thinned with ¼ cup of milk, avocado slices, and chopped cilantro. ❧

ROMPOPE, SWEETS, AND THE SISTERS OF THE SANTA CLARA CONVENT

The culinary skills of the sisters of the order of Puebla's Convento de Santa Clara, founded in 1607, were well known in Mexico by the beginning of the seventeenth century. Many *Clarisas*, as they are called, were even daughters of wealthy Spanish families and had been accustomed to dining well. The convent, which produced such Poblano culinary treasures as mole and *Chiles en Nogada* (see p. 257), was especially well known for its sweets. Today, on the Calle de Dulces (Sweet Street) in Puebla, you can find *Camote Santa Clara* produced just as it was almost three hundred years ago, as well as *rompope* for sale.

Known as "Mexican eggnog," rompope is a variation on egg punch (*ponche de huevo*) or *rompón*, a holiday beverage popular in Spain that migrated to Mexico during the time of colonization. While many Latin American countries have a similar concoction, the nuns of Puebla modified the recipe to create what would become a signature drink of Puebla and, eventually, of all of Mexico.

The story goes that each nun had a specialty, and that Sister Eduviges not only made the rompope, but was also responsible for its popularity, as her rompope was made with spirits. The nuns produced it for guests but were not permitted to drink it until Eduviges persuaded the Mother Superior to allow them to partake in moderation. Finding the smooth, sweet beverage intoxicatingly delicious, the nuns were soon preparing it daily. It wasn't long before, at Sister Eduviges's prompting, they began selling it to raise money for the Church. It was immediately in demand, and the convent began taking orders from families all over Puebla. Rompope quickly became known and popular in other parts of Mexico.

Puebla's nuns still make and sell rompope today. There are even online stores, and, although it is made all over the country, most know the drink as *Rompope de Santa Clara*. Mexicans drink rompope year-round for special occasions, and it is also a favored topping for *gelatinas* (see p. 193), Mexico's famous gelatin dessert, as well as for fruit.

Rompope with
Floating Islands /
*Islas Flotantes con
Rompope.*
Photo by Adriana
Almazán Lahl.

OLD-FASHİONED ROMPOPE

(SERVES 12)

½ gallon milk
Pinch of salt
2 vanilla pods, split in half lengthwise
¼ teaspoon nutmeg
4 cloves
1½ pounds sugar
30 egg yolks
1 cup cognac

BRING milk to a boil with salt, vanilla pod, nutmeg, and cloves. Once boiling, turn off and add sugar; mix well and let it cool.

Meanwhile, whip egg yolks until they turn light yellow. Once milk cools down, add yolks and place on stove over medium heat, stirring constantly in one direction only, and without stopping, until it thickens to a creamy consistency.

Remove from fire and let cool, stirring frequently to keep cream from forming on top. Place rompope in a metal bowl over a bath of ice to cool mixture quickly, stir frequently. Once cooled down but still warm, add cognac slowly and strain. Place rompope in glass bottles. It can be stored for 3 months at room temperature or 6 months if refrigerated. Serve at room temperature. 🐝

ALMOND OR HAZELNUT ROMPOPE

(SERVES 12)

1 cup almonds or hazelnuts
½ gallon milk
1 cup sugar
Pinch of salt
⅛ teaspoon nutmeg
4 cloves
1 cinnamon stick
⅛ tablespoon baking soda
1 vanilla pod split open in half
10 egg yolks
¾ cup brandy or cognac

SOAK almonds or hazelnuts in hot water for 5 minutes. Remove skins and blend nuts with 2 cups of milk until well blended and smooth. In a large pot, warm almond mix with the rest of the milk over high heat. Once it starts boiling, lower to medium-low and add sugar, salt, nutmeg, cloves, cinnamon, baking soda, and vanilla pod. Stir constantly in one direction with a wooden spoon to avoid sticking to the pan for 20 minutes or until the mix evaporates to half the quantity. Turn off fire and set aside.

In a separate bowl, whip egg yolks, add a cup of the warm milk, and whip vigorously until well incorporated.

Add egg yolks to the rest of the milk and place back on the stove over medium-low heat. Keep stirring until it acquires a thick, maple syrup consistency (20–25 minutes average). Remove from fire and strain.

Place rompope in a metal bowl over a bath of ice to cool mix quickly, stir frequently. Once cool, add cognac or liquor of your choice and mix well. Place rompope in glass bottles. It can be stored for 3 months at room temperature or 6 months if refrigerated. Serve at room temperature. 🐝

FLOATING ISLANDS IN ROMPOPE SAUCE / ISLAS FLOTANTES AL ROMPOPE

(SERVES 8–10)

2 cups milk
2 cups rompope of choice
1 vanilla bean pod or 1 teaspoon vanilla extract
2 cinnamon sticks
5 cups boiling water
6 egg whites
1½ cups powder sugar
½ tablespoon cream of tartar
3½ ounces quartered strawberries
Mint leaves to garnish
Dash of nutmeg for each portion

BRING milk to a boil with the rompope, adding the vanilla pod (split open in half and scrape the beans into the milk) or vanilla extract, and cinnamon sticks. Set on low heat and watch that the milk does not quite boil. Once hot, turn off heat, cover, and set aside.

Meanwhile in a different pot, boil water. Whip egg whites and cream of tartar on high speed until they become fluffy and firm, then and add sugar and keep whipping until they form stiff peaks. With a large serving spoon drop a generous spoonful of this meringue mix into the boiling water and cook 1 minute, flipping it around so it cooks uniformly. Remove carefully with a slotted spoon and drain water, set aside on a separate plate, or you can place meringue in large spoonfuls on a pregreased cookie tray and bake them at 400° for 10–15 minutes. Once cooked, let them cool completely.

Serve rompope sauce in a martini or margarita glass or a pretty bowl. Add meringue on top of the rompope sauce (removing any skin that may have formed on top of the rompope). Place a few strawberry quarters on the side, garnish with mint leaves, and add a dash of nutmeg.

Santa Clara Sweet
Potato "Cigars"
/ Camotes de
Santa Clara.
Photo by Adriana
Almazán Lahl.

SANTA CLARA SWEET POTATO "CİGARS" / CAMOTES DE SANTA CLARA

(MAKES 16 PIECES)

3 pounds sugar
3 cups water
4 pounds Vietnamese or white sweet potatoes, boiled, peeled, and puréed
Sugar Syrup (A)

PLACE sugar and water in a saucepan over medium heat until it reaches the hard-ball point (test readiness by dropping a little syrup in cold water; should result in a hard ball) 250–266° (you'll need a candy thermometer). Add sweet potato purée to the sugar and water mixture and continue cooking until you attain a thick paste and can see the bottom of the saucepan as you stir constantly. Remove from fire and keep stirring with a wooden spoon until it cools down completely. It is best if left overnight in refrigerator.

Roll the paste by hand to make cigar shapes, 1 inch thick and 4 inches long, and wrap them in wax paper. Let them rest overnight.

Unwrap cigar treats and dip into Sugar Syrup. Place them on a rack and allow to rest another day until completely dry, then rewrap individually with wax paper. 🐝

A. Sugar Syrup

15 ounces sugar
½ cup water or pineapple juice
Orange or lemon rind (optional)

PLACE sugar and water in a saucepan and bring to a boil; continue cooking until it reaches a thread point (test readiness by dropping a little syrup in cold water; should result in a thread of sugar forming) 230–233° (you'll need a candy thermometer). If you want to add flavor to the cigar treats, you can add orange or lemon rind to your syrup or use pineapple juice instead of water. Allow syrup to cool before using. 🐝

THREE KINGS' DAY / DÍA DE LOS REYES MAGOS
[JANUARY 6]

JANUARY 6, Day of the Wise Men, or Día de los Reyes Magos, is almost like a second Christmas in Mexico, coinciding with Epiphany. It celebrates the coming of the Three Wise Men and the presentation of the baby Jesus at the River Jordan for baptism, according to the Catholic religion. Los Reyes, as this popular holiday is called, marks the end of the period of a marathon of holidays that come one after another, beginning on December 12 with the Día de la Virgen de Guadalupe, informally known in Mexico today as the Guadalupe-Reyes Marathon.

Toys, Shoes, and Cake

This is the day Mexican children wait for all year long, as they anticipate the arrival of *Los Reyes Magos* (rather than Santa Claus on Christmas Eve). It is the Three Wise Men who will bring them toys, just as they came to ancient Bethlehem bearing gifts for the baby Jesus. (In Mexico, for Christmas, it is more traditional for children to receive clothing.) In many areas of Mexico, children leave out their empty shoes on the night of January 5, hoping that they will find them filled with treasures in the morning.

The holiday is also celebrated with the charming tradition of the *Rosca de Reyes*. This is the "Kings' Cake," a flour-based cake rich with butter and egg yolks, originally in the shape of a ring to echo a crown, but which has grown into an oval as it has "stretched" to accommodate larger crowds. As wheat flour was not introduced to Mexico until the invasion of the Spanish in the sixteenth century, the rosca likely became part of Mexico's holiday traditions sometime after that (originally, it was the Moors, invading Spain in the eighth century, who brought with them cakes rich in almonds, dried fruits, spices, and refined sugar—all key ingredients in the rosca).

Hidden inside the rosca is a figure of baby Jesus, either plastic or porcelain, to symbolize how Mary and Joseph had to hide Him from King Herod, who had been apprised of the signs that a new and rightful king of Jerusalem would born and ordered all male infants in Bethlehem be put to death. The deadly search is symbolized by the knife cutting the ring cake.

As with many Mexican holidays, on January 6, neighbors and family share the light evening meal, each having a chance to find the figure of baby Jesus in their slice of the rosca. The tradition of the Rosca de Reyes also extends the Christmas celebrations for another few weeks; the lucky guest who finds Him is designated to host a *tamalda*, a party at which tamales and hot chocolate are served, on February 2, Día de la Candelaria (see chapter 7).

> **MENU 6.1:**
> **THREE KINGS' DAY**
>
> Three Kings' Bread Ring /
> *Rosca de Reyes*
> Churros with Thick
> Chocolate Dipping Sauce
> Mexican Hot Chocolate

THREE KINGS' BREAD RING / ROSCA DE REYES

(SERVES 8–10)

3½ ounces sugar
¼ cup orange blossom water
1 envelope (1 teaspoon) yeast
¼ cup warm water
2 cups flour
½ teaspoon salt
1 ounce powdered milk
4 eggs
Rind of half a lemon
Rind of half an orange
3½ ounces butter
½ teaspoon anise seed
4 teaspoons vanilla extract
Small baby figurine or toy, porcelain or ceramic (or several)
Concha Bread Mix (for decoration) (A)

¼ cup candied figs, cut in strips
¼ cup candied orange rind, cut in strips
¼ cup candied pineapple strips
¼ cup candied cherries, cut in half
1 egg, beaten, to varnish rosca

COMBINE water, 1 tablespoon of sugar, and orange blossom water in a saucepan over a low flame and warm to 105°. Dissolve yeast in warm water and let it sit for 5 minutes or until it starts foaming. Place the flour on a clean, dry workspace and form a mountain with a valley in the middle or a "volcano." Place half the sugar, salt, powdered milk, and cracked eggs inside the "valley." Using this area as your work bowl, premix the ingredients carefully with your hands. Once ingredients are well mixed in the center, add water with yeast and start incorporating the flour dry ingredients and eggs from the area around until all ingredients are well mixed and become a pliable, elastic, and smooth dough. Add the lemon and orange rind, butter, and the remaining sugar, dry milk, and salt, and work the dough until all ingredients are well incorporated again.

Place in an 18-by-14-inch pregreased pan and cover with pregreased plastic wrap (spray the wrap with Pam or similar spray shortening to grease the wrap before placing it over dough). Wait 2 hours until the dough doubles in size, and punch once to deflate it. Cover again and wait an additional 25 minutes, punch

Rosca de Reyes.
Photo by Adriana Almazán Lahl.

again, and shape into a 10- to 14-inch oval wreath. Lift wreath carefully and place on a pregreased baking sheet. Insert small figurine(s) into the wreath. Cover and let it rise again to double the original size. Place concha dough strips across the wreath, and sprinkle concha dough only with sugar, alternating concha dough with candied fruit strips (cherries, orange, figs, and pineapple).

Varnish whole wreath with beaten egg and place in a preheated oven at 350° for 30 minutes until bread turns golden brown.

Warning: Be aware of small figurines in wreath. Supervise children while cutting and eating this bread. 🐝

A. Concha Bread Mix

3½ ounces powdered sugar
3½ ounces margarine
3½ ounces flour

CREAM margarine with powdered sugar. Once well mixed, add flour slowly, until incorporated completely. 🐝

Churros con Chocolate.
Photo by Adriana Almazán Lahl.

CHURROS

(MAKES 12)

1 cup water
½ cup butter
¼ teaspoon salt
1 cup all-purpose flour
3 large eggs
Vegetable oil, for frying
Cinnamon sugar
Chocolate Sauce (A)

IN a medium saucepan, combine water and butter; bring to a boil. When mixture is boiling, add flour all at once and stir vigorously with a wooden spoon until the dough forms. Continue to stir and cook the dough for about 1 minute. Transfer to a large mixing bowl and using a mixer on medium-high, beat in the eggs, one at a time, waiting until each has been well incorporated before adding the next. Keep mixing until smooth dough is formed. Transfer dough to a pastry bag fitted with a large star tip. Pour about 2 inches of oil into a deep saucepan. Once the oil reaches the desired temperature (365°), pipe 5- to 6-inch pieces of churro dough into the hot oil and cook until golden brown, flipping churro around so it browns evenly (about 3–4 minutes). Remove from oil and set on paper towel to drain. Dust with cinnamon sugar. Serve churros with small cups of chocolate sauce for dipping. 🪲

A. Thick Chocolate Dipping Sauce

2 cups milk (any kind)
¼ cup sugar (do not use if you use Mexican chocolate disc)
½ cup semi-sweet chocolate (chocolate chips) or 2 bars of Mexican chocolate disc, such as Abuelita or Ibarra
¼ teaspoon cinnamon (do not use if you use Mexican chocolate disc)
1 tablespoon cornstarch

WARM milk in a saucepan; do not bring to a boil. If using Mexican chocolate, add and dissolve or add semi-sweet chocolate, sugar, and cinnamon and mix well. Mix cornstarch with 3 tablespoons of warm chocolate milk in a cup, dissolving cornstarch to form a paste. Once the paste is well mixed, incorporate into hot chocolate and heat until it thickens. Serve hot with churros. 🪲

MEXICAN HOT CHOCOLATE

(SERVES 8)

2 discs (3 ounces each) of Mexican chocolate (Abuelita or Ibarra), finely chopped
8 cups of water or milk
½ tablespoon freshly ground cinnamon

PLACE a thick-bottomed pot on a medium-high flame, add water or milk, bring to a boil and add chocolate and cinnamon. Whisk vigorously with a molinillo or a whisk until frothy. Serve hot. 🐦

TRADITIONAL MEXICAN HOT CHOCOLATE

(SERVES 8)

8 cups water or milk
2 cinnamon sticks
1 vanilla pod, split open
8 tablespoons sugar
11 ounces chocolate of your choice, finely chopped
½ tablespoon ground Mexican cinnamon
1½ tablespoons cornstarch (optional)

NOTES FROM THE ALMAZÁN KITCHEN

Using a Molinillo

THIS hollow wooden stirrer is similar in use to a whisk, but so much more beautiful. Hand carved of solid wood and burnished in spots, which gives it a beautiful appearance with contrasting shades, the molinillo is designed to create rich, frothy pots of Mexican hot chocolate. To use, rotate the handle between your palms, and its smooth pestle bottom softens and grinds chocolate as it dissolves in hot milk. Loose rings in the middle of the molinollo (shake it, you'll be able to hear them rattle) facilitate "whipping" air into hot chocolate, which results in froth equal to any modern whisk or frother.

PLACE a thick-bottomed pot on medium-high flame, add water or milk, cinnamon stick, vanilla pod, and sugar and bring to a boil. Remove spices from the pot using a slotted spoon and add chopped chocolate and ground cinnamon. Stir and whisk vigorously until chocolate dissolves. (You can also use a handheld mixer to dissolve the chocolate and create a frothy drink.) If you prefer a thicker chocolate beverage, add cornstarch at this point and whisk for 3 minutes more, then, using a molinillo, froth milk until foam builds up. Serve hot. 🐟

Mexican Hot Chocolate and Churro.
Photo by Adriana Almazán Lahl.

THE FEAST OF SAN ANTONIO ABAD
(JANUARY 17)

Blessing of the Animals

J ANUARY 17 is the feast day of San Antonio de Abad, the patron saint of the animal kingdom. On this day the Catholic Church invites people to bring their animals to be blessed, ensuring their good health and long life. A mass takes place on the Sunday closest to the feast day of Saint Anthony. (January 17 is the date of his physical death but celebrated as his birth date in heaven.)

In Mexico's pueblos, there are processions as people bring their animals to church. As with many *días santos* (saints' days), street vendors find a ready and hungry crowd, and the marketplaces are crowded with vendors. *Tacos de Canasta* and *Elotes* are typical offerings.

Mazahuas preparing to begin a pilgrimage for the feast day of San Antonio. According to the 2010 Mexican census, 116,240 speakers of the language reside in the State of Mexico, (53 percent of all indigenous-language speakers in the state) and most are Spanish bilinguals. Smaller population groups inhabit parts of the Mexican states of Michoacán and Querétaro. Their folk religious practices combine elements of Catholicism and traditional, pre-Conquest beliefs, including the continuing practice of the New Fire Ceremony on March 19 (see p. 83). The Mazahua believe that the souls of the departed return on the Day of the Dead as monarch butterflies.

Mazahua women are easily distinguishable by their distinctive dress, the elements of which have specific meanings. For example, as the waist is considered to be the energy center, the sash is one of the most important pieces of clothing and is woven with varied designs: an abundance of birds signify beauty, freedom, and grace; a stylized star symbolizes the guardian of the night and is a protector of health. The traditional women's outfit, especially the version hand woven in wool, is in danger of disappearing, although there are ongoing efforts to save the skills and traditions needed to keep it.

Photo by Jorge Ontiveros.

TACOS IN A BASKET / TACOS DE CANASTA

THESE TACOS, TYPICAL TO CENTRAL MEXICO, WERE ORIGINALLY A SORT OF PEASANT FAST FOOD, COMMONLY SEEN IN A LARGE BASKET TIED ONTO THE BACK OF A BICYCLE, COVERED WITH PLASTIC AND A LARGE TABLE-CLOTH. TACOS DE CANASTA WERE A SIMPLE SOLUTION, ALLOWING WOMEN TO PREPARE AND BRING WARM FOOD TO THEIR HUSBANDS, LABORERS WHO WERE WORKING UNDER THE HOT SUN. WITH THE WAVE OF MIGRATION TO MEXICO'S URBAN CENTERS, TACOS DE CANASTA EVOLVED TO BECOME A STREET FOOD IN THE CITIES, WHERE THEY ARE VERY POPULAR.
(SERVES 8–10)

52 small (about 4½-inch) tortillas
    (see p. 236)
Chorizo oil from the drippings of one
    chorizo link (E)
Fillings of choice (these should be made a
    day ahead and kept in the refrigerator):
Mexican Sausage with Potatoes / *Chorizo
    con Papas* (A)
Pork Rind in Roasted Green Sauce / *Chicharrón en Salsa Verde* (B)
Beans with Pork / *Frijoles con Chilorio* (C)
Shredded Beef / *Carne Deshebrada* (D)
Mexican Chicken Fricassée / *Tinga de Pollo* (cook until liquid is almost gone or drain excess
    liquid before making tacos; see recipe, p. 133)

(see p. 236), (see recipe, p. 133)

> ## MENU 7.1: FEAST OF SAN ANTOIO ABAD
>
> **Small Plates / *Antojitos***
> Mexican Sausage with Potatoes
> Tacos / *Tacos de Chorizo con Papas*
> Fried Pork Rind in Roasted Green
> Sauce Tacos / *Tacos de Chicharrón
> en Salsa Verde*
> Beans with Pork Tacos /
> *Tacos de Chilorio con Frijoles*
> Shredded Beef Tacos /
> *Tacos de Carne Deshebrada*
> **Sides / *Guarniciones***
> Pickled Chiles or Chipotles
> and Vegetables / *Chiles o Chiles
> Chipotles en Escabeche*
> Mexican-Style
> Corn on the Cob / *Elotes*
> **Dessert / *Postre***
> Prickly Pear Popsicles /
> *Paletas de Tuna*
> **Beverage / *Bebida***
> Watermelon or Strawberry Water /
> *Agua de Sandía o Fresa*

TO ASSEMBLE THE TACOS: Heat all of the stews or fillings (*guisados*). Once warm, add 1 tablespoons of the previously prepared chorizo oil (E, below) to a saucepan and warm on medium-low heat. Dip each tortilla you are going to use to make the tacos into the oil, allowing it to soak up oil on each side as you are warming it (so be sure you dip and flip so as to allow both sides to make contact with the oil). Drain excess oil; add the stuffing of your choice. Repeat procedure until all your tortillas have been fried, adding oil when your pan is dry; the tortillas should be completely soaked in oil in order to prevent them from breaking.

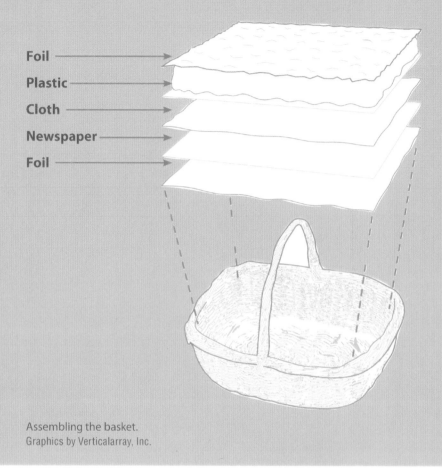

Foil ——————————→

Plastic ——————————→

Cloth ——————————→

Newspaper ——————————→

Foil ——————————→

Assembling the basket.
Graphics by Verticalarray, Inc.

TO PREPARE THE BASKET: Line the bottom of a woven or wicker basket with two layers of cloth with a few sheets of newspaper in between them. Make sure the cloths are larger than the basket, so as to allow them to drape over the sides of the basket. On top of the cloths, place a large plastic bag with the opening of the bag face up so you can fill it with tacos. Finally, prepare a sheet of foil long and wide enough to cover the basket once it is filled with tacos and place it inside the plastic bag so the tacos don't come in contact with the plastic bag.

Place tacos on top of the foil inside the plastic bag inside your basket, stacking them up in towers, separating by flavors. Close the plastic bag, cover basket by wrapping the foil on top of the tacos, and grab the cloth that is draped over the side, tucking it in all around the edges of the basket so as in to keep in the heat. Let tacos sweat or steam (see "Common Mexican Cooking Tools and Techniques," p. 337) this way for at least 1 hour before serving. 🐦

NOTES FROM THE ALMAZÁN KITCHEN

WHEN preparing your tacos, always keep a dry tortilla in your left hand and a fork in your right hand. As you dip each tortilla you are using to make a taco into the oil and then drain, this dry tortilla acts as a sort of shield, protecting you from burning yourself. As you drain its excess oil, place the fried warm tortilla on top of the dry tortilla on your left hand.

The fat you incorporate into the tortillas is an important component of *Tacos de Canasta* and you can't skimp on this element or make a low-fat version. The tortillas for the tacos must be well covered with fat in order for the tacos to hold together. If the tortilla is not well greased, the taco will disintegrate, leaving a mushy mess.

A. Mexican Sausage with Potatoes Tacos / Tacos de Chorizo con Papas

(MAKES 25 OR MORE TAQUITOS)

4 medium red potatoes, peeled and quartered
3 tablespoons oil
¼ Spanish white onion, finely chopped
7 ounces chorizo (previously cooked to prepare the fat for the taco, see E below)
Salt and pepper to taste

IN a saucepan cover potatoes with water and bring to a boil; add 1 tablespoon of salt and cook covered for 10 minutes. Drain water and mash potatoes; set aside. In a separate saucepan, add oil and sauté onion for 3 minutes; incorporate cooked chorizo and keep cooking for 3 minutes until warm. Add mashed potatoes and mix well with chorizo; season with salt and pepper if needed. Cook 2 more minutes and allow to cool and refrigerate overnight. Follow instructions on p. 109 to create your tacos.

Tacos in a Basket / *Tacos de Canasta*. Photo by Adriana Almazán Lahl.

B. Fried Pork Rind in Roasted Green Sauce Tacos / Tacos de Chicharrón en Salsa Verde

(MAKES 25 OR MORE TAQUITOS)

4 medium tomatillos (cleaned and with husk removed)
¼ white onion
4 guajillo chiles
1 garlic clove
3 tablespoons vegetable oil
1 cup chicken stock (see "Basic Recipes for Mexican Cooking," p. 11)
7 ounces chicharron, crumbled into 1-inch pieces
Salt to taste

DRY-roast the tomatillos, onion, chiles, and garlic on a comal (see "Common Mexican Cooking Tools and Techniques," p. 337) or dry grill pan. Once roasted, remove from heat and blend using a blender, mix to form a smooth salsa. Heat vegetable oil in a saucepan, add salsa (be careful not to burn yourself, salsa tends to splatter when added to hot oil), and cook over medium-high heat for 10 minutes; add chicken stock and cook for another 10 minutes over high heat. Add chicharron and season to taste with salt and pepper. Cook until there is no visible liquid left; let it cool and refrigerate overnight. Follow instructions on p. 109 to create your tacos. 🐛

C. Beans with Pork Tacos / Tacos de Chilorio con Frijoles
(MAKES 25 OR MORE TAQUITOS)

2 tablespoons vegetable oil
¼ onion, finely chopped
¼ cup Fresh *Salsa Roja* (red salsa; see "Salsas and Salsa Pairings," p. 20)
1 cup shredded pork butt
2 cups refried beans (see p. 152)

ADD vegetable oil to a saucepan and sauté onion for 3 minutes. Add *Salsa Roja* (be careful not to burn yourself, salsa tends to splatter when added to hot oil) and cook 4–5 minutes over medium heat. Now add shredded pork and refried beans, mix well, and cook for an additional 5 minutes or until mixture is dry. Let it cool and refrigerate overnight. Follow instructions on p. 109 to create your tacos. 🐛

D. Shredded Beef Tacos / Tacos de Carne Deshebrada
(MAKES 25 OR MORE TAQUITOS)

7-ounce skirt steak
1 bay leaf
7 ounces potatoes, diced
½ teaspoon salt, plus salt to taste
2 garlic cloves
¼ Spanish white onion
4 dry pasilla chiles, soaked in warm water and seeded and deveined
¼ cup chicken stock or water (see "Basic Recipes for Mexican Cooking," p. 11)
3 tablespoons vegetable oil

COOK skirt steak in 1 cup of water with bay leaf for 45 minutes to an hour; let it cool and shred beef thinly, tearing it apart with your hands (do not use a knife). Cook potatoes in 1 cup of water with ½ tablespoon of salt for 10 minutes. Drain water and set potatoes aside. In a blender, mix garlic, onion, pasilla chiles, and ¼ cup chicken stock or water to create a salsa. Heat oil in a saucepan, add salsa (be careful not to burn yourself, salsa tends to splatter when added to hot oil), and cook for 5 minutes, stirring frequently. Add meat and potatoes and mix well; continue cooking until liquid evaporates. Allow to cool and refrigerate overnight. Follow instructions on p. 109 to create your tacos. 🐛

E. Preparing the Fat for the Tortillas

1 cup vegetable oil
7 ounces chorizo link, casing removed (see recipe p. 131, or store bought)

HEAT oil in a saucepan, add chorizo, and heat on a low fire until well cooked (20 minutes). The intention is to flavor the oil and release the fat from the chorizo. Remove from heat and drain chorizo. Reserve fat, as you will use it to coat tortillas for the tacos, and use the chorizo for the *Chorizo con Papas* recipe. 🐛

PICKLED CHILES AND VEGETABLES I / CHILES EN ESCABECHE I

(MAKES APPROXIMATELY 1½ QUARTS)

¼ cup olive oil
5 carrots, peeled and cut in thin slices
2 zucchini, cut in slices
8 cauliflower or broccoli florets (optional)
1 large Spanish white onion, cut in large chunks
1 garlic head, cut in 4
15 cuaresmeños chiles or jalapeños, seeded, deveined, and quartered (see "Common Mexican Cooking Tools and Techniques," p. 334)
1 cup water
1 tablespoon salt
½ cup white vinegar
½ cup sherry wine vinegar
⅓ cup piloncillo, grated (see "Common Mexican Cooking Tools and Techniques," p. 336)
2 cloves
10 allspice berries
1 teaspoon mustard seeds
3 bay leaves
1 teaspoon fresh Mexican oregano or ½ teaspoon dry oregano
1 teaspoon cumin
1 teaspoon marjoram

HEAT oil in a large skillet and add all vegetables (cauliflower or broccoli florets can be added to this recipe), onion, garlic, and chiles, mustard seeds, allspice, bay leaves, cloves, and cumin. Sauté for 10 minutes, stirring constantly. Add water, piloncillo, and salt and allow to simmer for 5 minutes. Add both vinegars and salt and turn heat off. Save into sterilized glass jars and close lid tightly; allow to cool down with jars upside down. 🐛

Chiles en Escabeche.
Photo by Adriana Almazán Lahl.

PICKLED CHIPOTLE CHILES AND VEGETABLES II / CHIPOTLE CHILES EN ESCABECHE II

(MAKES APPROXIMATELY 1½ QUARTS)

7 ounces dried chipotles chiles, seeded
1 large carrot, peeled and cut in ¼-inch rounds
½ garlic head, cut in half
½ small white onion, sliced
1 cup water (or enough to cover chiles in a saucepan)
½ cup white vinegar
3½ ounces piloncillo, grated (see "Common Mexican Cooking Tools and Techniques," p. 336)
5 allspice berries
2 bay leaves
1 marjoram sprig
1 cinnamon stick (1 inch long)
¼ head cauliflower, florets only
Salt to taste
3 tablespoons olive oil

WASH chiles and vegetables thoroughly. In a large saucepan add water and all ingredients except oil; allow to simmer for 10 minutes until chiles are soft. Add oil and allow to simmer for another minute. Remove from heat. Remove cinnamon and bay leaves. Put in a sterilized glass container, close lid tightly, and flip upside down. Allow to cool completely. 🐝

MEXICAN-STYLE CORN ON THE COB / ELOTES

6 corn ears
Boiling water to cover corn
1 tablespoon tequesquite
3 sprigs Mexican or regular tarragon
3 Mexican limes
1 cup mayonnaise
1 cup grated Cotija cheese
Chile piquin or ancho chile powder
Salt to taste

PLACE corn with husk in a large pot with water to cover. Add tequesquite and Mexican tarragon. Cook covered for 15 minutes. Once corn cools down enough to handle, remove corn husk by cutting the thicker end and pulling husk toward the top; it should come out clean of any corn silk. Insert a wooden stick in the thicker end, rub lime around the corn while squeezing so as to release a little lime juice, spread mayonnaise, and sprinkle cheese and chile piquin. Add salt if needed. 🐝

PRICKLY PEAR POPSICLES / PALETAS DE TUNA

(SERVES 8)

3 cups fresh prickly pear, cubed
Juice of 2 limes
¾ cup sugar

BLEND all ingredients until smooth and pass through a sieve. Pour into 4-ounce paper cups or popsicle molds and freeze from 60 to 90 minutes, remove from freezer and insert wooden stick, return to freezer until completely set.

WATERMELON WATER / AGUA DE SANDÍA

½ ripe seedless watermelon, peeled and chopped
8 cups water
½ cup sugar or to your taste
Ice

IN a blender, add the chopped watermelon and 2 cups of the water. Blend well and strain. In a large glass jar, combine the watermelon mixture, sugar, the rest of the water, and ice. Stir well and serve. If you wish, you can add some extra chunks of fruit to the water for texture.

You can make this water with pineapple, papaya, mango, or your choice of fresh fruit.

STRAWBERRY WATER / AGUA DE FRESA

(SERVES 6–8)

2 pounds strawberries, hulled, cleaned, and chopped
2 quarts water
½ cup sugar or to your taste
1 cup fresh quartered strawberries (chunks)
Ice

COMBINE the 2 pounds of chopped strawberries and 2 quarts of water in a blender. Mix until very smooth. Strain and pour into a large glass jar, adding the rest of the water, sugar to taste, strawberry chunks, and ice. Stir well and serve. You can substitute any berry of your choice. 🦟

CANDLEMAS / DÍA DE LA CANDELARIA (FEBRUARY 2)

MEXICANS FINALLY wrap up the long Christmas holiday period with Día de la Candelaria (Candlemas), celebrated on February 2. This date also marks the onset of the planting season in central Mexico, a time for rituals and prayers in hope of a successful harvest. In this region there are local events marking the day, with rites beyond those celebrated across the country.

History of Candlemas and Mexican Traditions

Candlemas, so called because this was the day that all the Church's candles for the year were blessed, stems from Paganism. In pre-Christian times, it was the festival of light. This ancient festival marked the midpoint of winter, halfway between the winter solstice (shortest day) and the spring equinox. Día de la Candelaria commemorates the ritual purification of Mary and presentation of the baby Jesus to God in the Temple at Jerusalem. For forty days after giving birth to a boy, and for sixty days after giving birth to a girl, women weren't allowed to worship in the temple. At the end of this time, women were brought to the temple or synagogue to be purified.

La Tamalada, a Tamale Party

The tradition of the Rosca de Reyes on January 6 (see chapter 6) dictates that the guest who finds the figure of baby Jesus in a slice of the rosca is designated to provide tamales and Mexican hot chocolate, or atole, a traditional drink made of corn, on Día de la Candelaria.

THE making of the tamales followed a week of excitement for us as little kids. It was a festive feeling, going to the store to buy the corn, chiles, and spices and taking them to the mill in the Tacubaya neighborhood of Mexico City. Every year, we rushed to be in line at the mill before 7 a.m., early enough to beat the crowd and be some of the first ones to grind our ingredients, keeping them from mixing with the flavors of others. My aunts gave precise instructions to the clerks; each component had to be ground in a certain way. We would walk out with many bags of different sizes, aromas, and flavors.

The tamale preparation took days. The mole paste had to be made days in advance, as did the different stuffings. Even the task of getting the corn husk ready required special care and supervision, as all the pieces had to be sorted and selected so as to be similar in size, then washed and hydrated.

Then came la tamalada, a big tamal-making party. All the females in the family, between nine and twelve of us, crammed into in a small breakfast area next to the kitchen to make the precious tamales. Once the preparations were complete, we would wait for a couple of hours for them to cook. My cousin and I would always burn our tongues because we couldn't wait for those treasures to cool down, to put them in our mouths—the same happened with the atole. So, for the rest of the evening we would have scalded tongues but filled stomachs and spirits.

TAMALES

PREPARE tamale dough (*masa para tamales*) according to the recipe in "Basic Recipes for Mexican Cooking," p. 13).

For a tamalada you will want to choose several of the following fillings:

Tamales with Chicken Fricassée (A)
Tamales with Mole Filling with Chicken or Pork (B)
Tamales with Cheese and Chile (C)
Salsa Verde (Green Sauce) with Chicken or Pork (D)
Corn Tamales (see p. 37)
Tamales in Banana Leaf (see p. 39)
Sweet Tamales (see p. 38)

TAMALES

The name *tamale*, or more correctly, *tamal*—comes from the Nahuatl word *tamalli*, meaning "carefully wrapped"—and is masa steamed or boiled in a leaf wrapper, which is discarded before eating. Tamales in Mexico are typically filled with meats, cheese, or vegetables, especially chiles. Tamales date back to 8000 to 5000 BCE. Aztec and Maya civilizations as well as the Olmeca and Tolteca before them used tamales to feed their armies and hunters as they traveled. Tamales were initially disdained by the invading Spaniards in sixteenth-century Mexico, as food of the "lower class."

There are all kinds of stories and rituals around making perfect tamales. In some villages, the women swear that "*los tamales se hacen locos* [will come out crazy] if there is fighting; some will be done and others will be raw. . . . No doubt about it, it is true; we have seen it." In another pueblo, the poor outcome of tamales is blamed on other factors: "What was missing was for the cook to drink wine . . . or dance around the pot."[1] All agree on one tradition: One must tie ears of corn husk strips on the pot handles, which will protect the tamales from absorbing any strife so that they will cook perfectly.

Nahua woman preparing *el Zacahuil* (*tamal gigante*). Ethnographers report up to 370 different kinds of tamales, including el zacahuil, which is 3 feet long, weighs about 150 pounds, and requires most of the leaves of a banana tree to wrap it. While almost all tamales are steamed, a few are distinctive in that they are baked either in the ground or in a bread oven. Other unusual tamales include those made by the Otomi people near San Miguel de Allende, which are pastel-colored, and fresh fish *clapiques* of the coast, prepared since the time of Moctezuma II.
Photo by Jorge Ontiveros.

MASA

ASTOUNDINGLY, the process for getting the best out of corn, developed by the Mayans and Aztecs, is still in use today. It is called *nixtamalization*, or wet milling. First the corn kernels are brought to a boil in an alkali solution of lime/water (the lime is not the fruit but calcium hydrozide, labeled in Mexican groceries as "cal"), or wood ash/water, where they are left to steep and then hulled. This process softens the seed and liberates the nutrients, providing Mexicans with the basis for a balanced diet. Traditionally, Mexican woman faced the laborious task of grinding the kernels on a *metlapil* or metate, a three-legged stone, with a stone rolling pin to produce masa. Today, the basis of masa can be store bought, but many in Mexico still take their corn to the mill (*el molino*) and watch it being ground.

Otomi woman: Nixtamalization. In 2005, the Otomi language was spoken by 239,850 Mexicans (the Mexican census is etymological, in that it tallies people by the language they speak, not by bloodline). The highest concentration of Otomi is found in the Valle de Mezquital in the State of Hidalgo and in the southern portion of Querétaro, where over half the population speaks Otomi in some areas. Large populations also live in Puebla and Veracruz. The population dispersed during the Conquest, as the Spaniards employed Otomi warriors in their expeditions into northern Mexico, with Otomi then settling in some areas of Jalisco, Nayarit, and Guanajuato. However, many of this group assimilated and did not hold onto their language and therefore would not appear in the census data. As with many other indigenous groups, the Otomi practice a form of folk Catholicism, a hybrid of the teaching of the Roman Catholic Church with some of surviving pre-Hispanic religious beliefs and traditions.
Photo by Jorge Ontiveros.

A. Chicken Fricassée Filling

(MAKES 35 TAMALES)

2 tablespoons corn oil
½ onion, chopped
3 garlic cloves, finely chopped
1 tomato
2 pounds chicken breast, cooked and
    shredded (see "Basic Recipes for
    Mexican Cooking," p. 11)
2 apples, peeled, cored, and small-chopped
1 sweet plantain, chopped into ¼-inch
    pieces
½ cup chicken stock
1 whole clove
½ teaspoon cinnamon
2 tablespoons white vinegar
2 tablespoons sugar
Salt and pepper to taste

MENU 8.1: CANDLEMAS

Small Plates / *Antojitos*
Tamales with Chicken Fricassée /
Tamales de Picadillo de Pollo
Tamales with Mole Filling with
Chicken or Pork / *Tamales
de Mole con Pollo o Puerco*
Tamales with Cheese and Chile /
Tamales de Rajas con Queso
Tamales with Salsa Verde (Green
Sauce) with Chicken or Pork /
Tamales Verdes
Beverage / *Bebida*
Chocolate Atole / *Champurrado*

IN a saucepan, heat oil and add chopped onion and garlic. Cook for 3 minutes on medium-high heat, blend tomato with garlic and onion, and pass mixture through a colander into the saucepan. Continue cooking for 5 minutes. Add chicken, apples, plantain, chicken stock, and remaining ingredients. Cook for an additional 10 minutes to allow mixture to season or until liquid reduces. The consistency should be dry, as this will go into the tamales. Add salt and pepper to taste, set aside, and cool down completely before use. To assemble the tamales follow instructions in chapter 1 on how to fill, fold, and cook tamales (pp. 35–36). 🦐

B. Mole Filling

(MAKES 35 TAMALES)

Mole paste (see recipe, p. 306)
1 cup chicken or pork stock (see "Basic Recipes for Mexican Cooking," p. 11)
1 pulled chicken breast or 1 pound pulled pork butt (see "Basic Recipes for Mexican
    Cooking," p. 11)

PREPARE mole sauce (see recipe p. 306), add shredded chicken or pork. Continue simmering it until it thickens, and allow to cool completely. To assemble the tamales follow instructions in chapter 1 on how to fill, fold, and cook tamales (pp. 35–36). 🦐

C. Cheese and Chile Filling

(MAKES 35 TAMALES)

10 cuarezmeños or serrano chiles, quartered and deveined
1 pound queso fresco or panela, cut in thin, long slices
Epazote leaves, or substitute dry

SMEAR raw masa dough on the tamale to create a thin layer. Add chile sliver, 1 slice of cheese, and 1 or 2 epazote leaves; To assemble the tamales follow instructions in chapter 1 on how to fill, fold, and cook tamales (pp. 35–36). Option: add shredded, raw zucchini. 🦂

D. Salsa Verde Filling

(MAKES 35 TAMALES)

1 pound tomatillos, remove husk and clean tomatillos well
2–4 serrano chiles to taste
1 cup water
½ small onion
1 garlic clove
2 tablespoons vegetable oil
1 pulled chicken breast or 1 pound pulled pork butt (see "Basic Recipes Mexican Cooking,"
    p. 11)

BOIL tomatillos and serrano chiles in 1 cup water. Drain and mix well in a blender with ½ onion and 1 garlic clove to make salsa. In a saucepan heat oil and add salsa; cook for around 20 minutes until salsa thickens. Add pulled chicken or pulled pork and mix well, stirring constantly to avoid burning. Cook until you get a thick

---

TANCHUCUA

THERE is evidence of mixing atole, a traditional beverage made with corn and served warm, with chocolate as far back as the Mayan era. In the Yucatan today, where the strongest Mayan influence remains, they serve a thick, chocolate-flavored atole called *tanchucua*, to which allspice, honey, and black pepper is added.

---

mixture, about 10 more minutes. Let cool completely before you use. To assemble the tamales follow instructions in chapter 1 on how to fill, fold, and cook tamales (pp. 35–36). ▸🐟

CHOCOLATE ATOLE / CHAMPURRADO

(MAKES 6 SMALL CUPS)

1 cup prepared tortilla masa (Maseca brand) or fresh tortilla masa (not tamale masa)
5 cups water
1 cinnamon stick
3 ounces (90 grams) Mexican chocolate disc (Abuelita or Ibarra brand)
6 ounces sugar or 1½ piloncillo, grated
1 cup milk

BLEND masa with a cup of water by hand or with a blender; be sure there are no lumps left. Add a second cup of water gradually; continue blending. Heat the remaining water in a saucepan. Once boiling, lower to medium heat and add cinnamon, chocolate, and sugar or piloncillo. Once the chocolate is dissolved and starts to boil, add masa mixture and stir constantly to avoid lumps and to keep from sticking to the bottom of pan. Lower heat to medium and continue stirring until masa is cooked (30 minutes), then add milk and stir for 5 more minutes. ▸🐟

NOTES FROM THE ALMAZÁN KITCHEN

SOME recipes skip the milk. That is the traditional way. At home we added the milk, and it gives a little richer taste. You be the judge. Try it both ways and decide.

BENİTO JUAREZ DAY
[MARCH 21]

ON MARCH 21, Mexico celebrates the birthday of one of its most beloved leaders, Benito Pablo Juarez García. Born in 1806, he went from being a poor Zapotec Indian to serving five terms as Mexico's first (and only) full-blooded native president between the years of 1858 and 1872. Benito Juarez Day is a national holiday. Banks and businesses are closed and there is no school. His birthday coincides with the beginning of springtime, which is celebrated the same day by elementary schools, with spring parades.

Juarez is also known as *"Benemerito de las Americas"* ("Meritorious of the Americas"). Benito Juarez was responsible for resisting the French occupation of Mexico, ending the Second Mexican Empire (for more on the French Intervention, see chapter 15 on Cinco de Mayo). He is known for liberal reforms that would forever change the country, including the institution of free and obligatory education. In spite of, or maybe because of, his education in seminary school prior to studying law, Juarez was fiercely anticlerical, and he believed that the excessive power exercised by the Catholic Church in Mexico was one of the primary obstacles to the country's development. One of his most notable reforms was the secularization of Mexico, marked by separation of church and state.

A champion for respect and rights for all Mexicans, Juarez worked to affect a change in attitudes toward Mexico's indigenous people, against whom prejudice was so prevalent in the nineteenth century. For this, he is sometimes referred to as the "Mexican Abraham Lincoln." In a famous speech delivered in Mexico City on

Cazuelas de Comida Típica.
Photo by Adriana Almazán Lahl.

July 15, 1867, he said, *"Entre los individuos, como entre las naciones, el respeto al derecho ajeno es la paz"* ("Among individuals, as among nations, respect for each other's rights is peace").

While there are no special dishes specific to this day, we have chosen a menu of *Tacos de Cazuela*, typically served up by Mexican street vendors. These are soft tacos with various specialty fillings simmered in large earthenware casseroles (*cazuelas de barro*). This traditional presentation calls for serving up an assortment of stews, buffet style in the cazuelas in which they are prepared and inviting guests to make their own tacos with the filling(s) of their choice.

POBLANO CHILE WITH CORN IN CREAM SAUCE / RAJAS CON ELOTE Y CREMA

(SERVES 6–8)

2 tablespoons olive oil
1 onion, sliced
1 garlic clove
4 poblanos chiles, roasted, seeded, and
    cut into strips (see "Common Mexican
    Cooking Tools and Techniques," p. 334)
2 cups fresh corn kernels
1 epazote sprig or ¼ ounce dry epazote
2 cups Mexican sour cream
Salt to taste

IN a large skillet, heat the oil over medium-high heat. Add the onion and sautée for 4 minutes. Add garlic and cook 1 more minute. Reduce the heat to medium; add poblano chile strips (rajas), corn, and epazote. Cook 5 more minutes; add sour cream. Cook for an additional 5 minutes and salt to taste. Remove epazote sprig before serving.

MENU 9.1: BENITO JUAREZ DAY

Cazuelas
Poblano Chile with
Corn in Cream Sauce /
Rajas con Elote y Crema
Pork Rinds in Green Sauce /
Chicharrón en Salsa Verde
Green or Traditional Mexican
Sausage with Potatoes /
Chorizo Tradicional o Verde con Papas
Mexican Chicken Fricassée /
Tinga de Pollo
Sides / *Guarniciones*
Mexican Rice / *Arroz a la Mexicana*
(see p. 145)
"Clay Pot" Beans / *Frijoles de Olla*
(see p. 146)
Dessert / *Postre*
"Scribble" Cookies / *Garabatos*
Beverage / *Bebida*
Sweet Rice Water /
Agua de Horchata

PORK RINDS IN GREEN SAUCE / CHICHARRÓN EN SALSA VERDE

(SERVES 6–8)

2 tablespoons vegetable oil
1 medium onion, finely chopped
1 clove of garlic, peeled and finely chopped
2 cups Basic Green Salsa, Cooked I or II (see Salsa Recipes, pp. 17–18)
½ pound pork rind (chicharrones), broken to 1 ½" pieces
1 teaspoon salt
1 bunch cilantro, stems and leaves

IN a large skillet, heat oil and sauté onions and garlic until lightly brown (3–4 minutes). Add salsa and heat thoroughly, stirring occasionally. Add the chicharron and stir to combine. Cook for 5 more minutes; salt to taste. Remove from heat and serve with chopped cilantro. 🐟

MEXICAN SAUSAGE WITH POTATOES / CHORIZO CON PAPAS

(SERVES 6–8)

5 cups boiling water
1 tablespoon plus salt to taste
4 medium red potatoes
½ Spanish white onion, finely chopped
2 (4-inch) chorizo links (A) or store bought, casing removed
1 tablespoon parsley, finely chopped

IN a saucepan bring, 5 cups of water to a boil; add 1 tablespoon of salt and potatoes. Cook for 10–12 minutes over medium-high heat, until done but still firm. Let cool enough to handle; chop them into ¼-inch squares.

In a deep skillet, add onion and chorizo meat and cook over medium heat until brown (10 minutes). Add potatoes and cook for an additional 8 minutes or until potatoes are cooked but not mushy, stirring carefully so potatoes won't break. Season with salt to taste if needed. Let rest for 5 minutes before serving. 🐟

A. How to Make Traditional Mexican Sausage / Chorizo

(MAKES FOUR 4-OUNCE LINKS)

5 ancho chiles, seeded
2 pasilla chiles, seeded
4 garlic cloves
¼ onion
1 pound pork butt high in fat (25 percent fat at least, ask your butcher to grind the meat)
3 cloves, minced
½ tablespoon cilantro or use coriander seeds, toasted and ground
½ tablespoon black pepper, freshly ground
⅛ tablespoon cumin
⅔ cup white vinegar
½ tablespoon Mexican dry oregano, ground
2½ tablespoons salt
2 yards sausage casings or synthetic casings

I N a comal or cast-iron skillet, dry-roast chiles, garlic, and onion and set aside. Soak chiles in hot water for 10 minutes to hydrate. Place in blender with garlic and onion and purée with very little water until smooth.

In a large glass or a nonreactive container combine purée with ground meat and add the remaining ingredients (except the casings). Let rest in refrigerator for 1 hour. To be sure you have achieved the flavor your want, form a patty and fry in a hot skillet for tasting. Adjust seasonings if needed and proceed to stuff sausages into casings, or if you prefer, just make patties. 🪲

GREEN CHORIZO TOLUCA STYLE / CHORIZO VERDE DE TOLUCA

1 pound spinach
1 pound ground pork butt (25 percent fat, ask your butcher to grind the meat)
4 bay leaves, pulverized
½ tablespoon black pepper, freshly ground
½ tablespoon Mexican dry oregano, ground
1 garlic clove, minced
¼ cup Spanish white onion, finely chopped
2 poblano chiles, deveined, seeded, and peeled (see "Common Mexican Cooking Tools and Techniques," p. 334)
6 serrano chiles, finely chopped
5 teaspoons ground and peeled pumpkin seeds (*pepitas molidas*; grind using coffee or spice grinder or buy)
2 tablespoons salt
2 yards sausage casings or synthetic casings

W ASH spinach leaves and blanch them (see "Common Mexican Cooking Tools and Techniques," p. 334). Drain, and chop them very finely, also adding serrano chiles and poblano chiles, both finely chopped.

In a larger glass or nonreactive bowl, mix pork, bay leaves, black pepper, Mexican oregano, garlic, onion, chiles, spinach, ground pumpkin seeds (*pepitas*), and salt. Cover container with plastic wrap and place in the refrigerator for 24 hours, To be sure you have achieved the flavor your want, form a patty and fry in a hot skillet for tasting. Adjust seasoning if needed by adding salt and pepper. Proceed to stuff casings into links, or if you prefer, just make patties.

HOW TO STUFF SAUSAGES:

Here are two common methods to stuff sausages.

Manual method: Tie a tight double knot in the end of each casing. Cut off a desired length of the casing (we recommend using 1 yard at a time) and create a full

NOTES FROM THE ALMAZÁN KITCHEN

WHEN making sausages and chorizo, fat is what will keep your links moist and flavorful. If you try to make a leaner sausage, the flavor and moisture will be sacrificed. Unfortunately, you cannot reduce the fat and still make a good sausage or chorizo link.

Types of Casings

You can buy sausage casings from your butcher. This way they will be cleaned and ready to use. Sausage casings are available as synthetic, natural, or collagen. If using natural casing, the butcher most likely will give them to you in a brine mixture. Natural sausage casings are made from cleaned intestines of animals such as goats, sheep, cows, or pigs. Once the intestines are cleaned, they are kept refrigerated and covered with salt and need to be rehydrated in water before using. Nowadays you can even buy them pretubed. I usually use regular sheep or goat casings, as I prefer making smaller links. You can choose a pig or cow casing for larger links. Synthetic sausage casings are made from plastic or other inedible material. You will have to peel and dispose of the casings before cooking your sausage. Collagen casings are also an edible, natural casing. They are made of cow hide. Which casing you use is really a matter of preference. Experiment with different ones and choose the one of your liking.

If the casings become dehydrated, reconstitute them by placing them in warm water for at least 45 minutes.

Nahua woman preparing eggs in a *tequihl*, an outdoor Mexican kitchen; chorizo is hanging to dry overhead.
Photo by Jorge Ontiveros.

link by tying knots at the end of the casing and start stuffing the chorizo sausage by pushing the meat inside, with your fingers. Trying to pack tightly so no air is trapped inside the link, stuff meat into the sausage casings and twist. Tie a piece of twine between links to separate them. Continue stuffing, twisting, and tying-off until you have used all your sausage mix and/or casing. Check for air bubbles and pierce sausage with a needle to release any air.

Mechanical method: Use the sausage attachment on a KitchenAid sausage stuffer. (Note: This method works when two people work together, one controlling the sausage stuffer and the other stuffing the sausage mix into its casing.) Place sausage casing into the sausage attachment according to manufacturer's instructions. Person A should place meat into the grinder area and push meat through it. Person B should receive the meat as it goes into the casing and pull the sausage as it is being stuffed, extending the casing so as to facilitate the passing of the sausage meat mix into the casing. Check for air bubbles and pierce sausage with a needle to release any air. Once the desired length is achieved, twist and tie a piece of twine between links to separate. Continue stuffing, twisting, and tying-off until you have used all your sausage mix and/or casing. Use sausages within 3 days, keeping them refrigerated, or they will last 3 months in the freezer. 🐟

MEXICAN CHICKEN FRICASSÉE / TINGA DE POLLO

(SERVES 6–8)

2 tablespoons vegetable oil
2 Spanish white onions, thinly sliced
1 garlic clove, minced
4 tomatoes, medium size, peeled and chopped
1 small (1-inch) cinnamon stick
2 teaspoons adobo from canned chipotles
1 bay leaf
1 tablespoon white vinegar
½ cup chicken stock (see "Basic Recipes for Mexican Cooking," p. 11)
1 whole cooked chicken breast, shredded (see "Basic Recipes for Mexican Cooking," p. 11)
Salt to taste

PREHEAT a large skillet with 2 tablespoons of vegetable oil. Sautée onions and garlic on low heat until soft (3 minutes). Add tomatoes, cinnamon stick, chipotle sauce, bay leaf, and 1 tablespoon of vinegar and cook covered for about 10 minutes. Add ½ cup chicken stock and cook 5 more minutes. Add shredded chicken and season with salt to taste. Remove bay leaf and cinnamon stick. Serve warm with tortillas. 🐟

Garabatos.
Photo by Adriana Almazán Lahl.

"SCRİBBLE" COOKİES / GARABATOS

(MAKES 25 COOKIES)

1¼ cups butter or solid vegetable shortening
9 ounces confectioner's sugar
2 egg yolks
4 cups flour
Almond/Hazelnut Filling (A)
3 ounces melted chocolate

PREHEAT oven to 350°. Cream butter with confectioner's sugar, about 5 minutes until fluffy. Add egg yolks one at a time until well incorporated. Add flour; mix just until ingredients are well blended. Cover with plastic wrap and refrigerate for 1 hour, or allow to cool in the freezer for ½ hour.

Over a flour-dusted surface, spread dough with a rolling pin. Using a cookie cutter, cut 1½-inch rounds and place on pregreased baking sheet or silicon mat. Bake for 20 minutes until lightly brown; let cool completely.

Place a dollop of Almond Hazelnut Filling over the center of each cookie, cover with another cookie on top and gently press to form a "cookie sandwich." Drizzle melted chocolate over cookies, to simulate scribbling.

A. Almond/Hazelnut Filling

5 ounces dark chocolate
¾ cup whipping cream
⅛ tablespoon almond or hazelnut extract
2+ tablespoons confectioner's sugar

CHOP chocolate and in a saucepan heat whipping cream. Once cream starts to boil, add chocolate; mix well until chocolate is completely melted and both ingredients are well incorporated. Add almond or hazelnut extract and mix well. Allow to cool down completely. Once cool, add 2 tablespoons confectioner's sugar until consistency of mixture starts to thicken. You may need to add a little more confectioner's sugar to achieve the desired consistency, that of an Oreo cookie filling. 🐦

SWEET RICE WATER / AGUA DE HORCHATA

(SERVES 8)

1 cup of white rice
1 cup milk
2 sticks of cinnamon
8 cups water
1 teaspoon vanilla extract
¾ cup sugar or to taste
Ground cinnamon to taste
Ice

WASH rice and then soak it in 1 cup of milk with cinnamon sticks in a covered container; refrigerate overnight. In a blender, add rice, milk, and cinnamon sticks with some of the water; mix until completely blended. Strain though a coffee filter or a fine cheese cloth.

In a large pitcher, add the strained mixture, vanilla, sugar to taste, and the rest of the cold water. Stir well and add ice. Serve with a dash of ground cinnamon. 🐦

CARNIVAL / CARNAVAL
(DAY[S] BEFORE ASH WEDNESDAY)

CARNAVAL IS a celebration that, depending upon the locale, lasts anywhere from a single day (in which case it is the day before Ash Wednesday, and which we know as Mardi Gras, or Fat Tuesday, so named for the practice of eating fatty foods before the ritual fasting of Lent) to the entire week before Lent.

Carnaval in Colonial Mexico

Little concrete is known about how and when Carnaval found its way to Mexico. Mardi Gras was popular in both Spain and France during their respective occupations of Mexico, and records have emerged more from official attempts to eradicate the festivities than records of the festivities themselves. Consider this narrative as historians describe what Carnaval must have been like in Colonial Mexico City, based on edicts regarding bans and scanty writings:

> During the three days preceding Ash Wednesday, the city was gripped by an atmosphere of joy and liberty. There were dances, paseos [rides] and balls. . . . People threw eggshells and aniseeds at one another and everyone was tipsy. Many disguised themselves with masks and roved the city making fun . . . of the authorities . . . [and] men frequently put on women's clothing and vice versa, although the former was more common. . . . Young Indians dressed up as old men to do the dance of *huehuenches* (old men). On Mardi Gras, the Indians

Carnaval.
Photo by Jorge Ontiveros.

participated in the so-called ceremony of the hanged. In this parody of the judicial system, one of them is "hanged" from a tree.[1]

Carnaval was the epitome of the noisy, sometimes disruptive popular celebrations dominated by a combination of Mexicas and Mestizos that Mexico's elite looked to quash. In fact, and with good reason, the government feared such large gatherings as potential repositories for revolt and civil unrest. In Mexico City, in particular, the effort to eliminate Carnaval was the heart of a struggle for the very streets of the city, one that sought to create order by "civilizing" Mexico's native population and that would end with increased state regulation of popular celebrations in the country's most important urban centers. Authorities assumed control over many of the festivities, such as fireworks, and effectively transformed rowdy participants into somewhat more subdued spectators.

After an initial 1731 ban (coinciding with some similar bans and much controversy surrounding Carnaval in Spain and throughout Europe) and a subsequent order from the Spanish Crown in 1780, making Carnaval illegal, the celebrations and some of its most memorable ceremonies, in particular the "hanging" and the huehuenches, continued only in the more remote villages of the Valley of Mexico. Otherwise, the efforts of the Church and the Crown to civilize Mexico's cities by completely banning Carnaval were largely successful. Although it never regained its former glory after Independence, some vestiges survived with wide geographic

Mayo woman getting ready for a dance. As of 2005, 32,702 Mexicans spoke the Mayo language (Mexican census is language-based, counting how many people speak a given indigenous language, rather than how many identify with a specific tribe). The Mayo tribe has close resemblance to the Yaqui tribe in almost all aspects—the Mayos are, however, known for their dedication to work and their peaceful character. They live mainly in their two homeland states of Sonora and Sinaloa, and some Mayos have emigrated to southern Arizona. While much of their traditional costume has almost completely disappeared, the women still wear taffeta blouses decorated with lace, although this attire is more common among older people and in more isolated Mayo communities. Photo by Jorge Ontiveros.

differences. For example, the tradition of men dressing as women is still kept during various festivals, which the residents call "carnaval," celebrating the various patron saints of many of the towns of Central Mexico.

Records from Tlayacapan describe the history of the *chinelos*, traditional costumes reported to have been designed by hacienda workers for use during Carnaval to protest labor abuses. Created to mock the extravagant nightgowns worn by the wives of the wealthy *patrones* (bosses) with "awkward movements, sounds, ridiculous elbow-length gloves and plumed hats,"[2] the masks and costumes protected the identity of the wearer, permitting safe ridicule of the elite by the working class. This kind of parody is still seen in many Mexican parades today, with political figures typically the butt of the joke.

Revival of Carnaval and Its
Celebration in Mexico Today

Over a hundred years after it was banned, Carnaval was revived largely for political or commercial purposes and flourishes today in several Mexican cities. While the revival or birth of Carnaval in Mazatlán is murky, there are records of the festivities noted as early as 1864. During the 1880s and through the end of the century there too, people threw eggshells filled with glitter as well as perfumed flour, ashes, and dyes. In 1898 a committee was formed and Mazatlán's modern Carnaval was born. It included what were considered more civilized festivities, complete with a procession of bicycles and carriages, and confetti "to eradicate the immoral flour."[3]

The new, more refined Carnaval required the wearing of costumes and included a Carnaval Queen. Carnaval has been celebrated in Mazatlan every year since with the exception of six years leading up to and during the Mexican Revolution. Today, Carnaval in Mazatlán is reportedly the third-largest in the world after those in New Orleans and Rio de Janeiro.

In Veracruz the revival of Carnaval began around 1925 as a way to promote civic pride, and today it attracts over a million Mexican tourists, in no small part the result of promotion and significant investments by the state of Veracruz. Merida's Carnaval takes a cultural turn as floats representing the seven Mayan prophesies[4] as well a regional traditions, costumes, and dances populate parades with over 2,500 participants.

> ## VUELVE A LA VIDA
>
> A favorite for the day after the party is a dish called *Vuelve a la Vida* (Return to Life), a bracing seafood cocktail known as a cure for the dreaded hangover, *la cruda*. The same ingredients are also made as a soup of the same name, reported to be equally effective.

Aside from the carnival week celebrations that have emerged in Veracruz and Mazatlán, there are smaller but equally colorful events in Cozumel and Merida, among others. The party traditionally begins Tuesday of the week prior, with the burning of an effigy of the "Ill-Humored Man" (*Quema del Mal Humor*), a way to get the festivities off on the right note and make sure everyone is appropriately "happy." The festivities includes fireworks, dances, parades, and mischief, and it all ends with the funeral of "Juan Carnaval," where his widow mourns his death and a humorous testament, completely invented, is read. The more serious Lenten season then begins the following day with Ash Wednesday.

"RETURN TO LIFE" SEAFOOD COCKTAIL / VUELVE A LA VIDA (OSCAR ALMAZÁN RECIPE)

(SERVES 8)

4 ounces bay scallops, if using sea scallops
    cut in quarters
Juice of 5 Mexican limes
3 cups cooked octopus, cut in small
    pieces (A)
1 Spanish white onion, finely chopped
Cocktail Sauce (B)
½ pound cocktail shrimp
36 oysters, detached from shells/shucked
1 cup crab meat, minced
Salt and pepper to taste
2 avocados, sliced
4 whole Mexican limes cut in half
8 cilantro sprigs to garnish
Saltine crackers

MENU 10.1: CARNIVAL

Appetizer / *Botana*
"Return to Life" Seafood Cocktail
/ *Vuelve a la Vida*
Entrée / *Plato Fuerte*
Pork in Pibil Sauce with Pickled
Onions and Habaneros /
*Cochinita Pibil con Habanero
y Cebolla*
Sides / *Guarniciones*
Mexican "Red" Rice / *Arroz a la
Mexicana*
"Clay Pot" Beans / *Frijoles de Olla*
Dessert / *Postre*
Corn Custard with
Mexican Eggnog Sauce /
Flan de Elote con Rompope

ADD scallops and lime juice to a bowl, cover with plastic wrap, and reserve in refrigerator for 2 to 3 hours. Cook the octopus tentacles (directions below). To serve, add chopped onions and Cocktail Sauce to scallops. Add shrimp, oysters, octopus chunks, and crab meat; season with salt and pepper to taste and let rest from 10 minutes to a couple of hours in the refrigerator before serving. Serve in individual bowls garnished with a couple of slices of avocado, half a Mexican lime and a sprig of cilantro, with Saltine crackers on the side. 🐟

A. How to Cook Octopus

¼ cup white wine or beer
¼ cup water (if needed)
3 pounds octopus, cleaned (ask your fish market to do this for you, be sure they remove
    the beak)

WITH the sharpest chef knife, cut the octopus into 1-inch pieces; be careful, as the pieces are slimy and can be a little tough. Heat a large pan with a tightly fitting lid on the lowest heat—an enamel cast-iron pot is ideal, as the cast iron will distribute heat evenly—and cook octopus chunks for 20 minutes; no need to add anything else to the pan. After 20 minutes, stir gently and check liquid content; the octopus juices will turn into a red/purple thick sauce. When liquid gets low, add a quarter cup of boiling wine, cover again, and keep cooking until juices reduce, forming a very thick and syrup-like sauce (15–20 minutes). Once the liquid is reduced, taste a piece of octopus. If it's still tough, add a small splash of water and continue the slow cooking until the sauce has reduced again. Repeat the tasting and continue cooking until satisfied with the texture of the octopus. 🦟

B. Cocktail Sauce

1 cup ketchup
1 tablespoon Worcestershire sauce
½ tablespoon Maggi seasoning
½ cup white wine (substitute beer,
    vodka, tequila, or ⅛ cup of
    white vinegar if preferred)
Tabasco or Buffalo hot sauce (to taste)
¼ small onion chopped
1 teaspoon chopped cilantro
Salt and pepper to taste

"Return to Life" Seafood Cocktail / *Vuelve a la Vida*.
Photo by Adriana Almazán Lahl.

MIX ketchup, Worcestershire sauce, Maggi seasoning, wine or vinegar, Tabasco, onion, cilantro, salt, and pepper; cover and reserve in the refrigerator. 🦟

PORK IN PIBIL SAUCE WITH PICKLED ONIONS AND HABANEROS / COCHINITA PIBIL CON HABANERO Y CEBOLLA

(SERVES 8–10)

3½ ounces achiote paste (see "Basic Recipes for Mexican Cooking," p. 9, or use store bought)
½ cup bitter orange juice or substitute Bitter Orange Marinade (*narajana agria*) (A)
¼ cup white vinegar
2 medium garlic cloves, roughly minced
½ Spanish white onion, roughly chopped
¼ teaspoon cinnamon
¼ teaspoon Mexican oregano
6 pounds pork shoulder or butt, cut in large chunks
Salt and pepper to taste
2 large banana leaves
3 medium yellow onions, thinly sliced
Pickled Habaneros and Onions (B)
Habanero Salsa (see "Salsa Recipes," p. 22)

I N a blender mix achiote paste, orange marinade, vinegar, garlic, chopped white onion, cinnamon, and oregano until well blended. In a glass bowl, season pork with salt and pepper. Rub achiote mixture into the meat, coating it well. Cover with

Cochinita Pibil.
Photo by Adriana Almazán Lahl.

Pickled Onions and Habeneros.
Photo by Adriana Almazán Lahl.

plastic wrap and refrigerate for at least 3 hours—best if it is overnight. When ready to cook, remove pork from refrigerator and bring to room temperature (30 minutes).

Meanwhile wash banana leaves thoroughly and cut in half (horizontally), you will have 4 large pieces of banana leaf, each about 2-feet long. Soak these in hot water until they become soft and manageable.

Preheat oven to 350° or warm a Crock-Pot. Pat dry banana leaves with paper towels. In a heavy, large cast-iron pot or in the Crock-Pot place the banana leaves so they cover the bottom of the pot completely. Add pork with juices and sliced onions on top. Then fold in the sides of the banana leaves toward the center, covering meat completely, and tuck the leaves to the sides of the pot. Cover pot and cook in the oven's middle rack for 4 hours or 6 hours in the Crock-Pot.

Once cooked, place meat in a bowl and, using two forks, shred into bite-size pieces. Add cooked onions and pan juices and stir to mix thoroughly, adding salt and pepper if needed. Serve with Pickled Habaneros and Onions, and/or *Salsa de Chile Habanero,* warm corn tortillas, and limes. 🐟

A. Bitter Orange Marinade / Naranja Agria

½ cup sweet orange juice
Juice of 1 lime
½ cup white vinegar

Mix all ingredients. 🐟

B. Pickled Habaneros and Onions / Habaneros con Cebolla

2 habanero chiles, seeded and deveined and thinly sliced (use plastic gloves)
3 red onions, thinly sliced
¾ cup orange juice
¼ cup lime juice (made fresh from Mexican limes)
¼ cup white vinegar
Salt and pepper to taste

PLACE habanero chiles and sliced onions in a glass bowl, mix all ingredients, and let rest overnight in refrigerator. Bring to room temperature before serving to accompany Cochinita Pibil.

MEXICAN "RED" RICE / ARROZ A LA MEXICANA

(SERVES 6)

1 teaspoon olive oil
¼ onion, finely chopped
1 cup white rice
1 garlic clove, finely chopped
½ cup fresh tomato purée (see "Basic Recipes for Mexican Cooking," p. 15)
2 cups chicken stock (see "Basic Recipes for Mexican Cooking," p. 11)
½ teaspoon salt
2 sprigs fresh cilantro
¾ cup fresh carrots, peeled and diced
½ cup fresh peas

ADD oil to a hot skillet and sauté onion and rice for 2 minutes. Add garlic and cook for another minute over medium-high heat, stirring frequently. Add tomato purée and cook on high heat for 4 minutes. Add chicken stock, salt, and cilantro, then bring to a boil. Cover with tight lid and reduce heat to medium-low; cook 15 minutes. Add vegetables and cook another 10 minutes covered, or until rice is done and soft. Fluff with a fork before serving.

PAZOTE is a fragrant herb with a bright, almost lemony flavor that grows wild in Mexico and is even frequently found growing between the cracks in the sidewalks there. The name "epazote" comes from the Nahuatl *epazotl*, which means "skunk sweat," so-named, no doubt, for its pungent odor. It was used by the Aztecs for its medicinal properties as well as a culinary herb. Chopped epazote adds great flavor to *albóndigas* (Mexican meatballs, see p. 187) and a few sprigs not only enhance the flavor of pot of *frijoles de olla*, epazote is said to have gas-reducing properties as well. It is also the secret to a great quesadilla: a handmade tortilla, queso Oaxaca, and a couple of leaves of epazote!

"CLAY POT" BEANS / FRIJOLES DE OLLA

(SERVES 6–8)

2 pounds black beans (or substitute pinto or any beans you like)
5 cups water
½ Spanish white onion
3 garlic cloves
1 Serrano chile, small-chopped (optional)
1 bay leaf
1–2 sprigs of epazote, if available
Salt to taste

LEAN beans, removing debris, rocks, or broken beans. Once cleaned, add beans to a clay pot full of water and let them sit for 2 hours or overnight. (Note: You may, of course, make your beans in a traditional stainless steel pot. The flavor will be subtly but perceptibly different, though.) Be sure your pot is large enough to accommodate the beans as they expand. Your dry beans should not rise to past the ⅓ mark of your pot. Rinse beans and add 5 cups of water plus onion, garlic, chile, bay leaf, and epazote; cook covered for 2 hours on medium-low heat or until tender. For larger quantities of beans, this may take significantly longer. Make sure beans are constantly covered with water. No need to stir, but it is important that the beans never lack water or are allowed to become dry. If needed, add hot, not cold, water to bean pot. As you add more water, you may need to add more salt. It is important not to undersalt the beans. Once beans are cooked and tender, add salt and let them season for 15 more minutes. Remove onion, garlic cloves, epazote, and bay leaf before serving.

Corn Custard with Mexican Eggnog / *Flan de Elote con Rompope*
Photo by Adriana Almazán Lahl.

CORN CUSTARD WITH MEXICAN EGGNOG SAUCE / FLAN DE ELOTE CON ROMPOPE

(SERVES 6–8)

½ cup sugar
4 cups fresh corn kernels
5 eggs
1 (5-ounce) can condensed milk
1¼ cup milk

IN a saucepan cook sugar over medium-high heat until it caramelizes to medium-golden dark syrup; be careful not to let it burn. Pour caramel into an 8-inch round glass baking dish, tilt the pan to allow the caramel to cover the walls, and let it cool completely.

Meanwhile incorporate all remaining ingredients in a blender and mix well until kernels are completely integrated to the mixture. Pour mix into baking dish and cook in a Baño Maria (see "Common Mexican Cooking Tools and Techniques," p. 333) at 350° for 1 hour. Allow to cool for 30 minutes before unmolding. Serve topped with rompope, Mexican eggnog (see recipe, p. 94).

LENT / CUARESMA

[ASH WEDNESDAY TO HOLY SATURDAY]

THE FIRST DAY of Lent is Ash Wednesday and the forty-day holy interval ends with Holy Week (*Semana Santa*), which runs from Palm Sunday (*Domingo de Ramos*) through Easter Sunday (*Pascua*).

The Spanish word for Lent is *Cuaresma*, from the word *cuarenta* (forty), as this traditional period of abstinence corresponds to the forty days Jesus spent in the wilderness (the six Sundays are not counted). In Mexico, the custom had been that adults only ate one large meal daily, and meat is still not eaten on Fridays during Lent. Mexican households shop for and prepare what is known as *Comida Cuaresmeña* (Lenten foods), many of which are not well known outside of Mexico. Throughout the country, market stands (*puestos*) offer large dried shrimp for broths (*caldos*) and small dried shrimp for patties (*tortitas*), perfect heads of cauliflower for cauliflower fritters (*tortitas de coliflor*), seasonal *romeritos* (a spinach-like green), cactus paddles (*nopalitos*), lima bean soup (*sopa de habas*), as well as thick, dried slices of Mexican bread rolls (*bolillo*) for *capirotada*.

Viernes de Dolores

In a custom that was widespread in colonial Mexico but has survived only in the villages of the lowlands of central Mexico, the sixth and final Friday of Lent is Friday of Sorrows (*Viernes de Dolores*), a day of devotion to the pain and suffering of the Virgin Mary at the loss of her son. The secretary of the U.S. Legation to Mexico in 1841 described the festival of Mary as follows:

Fish vendor uses palm fronds for a distinctive Lenten presentation.
Photo by Huitzil Pedrero.

There is scarcely a house in the city where a little shrine is not erected and adorned with a profusion of glittering ornaments and blooming flowers. Glasses and vases of colored waters flash amid numerous lamps and wax candles: while the splendid jewels of the mistress of the mansion adorn the sacred image. The floors of the dwellings are strewn with roses, leaving a path for visitors, and music and refreshments welcome all. . . . In this gorgeous display, there is considerable rivalry.[1]

Today, where the custom is still observed (the following description is from the town of San Miguel de Allende), the *Virgen de los Dolores* is honored with beautiful altars on this day, many with images that show her hands clasped at her breast, her face streaked with tears. In some, she has a sword through her heart. With an icon of the Virgin at the center, the altars include flags or drapes in purple signifying mourning, white candles for purity, chamomile for her humility, bitter oranges for her sorrow, fennel signifying the betrayal of Jesus by his disciples, and gold foil representing her joy in the knowledge that Jesus will be reborn. These altars typically appear in the town plazas and churches as well as in homes. Some are small but others occupy an entire room, which has been cleared of furniture for this purpose. Often, similar to Día de los Muertos or the nativities of the Christmas holiday period, the entire family labors for days perfecting every detail, down to village scenes at feet of the icon of Mary.

Public fountains are cleaned and filled with fresh flowers, chamomile, fennel, and purple papel picado (Mexican cut-paper banners) and white and gold foil. Also, pots of pale wheat grass are grown without light to produce a pale yellow plant that is then exposed to the sun over the course of Cuaresma, turning it a bright green, a reminder of the Resurrection and renewal of life. Homeowners hand out treats, which include candied *chilacayote* (a kind of squash), which has been served on this day for nearly three hundred years.

> ## MENU 11.1: WEEK 1
>
> **Entrée / *Plato Fuerte***
> Mexican Greens with Shrimp Patties / *Romeritos con Tortitas de Camarón* (see p. 69)
> **Sides / *Guarniciones***
> White Rice Mexican-Style with Peas / *Arroz Blanco a la Mexicana con Chicharos*
> Refried Beans / *Frijoles Refritos*
> **Dessert / *Postre***
> Quince Paste with Cheese / *Ate de Membrillo con Queso*

WHITE RICE MEXICAN-STYLE WITH PEAS / ARROZ BLANCO A LA MEXICANA CON CHICHAROS

(SERVES 4–6)

1 teaspoon vegetable or olive oil
1 cup white rice
½ cup onion purée (see "Basic Recipes for Mexican Cooking," p. 13)
2 cups chicken stock (see "Basic Recipes for Mexican Cooking," p. 11)
¾ teaspoon salt
2 sprigs fresh cilantro
½ cup fresh peas

IN a hot skillet add oil and sauté rice for 2 minutes. Add onion purée, and cook for 3 minutes over medium-high heat, stirring frequently. Add chicken stock, salt, and cilantro and bring to a boil. Cover with tight lid and reduce heat to medium-low. Cook 10 minutes, then add peas and cook another 10 minutes, covered, or until rice is done and soft. Fluff with a fork before serving.

REFRIED BEANS / FRIJOLES REFRITOS

(SERVES 4–6)

4 cups cooked black beans drained, reserve stock (see p. 146 for cooking instructions)
2 teaspoons lard or oil of your choice
½ onion, finely chopped
1–1½ cups bean stock
½ teaspoon salt, or to your taste
½ cup Cotija cheese
Tortilla chips

MASH the beans into a purée with a potato masher. In a hot skillet warm lard or oil and add chopped onion; cook for 4 minutes or until lightly brown. Add beans, bean stock, and salt, and cook until purée has thickened enough to see the bottom of the skillet when stirred. Serve on a platter and garnish with cheese and tortilla chips.

QUINCE PASTE WITH CHEESE / ATE DE MEMBRILLO CON QUESO

2 pounds quince, peeled, cored, and quartered
4 cups boiling water
1 pound plus 12 ounces sugar
1 vanilla pod
10 ounces Manchego cheese (Mexican or Spanish)

IN a large saucepan, boil quince (*membrillos*) in water for 20 minutes; drain water and purée with a food mill or hand blender. Add sugar to the quince purée and split open vanilla pod; scrape vanilla seeds into the mixture leaving the pod in the mix. Cook for 40 minutes over medium-low heat, stirring constantly to avoid burning, until it changes color to a golden red-orange mix. Discard vanilla pod and pour into a flat glass pan. The thickness of your paste will be determined by how the liquid rises in the pan; select a pan accordingly. In Mexico, a thick paste is typical. Let it set and cool for a few hours, unmold, and serve ½-inch slices on top of ½-inch-thick slice of Manchego cheese. 🦂

MENU 11.2: WEEK 2

Appetizer / *Botana*
Tuna-Stuffed Cuaresmeño Chiles /
Chiles Cuaresmeños Rellenos de Atún
Entrée / *Plato Fuerte*
Seven Seas Soup / *Sopa Siete Mares*
Side / *Guarnición*
Toasted Tortillas / *Tostadas*
Beverage / *Bebida*
Hibiscus Water / *Agua de Jamaica*
Dessert / *Postre*
Plantains or Bananas with
Sour Cream / *Plátanos o Plátanos Machos con Crema*

TUNA-STUFFED CUARESMEÑO CHILES / CHILES CUARESMEÑOS RELLENOS DE ATÚN

(SERVES 4)

12 large cuaresmeño chiles
1 (5-ounce) can of tuna
½ Spanish white onion, finely chopped
½ red bell pepper, finely chopped
½ tablespoon mustard
5 tablespoons mayonnaise
2 tablespoons chopped parsley
1 cup corn or vegetable oil
Salt to taste
4 lettuce leaves
2 hard-boiled eggs, peeled and quartered lengthwise

WASH chiles and make a slit along one side. Boil chiles in water for 1 or 2 minutes. Carefully seed and devein chiles, removing skin. In a bowl, mix tuna with onion, bell pepper, mustard, mayo, parsley, and a pinch of salt and pepper to taste. Stuff chiles with tuna mix. Arrange 3 chiles over a lettuce leaf, alternating with hard-boiled egg slivers, and enjoy as an appetizer with crackers. 🦂

THE CUARESMEÑO CHILE

THE cuaresmeño chile, so-called because it is a popular meat substitute during Lent, closely resembles the jalapeño. As with all chiles, the seeds are the "hottest" part, and those of the cuaresmeño have the heat of a jalapeño, but overall, this chile has a mild flavor (see "Guide to Mexican Chiles," p. 339).

Seven Seas Soup / *Sopa de Siete Mares.*
Photo by Adriana Almazán Lahl.

SEVEN SEAS SOUP / SOPA SIETE MARES

(SERVES 4–6)

Guajillo Sauce Base (A)
¼ pound dry shrimp or pulverized shrimp (shrimp powder)
2 large sprigs epazote (or cilantro)
3 quarts fish or chicken stock (see "Basic Recipes for Mexican Cooking," pp. 11–12)
Salt and pepper to taste
1 cup fish stock (see "Basic Recipes for Mexican Cooking," p. 12) or 1 fish stock cube
6 small boiling potatoes, diced ¾ inch
1 cup carrots, finely chopped
1 onion, finely chopped
1 cup celery, finely chopped
12 ounces cod or halibut, cut into small chunks
4 large crab legs
1 pound oysters, cleaned
½ pound clams, cleaned
12 medium-large shrimp, deveined
⅔ cup finely chopped Spanish white onion
½ cup cilantro
2 large Mexican limes, cut into wedges

ADD the Guajillo Sauce Base (A), powdered or dry shrimp, and epazote to 3 quarts fish or chicken stock in a pot and simmer over medium heat, stirring occasionally, for about 30 minutes. Taste and season with salt and pepper; add 1 cup fish stock (or if you are using a cube, stir until well dissolved). At this point, if you added whole dry shrimp you may remove them. To finish the soup, add the potatoes, carrots, onion, and celery and simmer, uncovered, until potatoes are nearly tender, about 8 minutes. Add cod chunks, crab legs, oysters, and clams, and simmer until the shellfish open, about 3 minutes. Stir in the shrimp and cook 1 minute more, shrimp should turn color. Remove from the heat, cover and let stand 3–4 minutes. For garnishes, chop onion and cilantro, cut the lime in wedges, and place in a serving bowl. Serve the soup in large, warmed bowls, passing the garnishes separately.

ADRIANA'S MEMORIES

THIS is my Tio Ramon's recipe for *Caldo Siete Mares*—Seven Seas Soup. No one in my family loved good food and good wines more than my uncle Ramon, especially if we were talking seafood.

A. Guajillo Sauce Base

3 cloves garlic, unpeeled
6 medium-large guajillo chiles, stemmed and seeded
2 tablespoons oil
1 celery stalk, finely chopped
1 Spanish white onion
½ teaspoon Mexican oregano
⅛ teaspoon black pepper
1 tablespoon olive oil
3 tablespoons tomato purée (see "Basic Recipes for Mexican Cooking," p. 15)

ON a comal or hot griddle, dry-roast the unpeeled garlic until soft (10 minutes), turning so it cooks evenly; cool and peel. Meanwhile, dry-roast the chiles on another area of the comal; open them flat and press down firmly with a spatula so they are evenly toasted. After a few seconds, flip and press them down to toast other side as well. Place chiles in a small glass bowl, adding boiling water. Rehydrate for 10 minutes and drain water, reserving it. In a saucepan, heat oil and sauté celery and onions; cook for 5 minutes, stirring frequently. In the food processor, add sautéed onion, celery, oregano, black pepper, drained chiles, garlic (skin now removed) and ½ cup of chile water. Purée in blender, add water as needed to achieve desired consistency (paste should have the consistency of a thick salad dressing). Strain mixture and reserve. Heat the oil in a heavy, large pot over medium-high. Add the purée to hot oil (be careful about splatter), sauté, stirring for about 5 minutes. 🦈

HIBISCUS FLOWER WATER / AGUA DE JAMAICA

(SERVES 8)

10 cups water
2 cups dried hibiscus flowers
1 vanilla pod, split open
1 cup of sugar or to taste
Ice

IN a large pot bring 10 cups of water to a boil and add hibiscus flowers and vanilla pod, simmer on low heat for 10 minutes. Remove from heat and let cool. Strain cooked flowers from the water and vanilla, transfer liquid to a large pitcher. Add sugar to taste (if the taste is too concentrated, you can add more water) and ice cubes, but remember that the ice cubes will dilute the flavor as they melt; you will want to adjust the amount of water you add accordingly. 🦈

PLANTAINS WITH SOUR CREAM /
PLÁTANOS MACHOS CON CREMA

(SERVES 6)

1½ cups Mexican sour cream
3 ounces sugar
¼ teaspoon vanilla
Pinch of cinnamon
Pinch of nutmeg
6 plantains, sweet, ripe, and yellow (not green)
1 cup vegetable oil for frying

IN a medium bowl, combine cream, sugar, vanilla, cinnamon, and nutmeg. Mix well until sugar dissolves. Place in the refrigerator for at least 30 minutes. Meanwhile, peel and cut plantains into ⅛-inch rounds. In a large frying pan heat oil to 350°, fry plantains until they start to become golden brown, and flip them until they are evenly cooked on both sides. Drain excess oil by placing plantains on paper towels. Allow them to cool completely. To serve, place slices of plantains on a plate and drizzle a generous amount of the cream mix with a pinch of cinnamon. 🪲

BANANAS WITH SOUR CREAM / PLÁTANOS CON CREMA

(SERVES 6)

6 bananas
1½ cups Mexican sour cream
3 ounces sugar
¼ teaspoon vanilla
Pinch cinnamon
Pinch nutmeg

IN a medium bowl, combine cream, sugar, vanilla, cinnamon, and nutmeg. Mix well until sugar dissolves. Place in the refrigerator for at least 30 minutes. Once ready, peel and cut bananas into ⅛-inch rounds. Place bananas in a bowl and mix in cream. Refrigerate until serving. Dust with a pinch of cinnamon after serving in individual bowls. You can substitute strawberries for bananas. 🪲

FAVA BEAN SOUP / SOPA DE HABAS

(SERVES 6)

½ pound dry fava beans

4 cups water

2 cups chicken stock (see "Basic Recipes for Mexican Cooking," p. 11)

2 epazote sprigs (or ½ teaspoon dried epazote)

1 sprig fresh peppermint or ½ tablespoon dry peppermint

2 tablespoons olive oil

2 garlic cloves, finely chopped

1 small onion, finely chopped

1 serrano chile, finely chopped

2 tomatoes, diced

7 ounces tomato purée (see "Basic Recipes for Mexican Cooking," p. 15)

Salt and pepper to taste

MENU 11.3: WEEK 3

Soup / *Sopa*
Fava Bean Soup / *Sopa de Habas*
Entrée / *Plato Fuerte*
Hard-Boiled Eggs with Poblano
Chiles and Creamed Tomato
Sauce / *Rabo de Mestiza*
Sides / *Guarniciones*
White Rice Mexican-Style
with Peas / *Arroz Blanco a la
Mexicana con Chicharos*
(see recipe p. 151)
Refried Beans / *Frijoles Refritos*
(see recipe p. 152)
Dessert / *Postre*
Mexican Shaved Ice with
Fruit Syrup / *Raspados de Frutas*

PLACE dried fava beans in a pot with 2 cups of boiling water; cook for 2 minutes, turn off stove, and let them rest 2 hours. After 2 hours, drain water and top beans with chicken stock and 2 cups of fresh water. Add one sprig each of finely chopped epazote and peppermint, and cook covered for 45 minutes or until tender. Set aside, and remove foam that forms on top of the fava beans.

Warm olive oil in a skillet and sauté garlic, onion, chile, and tomatoes for 8–10 minutes. Add sautéed ingredients to the beans and let soup simmer covered for 15 minutes. Season to taste with salt and pepper and cook for 10 minutes more. Serve it as it is or purée with an immersion blender and serve hot.

Rabo de Mestiza.
Photo by Adriana Almazán Lahl.

HARD-BOILED EGGS WITH POBLANO CHILES AND CREAMED TOMATO SAUCE / RABO DE MESTIZA

"RABO DE MESTIZA" LITERALLY TRANSLATED MEANS "TATTERED CLOTHING OF A MESTIZA WOMAN" (A WOMAN OF MIXED INDIGENOUS AND SPANISH ANCESTRY), NOT AN APPETIZING IMAGE FOR FOOD, NECESSARILY. THE NAME IMPLIES THAT THIS IS A DISH THAT WAS CONSIDERED "PEASANT FOOD." DELICIOUS AND HEARTY, RABO DE MESTIZA IS ONE OF ADRIANA'S FAVORITE DISHES, AS IT BRINGS BACK FOND MEMORIES! (SERVES 6–8)

2 pounds tomatoes
1 garlic clove
3 cups boiling water
½ cup Spanish white onion, slivered or thinly sliced
3 tablespoons vegetable or olive oil
3 large poblano chiles, previously charred, sweated, skinned, stemmed, seeded, and cut in
    2-inch strips or rajas (see "Common Mexican Cooking Tools and Techniques," p. 334)
2 bay leaves
3 large fresh epazote leaves or ¼ teaspoon dry epazote
Salt and pepper to taste
½ cup Mexican sour cream
8 hard-boiled eggs

PLACE the tomatoes along with the garlic in a medium saucepan covered with 3 cups of boiling water over medium-high heat; simmer until thoroughly cooked (about 10 minutes). Place cooked tomatoes, garlic, and ¼ cup of the raw onion in the blender and purée until smooth.

In a large, heavy-bottomed pan over medium heat, pour in the oil. Once hot, add strips of poblano chile and remaining onion and sauté for 3 minutes, then add tomato purée. Add bay leaves and epazote, stirring well occasionally and continue cooking for about 8–10 minutes. Season with salt and pepper, remove from heat, and let mixture rest. Add Mexican sour cream and place back on stove at low heat. Remove herbs.

Peel hard-boiled eggs, and slice into ¼-inch-thick rounds. Add eggs to sauce and let rest 2 minutes to season in the sauce before serving. You can also substitute poached eggs. If you do, crack the eggs into a small bowl and slide them into boiling water with 1 tablespoon of white vinegar; cook 4 minutes and drain with a slotted spoon. Season with salt and pepper and slide them into the sauce for 2 minutes before serving. Serve with warm corn tortillas on the side. 🐗

MEXICAN SHAVED ICE WITH FRUIT SYRUP / RASPADOS DE FRUTAS

(SERVES 10)

10 cups shaved ice (see below)
Syrup of choice: Strawberry (A), Tamarindo (B), Mango (C)

TO make shaved ice, place ice cubes in blender until you get desired consistency, or you can use a snow cone machine. Grab a glass and fill with abundant shaved ice, cover generously with fruit syrup, and enjoy with a spoon. 🐗

A. Strawberry Syrup

4 cups water
2 cups sugar
2 pounds strawberries, cleaned, puréed, and strained

BRING 4 cups of water to a boil; add sugar and stir constantly until mixture thickens. Add strawberry purée, stir for 10 minutes over medium-low heat, and set aside to cool down, Place in refrigerator. Substitute any berries of your choice. 🐗

B. Tamarind Syrup

4 cups water
4 ounces peeled tamarind
2 cups sugar

IN 2 cups of boiling water, add peeled tamarind pulp; boil for 10 minutes over medium-low heat. In a separate saucepan, add 2 cups of water and sugar; cook until you get a light caramel. Strain tamarind mixture over caramel mixture and mix well. Cook over medium-low heat for 5 more minutes; set aside to cool in the refrigerator. 🪳

C. Mango Syrup

10 mangos
4 cups water
2 cups sugar

PEEL mangos and purée in a blender with 1 cup of water. Bring 3 cups of water to a boil in a saucepan; add sugar and create a light caramel. Strain and incorporate mango purée to the caramel mixture and cook for 10 more minutes over medium-low heat. Set aside to cool in the refrigerator. 🪳

FİSH ROLLS İN BANANA LEAF WİTH ACHİOTE SAUCE / ROLLOS DE PESCADO PİBİL

(SERVES 6–8)

3½ ounces achiote paste (see "Basic Recipes for Mexican Cooking," p. 9) or use store bought
2 garlic cloves, minced
½ onion, roughly chopped
½ teaspoon Mexican oregano
¾ cup bitter orange marinade (see "Basic Recipes for Mexican Cooking," p. 10)
¼ cup white vinegar
¼ teaspoon cinnamon

MENU 11.4: WEEK 4

Entrée / *Plato Fuerte*
Fish Rolls in Banana Leaf with Achiote Sauce /
Rollos de Pescado Pibil
Sides and Garnishes /
Guarniciones
Pickled Habaneros and Onions
(see p. 145)
Habanero Salsa (see p. 22)
"Green" Rice / *Arroz Verde*
Fried Sweet Plantains /
Plátanos Machos
Dessert / *Postre*
Mexican Chocolate Cake /
Pastel de Chocolate Mexicano

Fish in Banana Leaf with Pickled Onions and Habaneros / *Pescado Pibil con Cebolla y Habaneros*.
Photo by Adriana Almazán Lahl.

¼ teaspoon ground cumin
Pinch of nutmeg
2 pounds tilapia filets (6–8 fillets)
¼ pineapple, very thinly sliced (fresh preferred)
3 teaspoons olive oil
1 large banana leaf
¼ cup hot water

In a blender, add achiote paste, garlic, onion, oregano, bitter orange marinade, vinegar, cinnamon, cumin, nutmeg, and salt. Mix well, taking care that there aren't any chunks. Place filets in an ovenproof glass casserole dish, and pour the marinade over the top. Turn to coat. Refrigerate for 1 hour, covered with plastic wrap.

Wash banana leaves thoroughly and cut into eight 4-by-12-inch pieces; cover them with boiling hot water until they become soft and manageable. Place cooled banana leaves on a flat surface, add a tilapia filet and a couple of paper-thin slices of pineapple to the center of each leaf. Wrap banana leaf around fish, forming a taco, and secure with twine (or you may prefer to use a long, thin strip of the banana leaf). Place taco standing up in glass baking pan and add ½ cup of hot water to the bottom of the pan. Proceed to roll all the fish and drizzle with remaining sauce, and some olive oil. Place some pickled onion or pineapple on top; this will keep the fish moist as it bakes. Preheat oven to 375°. Bake for 20 or 25 minutes, serve with pickled onions and habanero salsa (see "Salsa Recipes," p. 22). 🦂

"GREEN" RICE / ARROZ VERDE

(SERVES 6–8)

1 tablespoon plus 1 teaspoon vegetable or olive oil
½ cup Green Purée (A)
1 cup white rice
2 cups chicken stock (see "Basic Recipes for Mexican Cooking," p. 11)
¾ teaspoon salt

IN a medium skillet, warm 1 tablespoons of oil and add Green Purée. Cook for 5 minutes, then set aside. In a separate hot skillet, add 1 teaspoon oil and sauté rice for 2 or 3 minutes until rice starts to brown lightly. Add fried Green Purée mixture to rice and cook for 3 minutes over medium-high heat, stirring frequently. Add chicken stock and salt; then bring to a boil. Cover rice with tightly fitting lid and reduce heat to medium-low. Cook 20 minutes, or until rice is done. Fluff with a fork before serving. 🐦

"Green" Rice / *Arroz Verde.*
Photo by Adriana Almazán Lahl.

A. Green Purée

1 small white onion, roughly chopped
5 ounces spinach leaves, cleaned
1 poblano chile, charred, seeded, and deveined (see "Common Mexican Cooking Tools
    and Techniques," p. 334)
1 cup fresh cilantro, chopped and rinsed
1 garlic clove
Generous pinch of salt

MIX ingredients well in a blender. Add ¼ or ½ cup water as needed to make a very smooth purée. Strain if desired. 🐦

FRIED SWEET PLANTAINS / PLÁTANOS MACHOS

(SERVES 6)

6 sweet plantains
1 cup vegetable oil for frying

PEEL and cut plantains into ¼-inch slices lengthwise. In a large frying pan heat oil to 350°, fry plantains until they start to become golden brown on one side, flip, and continue frying until they are evenly cooked on the both sides. Drain excess oil and place plantains over paper towels. To serve, place slices of plantains over rice, beans, or as a side dish. 🐦

MEXICAN CHOCOLATE CAKE /
PASTEL DE CHOCOLATE MEXICANO

(SERVES 6)

2 ounces (60 grams) Mexican chocolate disc (Abuelita or Ibarra brand)
⅓ cup plus 2 tablespoons cold whole milk
⅛ teaspoon ground cayenne pepper, for a less spicy cake, use Ancho chile powder
¾ cup flour
1 teaspoon baking powder
½ teaspoon baking soda
Pinch of salt
¼ cup melted butter or sunflower oil
¼ cup grated piloncillo or brown sugar
1 egg
Powdered sugar
Seasonal berries of choice

Mexican Chocolate Cake and Chocolate Disc.
Photo by Adriana Almazán Lahl.

PREHEAT oven to 350°. Roughly chop the chocolate. Place chocolate in a double boiler and melt. When chocolate begins to melt, add 1 tablespoon of cold milk, mixing constantly until chocolate has completely melted to a smooth texture. Remove from heat, add chile powder, and set aside

In a large bowl combine the flour, baking powder, baking soda, and salt; set aside. Pour the remaining cold milk into the melted chocolate, mix until well combined. Next add the melted butter or oil and sugar, mixing until well incorporated. Use a whisk to beat in the egg, until mixture begins to turn frothy.

Pour the dry flour mixture into the wet chocolate ingredients. Fold in until combined; do not over mix. Pour the cake batter into an 8-inch pregreased baking pan. Bake in center of oven for 30 minutes or until tester comes out clean. Allow to cool before placing on cake dish. Dust with powdered sugar as desired and decorate with your favorite berries. 🪲

MONTEZUMA'S GIFT OF CHOCOLATE

CACAO beverages dates back to 1900 BC. The first chocolate drink is thought to have been created around 2,000 years ago by the Mayans, and there is clear evidence of some form of cocoa beverage in Aztec culture by AD 1400. Recently, Mexico's National Institute of Anthropology and History announced that archaeologists have found, for the first time, traces of 2,500-year-old chocolate on a plate in the Yucatan peninsula, suggesting its use as a condiment or sauce as well.

Aside from being an ingredient in food and beverages, the seed of the cacao tree was a kind of currency. All of the territories that had been conquered by the Aztecs and grew cacao beans were ordered to pay them as a tax or, as the Aztecs called it, a "tribute." Chocolate also played a special role in both Mayan and Aztec royal and religious events. Priests presented cacao seeds as offerings to the gods and served chocolate drinks during sacred ceremonies. The Mayans sometimes mixed cacao with annatto, the most common food dye of that era, to form a sacred liquid resembling blood with ritual applications. There were several very specific recipes for combining the raw or roasted *cacåhoatl* with various grains to create many different beverages: some were believed to have aphrodisiac properties, others to address health concerns such as *"cachexia"*[2] (or wasting syndrome) as well as serious illness like dysentery or liver disease. Original texts include warnings against excessive consumption, which the Mexicas believed could lead to numerous illnesses.

In 1519, in a gesture meant to convey a great honor, Montezuma II presented explorer Hernán Cortés with the gift of a beverage made of ground cacao beans, vanilla, and chiles, known as *xo-xoatl* (in Nathuatl it is called *chocaltl*). When Cortés returned to Spain, xo-xoatl, what we know as chocolate, had been sweetened with sugar and was introduced to Europe.

What we call Mexican chocolate has a unique taste. Its texture is also quite different from that of any baking or cooking chocolate found in a typical American pantry; the sugar is grainier and the chocolate is quite sweet. A blend of cacao paste and piloncillo (hence the coarser texture) and cinnamon results in the signature Mexican chocolate flavor. It is sold in tablets. Two of the more popular brands are Ibarra and Abuelita.

SEAFOOD BUNDLES / MIXIOTES DE MARISCOS

(SERVES 6)

3 pounds white fish filet of choice (such as snapper), chopped in large chunks
10 clams, chopped
1 pound small shrimp, cooked
½ pound oysters
¼ cup capers
½ cup pitted olives
3 tablespoons lemon juice
1 tablespoon salt or to taste
Pepper to taste
2 tablespoons olive oil
1 Spanish white onion, finely chopped
2 garlic cloves, finely chopped
1 bell pepper
1 ancho chile, seeded, deveined, and soaked in warm water
3 teaspoons chopped parsley
1 cuaresmeño chile, deveined and chopped
6 banana leaves, cut into 12-inch squares, boiled for ½ hour, and cooled

IN a large bowl, mix fish chunks and seafood, capers, and olives; add lemon juice and season with salt and pepper and reserve in the refrigerator.

In a large skillet, warm 2 tablespoons of olive oil and, once hot, add onion and sauté for 3 minutes. Add garlic and cook until brown. Add bell pepper and ancho chile and continue cooking for 2 more minutes, then add parsley and cuaresmeño chile. Stirring constantly, cook mixture for 4 more minutes. Place all ingredients in blender. Add ½ cup of water and ½ tablespoon salt and blend all until smooth. Add warm mix to seafood.

Working on a flat surface, place each banana leaf square on top of a square of aluminum foil, preparing to create six "pockets." Distribute the seafood evenly among the six squares. Gather each banana leaf square and tie with cooking twine, forming a little "purse" or "bundle" and then wrap with aluminum paper.

Place the six bundles in a large tray and cook, creating a Baño Maria by adding ¼ inch of boiling water in the tray. Bake at 350° for 25–30 minutes in a preheated oven. To serve, remove aluminum foil carefully and serve banana leaf bundles in a bowl with warm tortillas and a wedge of lemon. Sprinkle the opened bundles with fresh parsley. 🐟

Cactus Paddle Salad / *Ensalada de Nopalitos*.
Photo by Adriana Almazán Lahl.

CACTUS PADDLE SALAD / ENSALADA DE NOPALITOS

(SERVES 6–8)

1 pound nopales, cleaned and medium diced (see below)
Salt to taste
1 teaspoon baking soda
1 small Mexican onion with greens
¼ red onion, finely diced
¼ cup cilantro, finely chopped
2 tomatoes, seeds removed and finely chopped
1 or 2 serrano chiles
1 tablespoon white vinegar
Juice of 2 Mexican limes
2 tablespoons olive oil
Queso fresco (optional)

WASH and prepare nopales, following the instructions below, then dice, or you may be able to purchase them already cleaned and diced in a Mexican market. Boil in water for 20 minutes with salt and baking soda. Once cooked, rinse with cold water. Nopales naturally produce a gooey liquid (sap), which you will want to clear by repeated rinsing in a colander. Then, mix all ingredients in a large bowl. Season with vinegar, lime juice, and oil; add salt and pepper to taste. Top with queso fresco. 🌵

To clean nopales it is best to wear thick gloves to protect hands from tiny spines. Trim off the outside edge that outlines the cactus (paddles). Then, scrape off the tiny spines from both front and back sides by holding the nopal at the bottom (where it was attached to the cactus plant; this is the narrowest part) against a flat surface. Cut spines with a sharp knife on a 30-degree angle and carefully scraping needles from front and back of the paddle. Rinse thoroughly to remove any needles and some of the sticky sap. You can leave the paddles whole, cut in slices, or dice the nopalitos, depending on the recipe you are using.

CAULIFLOWER FRITTERS / TORTITAS DE COLIFLOR

(SERVES 6)

1 small head cauliflower
2 cups vegetable oil
4 eggs, separate yolks from whites
½ pound Panela cheese, small diced
½ cup flour
½ teaspoon salt plus salt to season
½ teaspoon pepper
Tomato stock (see "Basic Recipes for Mexican Cooking," p. 14)

IN a medium-size pot steam cauliflower for about 10 minutes. It should be al dente, so be careful not to overcook (if florets are soggy, they will not do well in the frying stage of this recipe). In a cast-iron skillet, heat oil to 350°. Add 2 cups of vegetable oil to a frying pan and bring to 350°.

Meanwhile, in a mixing bowl, whisk egg until stiff peaks form, then add egg yolks slowly, and mix well. Separate the florets (creating small "bunches," resulting tortitas should be ½ to 2 inches in diameter) and insert some cheese inside the cavities between florets. Mix flour with salt and pepper. Drench stuffed florets in flour and then cover with foamy egg mixture. Carefully fry cauliflower in preheated oil until golden brown. Drain excess oil on paper towel and set aside.

Meanwhile make tomato stock. Add cauliflower patties to the sauce and let them simmer 5 minutes. Serve in a soup bowl with white rice and tortillas.

VANILLA FLAN / FLAN DE VAINILLA

(SERVES 6–8)

Caramel (A)
4 eggs
1 (12-ounce) can condensed milk
1 (14-ounce) can evaporated milk
1 tablespoon vanilla essence
½ tablespoon orange rind
Dash of nutmeg

PREPARE caramel. Once caramel is done, pour into a 8- or 9-inch round oven-proof glass pan and tilt pan so as to cover all surfaces with caramel; set aside. In a bowl, combine eggs, condensed milk, evaporated milk, vanilla, orange rind, and dash of nutmeg. Pour mixture into glass container and bake in a Baño Maria (see "Common Mexican Cooking Tools and Techniques," p. 333) at 375° for an hour, or until a toothpick inserted comes out clear. Let it cool completely and refrigerate before serving (about 4 hours or overnight). 🌶️

A. Caramel

5 tablespoons sugar
3 tablespoons water

IN a small saucepan over medium heat add sugar and water, stirring constantly until sugar dissolves and you achieve a thick caramel. 🌶️

VERACRUZ-STYLE FISH / PESCADO A LA VERACRUZANA

(SERVES 6)

1½ pounds red snapper or similar fish fillets
Juice of 1 lemon
2 tablespoons olive oil
½ Spanish white onion, sliced thin

> ### MENU 11.6: WEEK 6
>
> Entrées / *Platos Fuerte*
> Veracruz-Style Fish /
> *Pescado a la Veracruzana*
> or
> Fish Zarandeado /
> *Pescado Zarandeado*
> Side / *Guarnición*
> *Chayotes con Crema*
> (see recipe, p. 246)
> Salad / *Ensalada*
> Green Salad / *Ensalada Verde*
> Dessert / *Postre*
> Pound Cake Cupcakes
> with Lime-Apricot Glaze and
> Nonpareils / *Garibaldis*

Veracruz-Style Fish / *Pescado a la Veracruzno.*
Photo by Adriana Almazán Lahl.

1 large garlic clove, finely chopped
2½ cups chopped fresh tomatoes
1 bay leaf
1 sprig cilantro
¼ tablespoon ground cumin
1–2 jalapeño chiles escabeche-style, cut in strips (see recipe pp. 114–15)
2 tablespoons capers
¼ cup pitted green olives
Salt and pepper to taste
½ cup good white wine or tequila
Chopped parsley
Lemon wedges

MARINATE fish fillets with lemon juice; let rest for 15 minutes. In a large skillet, heat oil and add fish fillets. Cook for 2 minutes on each side, remove from pan, and reserve. In the same pan, add onion and cook for 4 minutes. Add garlic and cook another minute. Add tomatoes, bay leaf, cilantro, cumin, chiles, capers, and green olives and cook for another 3 minutes, or until tomato juice has almost evaporated. Deglaze pan with wine or tequila and cook 2 more minutes. Return fish filets into the pan and cook 6 more minutes; season to taste with salt and pepper. Remove bay leaf and serve fish, pouring sauce on top. Garnish with chopped parsley and lemon wedges. 🐟

FISH ZARANDEADO / PESCADO ZARANDEADO

(SERVES 4–6)

½ cup mayonnaise
¼ cup yellow mustard
1 cup butter
Blackened Tomato Salsa (see recipe, p. 19)
1 whole red snapper (4–6 pounds) cleaned
Salt and pepper to taste

IN a bowl mix mayo, mustard, and butter and incorporate salsa; mix well. Split fish open (butterfly style) and sprinkle salt and pepper to taste. Grill over medium-high flame, skin down, for 8–10 minutes (depending on size of the fish), placing it close to grill with the grill cover opened. Spread salsa mix evenly over fish, close grill, and cook for 8–10 minutes more, or until fish is completely cooked (it should be moist and flaky. Alternatively, place fish in a large nonstick rectangle grilling basket, cover with sauce, and grill skin side up, flip after 5–7 minutes and continue cooking for an additional 5 minutes; do not close grill cover. Enjoy with fresh tortillas and your favorite homemade salsa and fresh-squeezed lemon juice. Serve with white rice and frijoles de olla.

GREEN SALAD / ENSALADA VERDE

(SERVES 6–8)

1 large head of romaine lettuce, chopped
2 tomatoes, cut in wedges
1 avocado, skin removed and cut in wedges
¼ Spanish white onion, cut in thin slivers
Classic Mexican Vinaigrette (A)

TO serve, mix all vegetables in a large salad bowl and drizzle with dressing; toss.

A. Classic Mexican Vinaigrette

¼ cup olive oil
¼ cup white vinegar
⅛ cup water
Juice of 1 Mexican lime or lemon
1 tablespoon sugar
Salt and pepper to taste

MIX all ingredients and refrigerate for ½ hour before serving. Mix well before serving. 🐦

POUND CAKE CUPCAKES WİTH LİME-APRİCOT GLAZE AND NONPAREİLS / GARİBALDİS

(MAKES 30 MEDIUM-SIZE CUPCAKES)

½ pound butter, at room temperature
¾ cup sugar
3 eggs, at room temperature
2 cups all-purpose flour
1 tablespoon baking powder
Pinch of salt
⅔ cup heavy whipping cream
Apricot-Lime Glaze (A)
Nonpareils (*chochitos blancos*)

PREHEAT oven to 375°. Butter 2 sets of cupcake molds (makes 24 cupcakes total). In a mixer, cream remaining butter on high speed. Add sugar and keep mixing until it is well incorporated. Add the eggs, one by one; mix well until well incorporated. In a mixing bowl, combine the flour with baking powder and a pinch of salt. Bring the speed of the mixer to low and slowly add the flour mix, alternating with the heavy cream until well combined.

Spoon the batter into the molds to just under the rim, as they will puff. Place molds in the oven and bake for 12 to 15 minutes for normal cupcake molds and about 10 minutes for mini cupcake molds. A toothpick inserted should come out clean, indicating they are ready. Remove from the oven. Once cool enough to handle, remove them from the molds and place them on a plate or cooling rack.

Garabaldis.
Photo by Adriana Almazán Lahl.

Place nonpareils in a large plate or bowl. One at a time, dunk the top of the cupcakes, up to half their height, into the apricot glaze, then gently roll the glazed part in the nonpareils. Place them on a platter, let cool, and cover. They taste even better the next day. ❧

A. Apricot-Lime Glaze

1 cup soft apricot preserves
1 tablespoon sugar
5 tablespoons fresh-squeezed lime juice

IN a saucepan set over medium heat, combine apricot preserves, sugar, and lime juice. Stir occasionally for a couple minutes until the ingredients are well dissolved. ❧

HOLY WEEK / SEMANA SANTA (PALM SUNDAY TO EASTER SUNDAY)

HOLY WEEK (*Semana Santa*) begins with Palm Sunday (*Domingo de Ramos*) and lasts until Easter Sunday, or *Pascua*. Holy Week is one of the most important holiday seasons in Mexico. It is also the release from the sacrifices of Lent, which began on Ash Wednesday.

Early Celebrations

In this late 1700s description of Palm Sunday in Nueva España, a ceremony blessing the palms takes place at the cathedral: "There appears a long line of Indians, each bearing a palm at least seven feet high. Some . . . have travelled many a weary mile bearing their strange burden, which of course has lost all vitality by the way and is now carried with its leaves curiously plaited together." It goes on to paint a picture of the festivities in general.

> The occupation of the Mexicans at this season is to hurry from church to church, kneeling a few minutes before some altar in each and then passing to another. . . . Large images of the Virgin Mary, dressed in magnificent robes of silk and embroidered with lace and jewels are conspicuous in almost every edifice. In some [chapels] a large wax figure of the Savior is surrounded by other figures to represent some occurrence in the Life of Christ . . . large flowering shrubs of exquisite beauty, roses in full bloom, orange trees laden with fruits and blossom and immense vases of cut flowers."[1]

Each day had its ritual: On Holy Thursday, no carriages were permitted and the ladies walked in their finest clothes among a crowd that included "Indians and Poblano peasants in their picturesque costume," and in the evening, the reenactments of the Agony in the Garden.[2] Holy Saturday was "devoted to the death and disgrace of Judas" as described by Fanny Chambers Gooch in *Face to Face with the Mexicans*, written in 1887:

> Effigies of the traitor are hung all over the streets, and, being filled with powder, burst as they fall to the ground. This catastrophe is celebrated by the rattling of myriads of matracas, wooden rattles, that make the head ring, mingled with the shout of the populace. Numerous and grotesque paper effigies hung across many of the most prominent streets, and the Judases, filled with bamboos of powder, were tied to the balconies, roofs of buildings and lamp-posts. Many of them had silver coins pasted on them, representing the thirty pieces of silver for which Judas sold Christ. When the Judases burst,

Nahua man at altar during Semana Santa. The Nahuas live in every state of Mexico and form the largest group of indigenous peoples (over 20 percent) in the country. An estimated 1,376,026 Mexicans spoke one of the 28 Náhuatl languages as of 2005; including some 190,000 Nahuatl speakers who are monolingual. Some of the most important Mesoamerican civilizations were of Nahua ethnicity, including the Toltec and Aztec cultures. As the Spaniards sought to extend their political dominance into the most remote corners of Mesoamerica, the Nahua accompanied them as foot soldiers, often forming the bulk of the Spanish military expeditions that conquered other Mesoamerican peoples, such as the Maya, Zapotecs and Mixtecs. In contrast with the photo on p. 178 of a Cora man during Semana Santa, the photo below reflects the degree to which Catholic practices permeate the Nahua culture today.
Photo by Jorge Ontiveros.

the eager crowd gathered up the coins and then proceeded to tear into shreds the effigies, in order to avenge the treachery of Judas.[3]

On Easter Sunday, the sound of booming cannon celebrated the triumph over death, as Jesus rose.

A description of a Passion Play from the early 1900s,[4] performed in the town of Taxco (in the state of Guerrero), recounts a scene in which a small company playing the role of Roman soldiers complete with torches, lanterns, clubs, and spears and directed by "Judas," seize a life-sized statue of Christ, "clothed in soiled and torn garments," which was tied with ropes and chains and hoisted onto a frame then carried by six men. This all began shortly after 6 p.m., and continued until midnight with a candlelit procession of two thousand to the sound of drums and *chirimias* (a musical instrument with a sound like a fife).

Semana Santa in Modern Mexico

Holy Week is a truly a beautiful time of year to be in Mexico. Important religious images are displayed, altars are decorated at homes and in the streets, and floral decorations and palm crosses are everywhere. Each region celebrates a little differently, but pretty much the whole country participates in the tradition of breaking *cascarones*, colored eggshells filled with confetti—or, for the more mischievous, with flour—on the heads of friends and family. Churches everywhere are crowded for Easter Sunday Mass.

On Palm Sunday palm weavers (*tejadores de palmas*) sell their woven leaves outside the church, of which people buy several to fashion into the shape of a cross, which are blessed inside the church. Holy Thursday commemorates the Last Supper, and the traditional reenactments of the Agony in the Garden continue today. On Good Friday, the rites depict the events leading up to the Crucifixion, with an evening visit to the mourning Virgin (*pesame a la Virgen*) and end with the reenactment of Christ's burial service. As with so many Mexican festivities, the Passion plays (reenactments of the Passion of Christ) are fully staged and colorful, with amazing costumes; processions of penitents, sometimes on their knees; a portrayal of the Last Supper; and the Crucifixion itself. Participants are chosen before Lent begins and even practice for their roles.

Holy Saturday (*Sábado de Gloria*) is a time of purification through water, evoking the purification of Jesus. There are a lot of baptisms at this time in the Catholic faith. The holy water serves as a reminder that people all belong to the same spiritual family. This expression of water as a unifying medium was, at one time, celebrated as a sort of neighborhood party with water fights involving hoses, buckets, water balloons, and pots, and everybody got wet. However, the tradition has been banned since the water supply is now limited and the cost of supplying water to the Mexico's big cities is too high.

Cora man during Semana Santa. As of 2005, there were 17,086 persons who were members of Cora-speaking households. Unlike many of Mexico's other indigenous people, until 1722 the Cora had never permitted Catholic missionaries to live among them. In 1716, a Spanish expedition that attempted to bring the Cora under Spanish control failed. However, in 1722, the Spanish returned in force and the Cora yielded. According to Spanish accounts, many became Christian, but they still maintain a strong folk Catholic tradition, represented in this photo of a man dressed for Semana Santa celebrations, taken in 2012. The Cora practice a family and community ceremony several times a year known as *mitote*; obligations include fasting, sexual abstinence, and a period of activity such as special cooking, dancing, singing, praying, as well as blessing the *maíz* (corn). The celebration is unique to the Cora and continued after Spanish gained control of Cora lands.
Photo by Jorge Ontiveros.

Holy Week in Iztapalapa

In 2010, the reenactment of the Holy Week events in Iztapalapa was nominated to UNESCO's World Heritage List. More than two million people from all over Mexico come annually to this poor district south of Mexico City. The Passion of Iztapalapa was first performed in the year 1833 when a cholera epidemic struck the region, wiping out most of the population. A group from the area went on a pilgrimage to *El Señor de la Cuevita* (the Lord of the Little Cave) asking for God's intercession, praying for an end to the outbreak, in return for which they promised to perform a Passion play every year. Annually, for over 150 years, the promise has been fulfilled. Today, this event is closely tied to the identity of the district. The area where the passion play is performed incorporates the hill that was once home to the sacred Aztec New Fire ceremony (see p. 83).

Every year, men prepare themselves, hoping to be selected for the honor of playing the part of Jesus. Besides character requirements that insist upon no vices (or piercings or tattoos), the role requires excellent physical conditioning as it includes sporting a crown of real thorns, and dragging a two-hundred-pound cross for more than five miles through the streets. The actor is actually tied to a cross late in the afternoon on Good Friday on a hill overlooking Mexico City.

LAMB BUNDLES / MIXIOTES DE CORDERO

(MAKES 10)

3½ ounces guajillo chile
1 cup boiling water
4 garlic cloves
¼ teaspoon cumin
½ onion
¼ cup white vinegar

MENU 12.1: HOLY WEEK

Entrée / *Plato Fuerte*
Lamb Bundles /
Mixiotes de Cordero
Side / *Guarnición*
Chiles Stuffed with Beans,
Plantain, and Cheese /
*Chiles Rellenos de Frijoles,
Plátano Macho y Queso*
Salad / *Ensalada*
Beet Salad with Oranges and
Peanuts / *Ensalada de Betabel
con Naranja y Cacahuates*
Dessert / *Postre*
Mexican Bread Pudding /
Capirotada

Lamb Bundles / *Corderos.*
Photo by Adriana Almazán Lahl.

1 tablespoon salt or to taste
3½ pounds lamb or goat meat cut into 1-inch squares
Plantain leaf, cut into ten 12-inch squares
10 avocado leaves
Chopped Spanish white onion
Cilantro
Lemon juice
Marinated Onions with Habanero (A) (optional)

SOAK guajillo chiles in boiling water for 10 minutes. In a blender, mix chiles, garlic, cumin, onion, vinegar, and salt. Strain and marinate meat in mixture overnight in the refrigerator.

Grill or boil plantain leaf squares until pliable. Place about 4½ to 5 ounces of meat at the center of the leaf. Add an avocado leaf. Fold corners of the plantain leaf toward the center and tie with twine, forming a little sack. Cover mixiotes with 11-inch wax paper squares by placing mixiotes on top of your wax paper squares, gathering the wax paper square together, and tying both with twine, creating a double-layered cover for your mixiotes (outside layer will be the wax paper). Place mixiotes in a large tray. Cook mixiotes over Baño Maria (see "Common Mexican Cooking Tools and Techniques," p. 333) for 2 hours. Serve over warm tortillas with chopped onion and cilantro and a few drops of lemon juice or with Marinated Onions with Habaneros. 🦃

A. Marinated Onions with Habaneros

⅛ cup lemon juice
¼ cup white vinegar
½ onion, thinly sliced
1 habanero chile, thinly sliced, seeded, and deveined (use gloves while handling this type of chile)
1 tablespoon finely chopped cilantro
½ tablespoon salt

MIX lemon, vinegar, onion, and habanero chile; refrigerate overnight. Add chopped cilantro and salt before serving with mixiote. 🦃

CHILES STUFFED WITH BEANS, PLANTAIN, AND CHEESE / CHILES RELLENOS DE FRIJOLES, PLÁTANOS MACHOS Y QUESO

(SERVES 6)

6 ancho chiles, poblano chiles, or dried puya Chiles (for poblano chiles see "Common
    Mexican Cooking Tools and Techniques," p. 334).
3 cups boiling water
1 pound refried black beans (see recipe p. 152)
5 sweet plantains, ripe, medium sliced, fried
8–9 ounces Panela cheese, thinly sliced
2 cups flour
4 egg whites
Corn or vegetable oil for frying
Tomato stock (see "Basic Recipes for Mexican Cooking," p. 11)

DIP chiles in hot water for 10 minutes, pat them dry, and open a side slit on each. Devein and seed the chile, being careful not to break the flesh. Stuff with a table-spoon of beans, a slice of fried plantain, and a slice of cheese. Preheat oil to 350°. Close chile and dredge in flour. Whisk egg whites in a deep bowl until they peak and dip chile with the egg white to cover. Deep-fry in the oil and drain on paper towel or brown paper bag to remove excess oil. Serve warm over tomato stock. Note: You can also skip deep-frying the chile and serve it after stuffing it with beans, plantains, and cheese.

Chile relleno.
Photo by Adriana Almazán Lahl.

BEET SALAD WİTH ORANGES AND PEANUTS / ENSALADA DE BETABEL CON NARANJA Y CACAHUATES

(SERVES 8–10)

1 large orange
1 beet, boiled, skin removed, and thinly sliced
1 quarter red onion, sliced into thin rings
1 head romaine lettuce, washed and chopped in small pieces
Orange Vinaigrette (A)
¼ cup toasted peanuts

CAREFULLY cut the orange peels off with a small paring knife and thinly slice the oranges. On a serving platter, lay a handful of lettuce. Place orange slices, beet slices, and red onion rings over the lettuce. Drizzle Orange Vinaigrette over the salad; garnish with toasted peanuts. 🐝

A. Orange Vinaigrette

3 teaspoons orange juice
1 teaspoon olive oil
1 teaspoon sherry vinegar
1 teaspoon sugar
¼ teaspoon Mexican oregano
Salt and pepper to taste

IN a small bowl mix the orange juice, olive oil, vinegar, sugar, oregano, salt, and pepper until it is well mix. 🐝

MEXİCAN BREAD PUDDİNG / CAPİROTADA

TRADITIONALLY SERVED ON GOOD FRIDAY (ALTHOUGH IT IS ALSO EATEN YEAR-ROUND), *CAPIROTADA* IS A SYMBOLIC FOOD FOR MEXICAN CATHOLICS, A VIRTUAL BODY OF THE PASSION OF CHRIST IN A PUDDING, WITH THE CLOVES REPRESENTING THE NAILS, THE BREAD THE BODY OF JESUS, THE CINNAMON STICKS THE WOOD, THE SYRUP HIS BLOOD, AND THE MELTED CHEESE THE HOLY SHROUD. (SERVES 6)

2 piloncillo pieces
2 cloves

Capirotada.
Photo by Adriana Almazán Lahl.

1 cinnamon stick
2 cups water
1 teaspoon vanilla extract
2 cups vegetable oil for frying
4 bolillos or French baguette, sliced (best if it has been left to air for a day)
½ cup peanuts or chopped pecans
½ cup raisins
1 cup of queso añejo or Cotija

PLACE piloncillo, cloves, and cinnamon with water in a medium saucepan over medium heat until piloncillo dissolves and forms a syrup. Stir in vanilla, remove cinnamon and cloves from syrup, and set aside. Meanwhile heat oil in a frying pan. Add and deep-fry bread slices to a light golden brown; place them on paper towel to drain excess oil. Place bread in a baking pan and distribute half of the peanuts, raisins, and cheese on top; add another layer of bread and again distribute raisins, peanuts, and cheese. Drizzle syrup over the bread and bake covered for ½ hour at 300°; serve cold or warm.

CHİLDREN'S DAY / DÍA DEL NIÑO
(APRİL 30)

İN 1924, Mexican president Alvaro Obregon declared April 30 *Día del Niño*, or Day of the Child, following the League of Nations' Declaration of the Rights of the Child in the same year. Although it is not an official holiday on the school calendar, activities at school may include special presentations for the parents, with many schools celebrating the day before so that the children can have a day off.

Mazahua girls dressed in traditional clothing, a custom and handcraft that is in danger of disappearing (especially the version hand woven in wool, although through women's collectives efforts are being made to save the skills and traditions). The pleated skirt, usually made with satin and lace, is called a *chinche*, under which an underskirt with an embroidered edge is worn.
Photo by Jorge Ontiveros.

For those schools that do remain open on April 30, there are no classes and children are not required to wear their school uniforms. The day is always filled with activities, and children look forward to this holiday that is all their own.

While there is no specific menu traditionally served on this day, we have selected dishes that are favorites with Mexican children and added a selection of sweets and treats.

MENU 13.1: CHILDREN'S DAY

Soup / *Sopa*
Mexican Meatball Soup / *Sopa de Albóndigas*
Side / *Guarnición*
Warm Corn Salad / *Esquites*
Entrée / *Plato Fuerte*
Open-Faced Refried Beans and Melted Cheese Sandwiches / *Molletes*
Dessert / *Postre*
Choose from sweets and treats listed below

WARM CORN SALAD / ESQUITES

(SERVES 6–8)

6 corn cobs, shucked and degrained
3 tablespoons butter
2 cups chicken stock (see "Basic Recipes for Mexican Cooking," p. 11)
Salt to taste
1 serrano chile, deveined, seeded, and cut in thin strips
1 epazote sprig or ½ teaspoon dry epazote
Piquín chile or ancho chile powder
Juice of 3 Mexican limes
6 tablespoons of queso fresco or crumbled Cotija
Mayonnaise (optional)

USING a knife, remove corn kernels from cob. In a large skillet, melt butter and add kernels; cook over low heat, adding 1 cup of chicken stock, salt, serrano chile, and epazote. Allow to simmer for 15 minutes and adding extra stock as needed. This stew is served soup style, with ¾ kernels to ¼ broth. Serve hot in a cup or mug and sprinkle with piquín chile or ancho chile powder, the juice of half a lime, and 1 tablespoon of queso fresco or crumbled Cotija. Some people like to add a dollop of mayonnaise.

Albdónigos.
Photo by Adriana Almazán Lahl.

MEXICAN MEATBALL SOUP / SOPA DE ALBÓNDIGAS

(SERVES 6)

1½ pounds ground beef
4 sprigs fresh mint, finely minced, or epazote
2 garlic cloves, minced, plus 1 whole garlic clove
1 raw egg
½ cup breadcrumbs
½ white onion, finely chopped
Salt and pepper to taste
2 medium tomatoes
½ Spanish white onion, chopped
3 chipotle chiles in adobo sauce, canned (optional)
2 tablespoons canola or vegetable oil
2 cups chicken stock (see "Basic Recipes for Mexican Cooking," p. 11)
3 cilantro sprigs
2 hard-boiled eggs, quartered

IN a bowl, mix ground beef, mint, minced garlic, lightly beaten raw egg, bread crumbs, finely chopped onion, salt, and pepper; mix well and cover with plastic wrap. Place in the refrigerator for a half hour. Meanwhile, mix tomatoes, ½ onion, garlic clove, and chipotle chile in blender until smooth. (For a kid's version, we recommend adding ½ seeded chile only, or you can omit chipotle.) Strain mixture.

Heat oil in a saucepan; add strained, blended sauce; and let it cook covered for 5–7 minutes over high heat. Add chicken stock and cilantro, bring to a boil and set aside.

Meanwhile, peel and chop boiled eggs. Make meatballs 1 inch in diameter from the ground beef mixture. Make a hole with your thumb in the middle of each meatball and place a piece of hard boiled egg in the cavity. Seal very carefully with a little more ground meat and roll until smooth.

Add meatballs into stew and let them cook for 25 minutes on medium heat; add additional stock if needed. Remove cilantro sprigs before serving. Serve hot with broth. If you are not following menu 13.1, serve with rice and beans on the side. 🐦

OPEN-FACED REFRIED BEANS AND MELTED CHEESE SANDWICHES / MOLLETES

(SERVES 6)

6 French bread rolls or bolillos
2 teaspoons butter
1 large chorizo link (optional, see recipe p. 130) or 4 bacon strips (optional)
½ Spanish white onion, chopped
2 cups refried beans (see recipe p. 152)
8 ounces shredded Mexican or Oaxaca cheese
Pico de Gallo (see "Salsa Recipes," p. 24)

CUT bread in half; spread butter and toast on a hot skillet. In a separate skillet, sauté chorizo with onion and set aside, or fry bacon. Warm refried beans and set aside. Place bread on a serving platter and spread 2 tablespoons of beans on each piece, then add the chorizo with onion or bacon and 2 tablespoons shredded cheese. Place under broiler until cheese melts and starts browning. Serve with Pico de Gallo on top.

You can also make *molletes* just with beans and cheese. 🐦

Molletes.
Photo by Adriana Almazán Lahl.

MANGO POPSICLES WITH PIQUIN CHILE / PALETAS DE MANGO CON CHILE PIQUÍN

(SERVES 8)

2 ripe mangos
¾ cup sugar
2½ cups water
Piquin chile powder to garnish

BLEND all ingredients, except piquin chile, until smooth. Pour into 4-ounce paper cups or popsicle molds and freeze from 60 to 90 minutes. Remove from freezer and insert wooden stick. Return to freezer until completely set. Peel cup, dip popsicle in piquin chile powder, and enjoy. 🐝

SWEETS AND TREATS

Mango Popsicles with Piquin Chile /
Paletas de Mango con Chile Piquín
Lemon Chia Popsicles /
Paleta de Limón
Pineapple Popsicles /
Paletas de Piña
Fruit and Veggies Snacks with
Lime and Chile Piquin / *Frutas
y Vegetales con Chile y Limón*
Mama's Orange Cinnamon
Cookies / *Galletas de Naranja
y Canela de mi Mamá*
Mexican Peanut Brittle /
Palanquetas
Layered Fruit Gelatin Dessert /
Gelatina de Frutas
Happy Amaranth Cakes / *Alegrías*

Paletas.
Photo by Adriana Almazán Lahl.

LEMON CHIA POPSICLES / PALETAS DE LIMÓN

(SERVES 8)

5 Mexican limes, rind and juice
2½ cups water
¾ cup of sugar (or sugar substitute) or to your taste
2 tablespoons chia seeds

WITH a potato peeler, remove skin from limes and juice them, reserving rind. Add liquid and rind to blender with water and sugar; blend well until rinds are puréed completely. Mix in chia seeds and pour inside 4-ounce paper cups or popsicle molds and freeze from 60 to 90 minutes. Remove from freezer and insert wooden stick; return to freezer until completely set.

PINEAPPLE POPSICLES / PALETAS DE PIÑA

(SERVES 8)

3 cups fresh pineapple, roughly chopped
Juice of 2 Mexican limes
¾ cup sugar
1 sprig, mint finely chopped

BLEND all ingredients until smooth, pour in 4-ounce paper cups or popsicle molds, and freeze from 60 to 90 minutes. Remove from freezer and insert wooden stick; return to freezer until completely set.

Instead of mint and pineapple, you can substitute with basil and watermelon or tarragon and cantaloupe, or you can skip the herbs for a more purist flavor. 🦟

FRUIT AND VEGGIE SNACKS WITH LIME AND CHILE PIQUIN / FRUTAS Y VEGETALES CON CHILE Y LIMÓN

(SERVES 6–8)

1 cucumber, peeled
1 jicama, peeled
1 carrot, peeled
¼ watermelon, rind removed (seedless preferable)
1 large green mango, peeled
Ancho chile powder or piquin chile
Juice of 2 Mexican limes
Salt to taste

CUT fruit and vegetables in large long wedges; place mixed fruits and vegetables in large glasses and sprinkle with lime juice. Mix the chile powder with the salt and then dust the fruits and vegetables. 🦟

MAMA'S ORANGE CINNAMON COOKIES / GALLETAS DE NARANJA Y CANELA DE MI MAMÁ

(SERVES 8–10)

2 cups vegetable shortening
1 pound sugar plus 3½ ounces sugar
Rind of one orange
1 tablespoon cinnamon plus 3½ ounces freshly ground cinnamon
4 cups flour
2 egg whites
10 egg yolks

WITH an electric mixer, whip vegetable shortening for 5 minutes on high speed until creamed. Add 2 cups sugar and whip additional 5 minutes; add orange rind and 1 tablespoon cinnamon. Add eggs yolks, one at the time until well mixed, then mix in egg whites. Once well combined add flour slowly until dough becomes uniform and one whole piece. Place dough on a flat floured surface and knead it by hand for 5 minutes more, then allow to rest for ½ hour to an hour

With a rolling pin, work dough to ¼-inch thickness. Cut the dough into cookies, place on greased baking sheet, and bake at 350° for 20 minutes, or until edges of the cookies start to brown.

In a separate bowl, mix 3½ ounces of sugar and 3½ ounces cinnamon. Set aside. Once cookies are baked, dust with the sugar-cinnamon mix as soon as they come out of the oven. 🐛

MEXICAN PEANUT BRITTLE / PALANQUETAS

(SERVES 6)

¼ cup water
1 cup sugar
2 tablespoons piloncillo
2 ounces butter
½ cup fresh shelled peanuts
¼ tablespoon food-grade citric acid powder or baking soda

PREPARE a baking sheet by greasing it or placing a silicon baking sheet on top. Set aside. In a copper saucepan or a regular saucepan bring water to a boil, add sugar and piloncillo, and cook over medium flame, stirring constantly with wooden spoon until you get caramel and the caramel reaches 300° on a candy thermometer.

Add butter and stir again. Add peanuts and keep stirring until all peanuts get coated. Meanwhile dissolve citric acid or baking soda with one tablespoon of hot water, add it to the caramel-peanut mixture and mix well.

Pour peanut mixture onto baking sheet and spread evenly. With a wet knife, make 3-by-1-inch rectangle cuts and let cool completely. Once cold, separate and wrap with plastic wrap. 🐟

GELATIN DESSERTS / *GELATINAS*

IF you've traveled to Mexico, or live in a city with a large Mexican population, you've probably seen them in push carts: pretty little gelatin desserts with raisins, nuts, or fruit fillings, usually layered. Gelatin desserts are eaten almost daily in nearly 90 percent of Mexican homes. Mexicans consume more gelatin desserts than nearly any other country in the world. Whether it's a birthday party, baptism, or quinceañera, the dessert selection usually includes a beautifully crafted gelatin.

Gelatin artists take their gelatin desserts to a whole other level. (Yes, there are many señoras who are famous for their *Gelatina Artistica* in Mexico—they even give classes and are quite competitive about who is the queen, or *reina de la gelatina*.) Using a fine flavor-injection tool, three-dimensional creations are set in a transparent gelatin base, all 100 percent edible, including the intricate flowers. *El Arte Floral en Gelatina* is originally from France and doubtless is an import that arrived along with *La Comida Afrancesada* (see p. 219), introduced in the 1800s by the brief yet important colonization of Mexico by the French.

LAYERED FRUIT GELATIN DESSERT /
GELATINA DE FRUTAS

(SERVES 8–10)

FOR THE FRUIT GELATIN LAYER

3 gelatin envelopes
4 cups water
10 ounces sugar
½ tablespoon citric acid

HYDRATE gelatin by mixing with ¼ cup cold water. Once the gelatin is hydrated, dissolve over a Baño María (see "Common Mexican Cooking Tools and

Gelatina Artistica by Sweets Collections,
San Francisco.
Photo by Michelle Edmunds.

Techniques," p. 333) for 5 minutes. Place remaining water and sugar in a saucepan over medium-high heat until it boils. Add gelatin and cook for 8–10 minutes, incorporate citric acid, and remove from heat; stir well and allow to cool for 20 minutes. ❦

ASSEMBLE FRUIT

3 ounces peaches in syrup, sliced (see recipe, p. 247)
2 ounces large strawberries, sliced
1 kiwi, peeled and sliced

USING a gelatin mold, arrange each fruit nicely at the bottom of the mold. With a ladle, carefully spoon clear liquid gelatin on top of the arranged fruits, taking care not to disturb the fruit arrangement (mold should not be filled up to the top at this point). Place in the refrigerator overnight or until completely set. ❦

FOR THE MILK GELATIN LAYER

1 egg yolk
1 gelatin envelope
2½ cups milk
½ cup sugar
1 cinnamon stick
1½ tablespoons vanilla extract

SEPARATE yolk and whisk in a medium mixing bowl. Dissolve gelatin in ¼ cup milk in a saucepan, let it hydrate 3 minutes, and then combine with remaining milk, sugar, and cinnamon stick. Bring to a simmer over a medium-low flame. Continue simmering for 5 minutes. Combine with egg yolk by adding a little hot milk to the egg yolk, then add the egg yolk/milk mix to saucepan slowly, stirring rapidly to avoid lumpy, scrambled eggs. Simmer mixture for 3 additional minutes and add the vanilla extract; stir well for 2 minutes more, remove from heat, and let it rest for 25 minutes.

Take prepared fruit gelatin out of the fridge and pour liquid milk gelatin on top with a ladle; place in the fridge for at least 3 more hours or overnight. Remove from mold by placing mold into a bowl of hot water for 10 seconds, taking care not to allow any of the hot water to find its way into the mold, and flip over a large serving plate. 🐦

AMARANTH

ONCE a staple of the Aztec diet, this grain was used in indigenous religious ceremonies. One ceremony particularly irked the Church, in spite of, or maybe because of its similarity to the Christian ritual of communion. The Aztecs formed sculptures of their gods out of amaranth and honey and broke them into pieces and ate them. Amaranth was subsequently banned by the Catholic Church but continued to grow as a weed throughout Mexico. Today, amaranth is widely available in Mexico, and in the United States it has gained prominence as a "super food" for its health benefits.

Alegrías.
Photo by Adriana Almazán Lahl.

HAPPY AMARANTH CAKES / ALEGRÍAS

(MAKES 20 PIECES)

2 cups sugar
½ cup honey
2 cups water
1 pound toasted amaranth
4 galvanized metal rings or empty tuna cans (washed and open at both ends) or baking pan
½ cup mix of raisins and almonds or peanuts (both optional)

IN a large pot add sugar, honey, and water and stir until the mix becomes a syrup and has reached the hard-ball stage, 245° on a candy thermometer. Remove from heat and add amaranth and raisins and nuts (if desired). Mix well with a wooden spoon until you get a paste-like consistency. Place mix inside clean prepared tuna can molds or metal rings and press them down to form tight patties. Remove metal ring and cut patties in four pieces. Allow to cool completely and wrap cakes with plastic wrap.

You can also spread the mixture on a large baking sheet or wooden board. Press it to a uniform thickness of ½ inch, using a rolling pin. Cool the mixture for about 2 minutes, until partially set, then cut it into finger-size strips or squares. Wrap the pieces individually in plastic wrap and store in an airtight tin for up to 1 month. 🦗

DAY OF THE HOLY CROSS / DÍA DE LA SANTA CRUZ
[MAY 3]

MAY 3 is Day of the Holy Cross (*Día de la Santa Cruz*). It is also *El Día del Albañil* (the Day of the Mason Worker) the most important of several Mexican holidays celebrated to acknowledge various trades and professions (like *Día del Maestro*, the teacher). These two celebrations are connected, as mason workers were credited with locating the cross on which Jesus was crucified.

Origins of the Day of the Holy Cross

By the time Spain conquered Mexico, *The Golden Legend*, written by Jacopo de Voragine, Bishop of Genoa in 1260, was widely accepted as doctrine regarding many issues of faith, including the origins and history of the True Cross (*Vera Cruz*). Interestingly, *The Golden Legend* contains two different accounts of the origin of the True Cross. In one section of the book, "The Life of Adam," Voragine talks about three seeds from which three trees grew and goes on to explain that it was from these three trees that the cross on which Jesus was crucified was made. In a chapter titled "Of the Invention of Holy Cross, and First of This Word Invention," Voragine traces the origins of the cross to the Tree of Knowledge of Good and Evil, from which Adam ate.

Other traditions persist as well. The Eastern Orthodox Church interprets this Bible passage as referring to the True Cross, made of three different kinds of wood, being the place Christ's feet were nailed: "Isaiah 60:13: The glory of Lebanon shall come unto thee, the fir tree, the pine tree, and the box together to beautify the place of my sanctuary, and I will make the place of my feet glorious."

There are many versions of the story of the rediscovery of the cross, but the most widely accepted, from year AD 326, recounts how Roman Emperor Constantine sent his mother, Saint Elena, to Jerusalem to look for the remains of the cross upon which Jesus had been crucified. A cross was located with the assistance of a crew of masons, its authenticity determined when a very ill person in the group touched it and was healed, thus identifying it as the real cross, or *cruz verdadera*.

During first years of Christianity, the cross alone was the center of Christian altars. (In the year AD 432, the sculpture of Christ was first placed on the Cross.) According to the Christian liturgical calendar, there are several different days commemorating the cross used in the crucifixion of Jesus. In 1960, Pope John XXIII changed the holiday to September 14, but the May 3 tradition was well rooted and remains strong in Mexico.

The Day of the Mason Worker
(El Día del Albañil)

All construction, especially in Mexico City and surrounding areas of Central Mexico, is suspended on May 3 and laborers celebrate a Mass at the construction site in front of a handmade cross, configured with devotion by the chief contractor and his team. Some smaller building sites may not have a Mass hosted at the spot, but prayers are always said and the cross taken to the nearby church to be blessed. Early that morning the site is decorated by the masons (*albañiles*) with ribbons and flowers, which will stay until the end of the project. The cross is placed at the highest spot of the construction.

The architect, engineer, or owner of the house under construction hosts a *taquiza* (taco party), for this, the Day of the Mason Worker. *Guisados* (roasts), typically *barbacoa* or *carne asada*, along with an abundance of tortillas and salsas, are consumed at the construction site without plates and cutlery. Everyone involved in the building project is invited to this party, where music and firecrackers are part of the celebration, along with beer and *pulque* (fermented sap of the maguey plant).

BARBACOA

COOKING in pits is a technique that remains from pre-Hispanic times. There are records describing the Chichimeca, a fierce tribe living in central Mexico, who, when they prepared meat, hollowed out a hole in the ground which they filled with hot stones. The original ingredients were deer, armadillo, rabbit, or turkey, which were wrapped in maguey leaves. The traditional dressing is a "drunken" salsa made with pulque, and flavored pulque is offered as a drink.

As we can see from Fanny Chambers Gooch's 1887 text, *Face to Face with the Mexicans*, preparation of the Mexican specialty has changed little since colonial times:

> [Barbaoca] is one of the principal articles of food known to the Mexican market—and is good enough for the table of a king. The dexterous native takes a well-dressed mutton, properly quartered, using head and bones. A hole is made in the ground and a fire built in it. Stone slabs are thrown in, and the hole is covered. When thoroughly hot, a lining is made of maguey leaves, the meat put in, and covered with maguey. The top of the hole is also covered, and the process of cooking goes on all night. The next morning it is put in a hot vessel, ready to eat—a delicious, brown, crisp, barbecued mutton. As the process is difficult and tedious, it is generally prepared in the families, and even the wealthiest patronize the market for the delicacy, ready cooked.[1]

This is still the case in Mexico. Visiting the valley of central Mexico, one of the first foods your host will insist that you try is barbacoa, found in the marketplace. The broth is a special source of Mexican pride as well.

Mixtecos preparing barbacoa. Known as the "People of the Cloud," the Mixtec live primarily in the southern Mexican states of Oaxaca, parts of Guerrero, and Puebla. However, they are unique among Mexico's indigenous people in that significant populations can be found in almost every part of Mexico as well as in areas in the United States. According to a 2005 language survey, it was believed that 423,216 spoke one of the 57 Mixtec dialects. The language and culture predates the Spanish conquest by hundreds of years, and in pre-Columbian times, the Mixtec were one of the major civilizations of Mesoamerica. Much of their history has been recorded in codices (pictograph manuscripts) such as *Codex Nuttall*, written on deer hide or tree bark.

The Mixtecs' economy was traditionally based on farming the steep, mountainous terrain of central southern Mexico, planting corn, beans, and squash (the basis of the pre-Columbian diet in many areas of the country). With the introduction by Europeans of hoofed animals, as well as the plow, the delicate environmental balance of the area was disrupted, and today soil erosion has left the Mixteca region one of the most geographically devastated in the world. The Mixteco/Indigena Community Organizing Project noted on its website that "current Mixtec societies in Mexico are able to grow only [about] 20% of the food they need to sustain their populations."

Fiestas, during which hundreds of people participate in processions, a Mass, and communal meals, are an integral part of Mixtec communal life. Many fiestas are centered around the saints introduced by the Catholic Church during the Conquest. Almost every Mixtec town has a Catholic church at its center and folk Catholic practices prevail, such as nature worship and personal sacrifices for the well-being of the earth.
Photo by Jorge Ontiveros.

SLOW-COOKED LAMB (OR GOAT) SOUP / CALDO DE BORREGO

THE soup is basically all the drippings from your barbacoa and the vegetables at the bottom of the pan, all of which create a flavor-packed stock. To serve, remove herbs and lemons; serve stock and vegetables in a soup bowl; and garnish with some raw chopped onion, chopped cilantro, and a wedge of lemon to drizzle over the soup. 🐟

SLOW-COOKED LAMB (OR GOAT) WITH DRUNKEN SALSA / BARBACOA CON SALSA BORRACHA

(SERVES 24)

1½ gallons beer or pulque
6–8 pounds leg of lamb or goat meat
¾ cup garbanzo beans, previously soaked overnight and drained
2 pounds carrots, diced
10 garlic cloves
10 tomatillos
2 large tomatoes, chopped
2 tablespoons salt
1 teaspoon black pepper
2 Spanish white onions, quartered
1–2 Persian dry lemons
12 avocado leaves (dehydrated)
6 bay leaves
6 serrano chiles (optional)
8 banana leaves
1–2 cups of masa harina (tortilla flour can be substituted for a mixture made with 1¼ cup of tortilla flour and water, to create a thick paste)
Drunken Salsa (A)

MENU 14.1: DAY OF THE HOLY CROSS

Soup / *Caldo*
Slow-Cooked Lamb (or Goat) Soup / *Caldo de Borrego*
Entrée / *Plato Fuerte*
Slow-Cooked Lamb (or Goat) with Drunken Sauce / *Barbacoa con Salsa Borracha*
Side / *Guarnición*
Grilled Cactus Paddles with Beans au Gratin / *Napolitos Asados con Frijoles y Queso Gratinado (Volcanes)*
Dessert / *Postre*
Corn Cake / *Pastel de Elote*

IN a deep foil cooking pan, add beer or pulque, garbanzo beans, carrots, garlic, tomatillos (prepare tomatillos first by removing husks, washing tomatillos well, and quartering them), tomatoes, salt, pepper, onions, dry lemons, and 4 avocado leaves. Place a wire rack in the pan on top the vegetables and beer, leaving space below for the meat juices to drain into the pan. Place banana leaves on the wire rack and then place the meat on top of the banana leaves. Cover the meat well with the rest of the banana leaves and place a second foil cooking pan upside down over the first as a lid, sealing it with a mixture of masa harina or a mixture of flour (cover masa harina or flour mixture with foil paper taking care to wrap the edges of the pans to protect the "package" from burning and falling apart. This procedure will prevent steam from escaping from the cooking pans and will create sort of a pressure cooker, effectively locking the juices inside the pans). Place in oven at 375° and cook for 6 hours.

Serve meat with corn tortillas as tacos and the stock with vegetables with a wedge of lime; garnish soup and tacos with diced onion, cilantro, and Drunken Salsa. 🐟

ADRIANA'S MEMORIES

THE original barbacoa was baked in a pit underground. It is an amazing process. My uncle used to have this big feast once a year and he had a whole goat, *un chivo*, cooked this way. They dug a deep hole into the dirt in a wide open space, where they made a huge fire, placing some deep pots with cut vegetables(tomatoes, garbanzo beans, onions, garlic, and spices), and arranged a metal rack on top where they placed the whole goat, opened. Then they covered everything very well with banana leaves. Next, they covered everything back with dirt and left it there to cook for hours. When they dug out the dirt and pulled the meat out, the juices from the meat drained into the pot below, making the most delicious soup you could imagine, and meat so tender it would fall apart. It was a very messy process but fascinating. The smell, when they were digging out the dirt, was so disgusting, you would think you could never eat something that comes out of that place, but the final results were incredible.

A. Drunken Salsa / Salsa Borracha

6 dried pasilla chiles
10 tomatillos, remove husks and wash tomatillos well
1 tablespoon vinegar
2 tablespoons olive oil
1 garlic clove
4 ounces beer (Indio, Tecate, or Carta Blanca preferred) or pulque if available
Salt to taste
½ teaspoon dry Mexican oregano
3½ ounces queso añejo, feta cheese, or any dry aged cheese

YOU can substitute ¼ cup of orange juice for beer or pulque for a nonalcoholic version. Toast dried chiles on a comal or directly on the flame, watching so as not to burn them. Place chiles in a container with hot water to soften. Working with gloves, remove seeds and veins from chiles. In a blender, purée tomatillos, vinegar, oil, and garlic. Add beer and salt; lastly add chiles. Blend until smooth. Place in serving dish. Stir in dry oregano and mix well. Sprinkle with dry cheese before serving. ✤

Grilled Cactus Paddles with Cheese / *Nopales Asados con Queso*, called *"volcanes."*
Photo by Adriana Almazán Lahl.

GRİLLED CACTUS PADDLES WİTH BEANS AU GRATİN / NOPALES ASADOS CON FRİJOLES Y QUESO GRATİNADO *(VOLCANES)*

(SERVES 6–8)

8 paddles of nopal (baby cactus)
1 cup refried beans (see recipe p. 152)
4 ounces queso Oaxaca or Mexican Manchego
Fresh Green Salsa (see "Salsa Recipes," p. 19)
¼ cup chopped cilantro
¼ cup white onion, finely chopped
Salt to taste

B UY the nopales clean of thorns (or prepare following instructions on p. 168). Place nopales on a plate full of salt and let them cure, covered with salt for 45 minutes; this will reduce the mucilage (slime). Rinse well and pat dry with a paper towel. Cook nopales on a dry comal or cast-iron pan on high heat for 5 minutes on each side or until you see dark spots.

Corn Cake / *Pan de Maiz*.
Photo by Adriana Almazán Lahl.

Once the nopales are cooked, place on a baking sheet; add a spoonful of beans and a thick slice of cheese on top of each nopal. Broil in an oven at 400° until cheese is melted and starts to brown. Serve each nopal in a pond of salsa with warm tortillas; sprinkle with fresh cilantro and raw onions and season with salt. 🐝

AUNT MARGARITA'S CORN CAKE / PASTEL DE ELOTE DE TÍA MARGARITA

(SERVES 16–24)

Kernels of 6 large sweet corn cobs
3 eggs
¼ pound (1 stick) butter, melted
1 (14-ounce) can condensed milk
1 tablespoon baking powder
Pinch of salt

PREHEAT oven to 350°. In a blender, combine all the ingredients on high speed. Place batter in a pregreased, 9-inch cake mold, and bake for 40 minutes. Allow to cool for at least 45 minutes before removing from cake pan. 🐝

CINCO DE MAYO
(MAY 5)

CINCO DE MAYO is much more widely celebrated in the United States than in Mexico, where it is really only observed in Puebla. There, it is commemorated with military maneuvers reenacting the Battle of Puebla, a parade, and other festivities. Several theories and stories combine to explain the popularity of the Cinco de Mayo holiday in the United States, one that actually commemorates the Mexican victory against the French on May 5, 1862.

An Unlikely Mexican Victory

Cinco de Mayo is a celebration of a surprising victory, a secret alliance, and a battle that changed history in three countries on two continents. The French invasion of Mexico, known as the French Intervention (1862–1867), occurred concurrently with the American Civil War. With the United States divided and distracted by civil war, Napoleon saw an opportunity to expand French territories in North America, and with the pretext of collecting a debt owed France by previous Mexican administrations, sent his troops to remove Mexican president Benito Juarez from power and in his place install his own cousin Prince Maximilian of Austria as ruler. But, as the French Army marched across the country from the port of Vera Cruz, they first had to pass through the city of Puebla, defended by a ragtag, poorly equipped Mexican Army.

The Mexicans fought back and were victorious against what at the time was the mightiest army in the world, one that had not seen defeat in over fifty years. The eight-thousand-strong French army attacked the Mexican army of four thousand just outside of Puebla and yet was decisively crushed. This was the last time a European military force invaded the Americas.

The Battle in Mexico That Changed the Outcome of the American Civil War

The Confederacy had appealed to Napoleon III for support, and there was talk of French recognition for the breakaway Southern states. According to some historians, the French had a plan that involved using Mexico as a base from which they could provide military support to the Confederacy. The Confederacy, having just won several impressive victories over the Union forces, was gaining ground at the very time that French forces were engaged by Mexico in the Battle of Puebla.

However, the defeat at Puebla on May 5 was a major setback for Napoleon, and while France's forces regrouped and recovered, the Union army was able to gain momentum. Some contend that had the French won at Puebla the outcome of the American Civil War would have been much different, that the French and Confederates together could have taken control of the North American continent, from the Mason-Dixon Line to Mexico's border with Guatemala.

Tipping the Scales: Mexican Americans Write Antislavery Laws into California Constitution

What is now the state of California was part of the Republic of Mexico when slavery was outlawed in that country in 1820, decades before it was abolished in the United States. As California prepared to enter the Union, the Latinos who helped write the California Constitution in 1849 were insistent that slavery be kept out of the state. California's subsequent admission to the Union tipped the balance between free and slave-holding states, thwarting the original Union strategy to create a territory where slavery was legal all across the United States to the Pacific coast.

If the French had been victorious on that Cinco de Mayo over 150 years ago, it is very possible that two treacherous allies, Napoleon and the Confederacy, would have been successful in their plans and much of North America to the Guatemalan border would have been become slave-holding territories under French rule.

A Holiday Is Born in California

In his book *El Cinco de Mayo: An American Tradition*, David Hayes-Bautista, whose great-great-grandfather fought in the Battle of Puebla, explores the roots of Cinco de Mayo celebrations in the United States and makes a little-known connection between the Civil War and the Battle of Puebla: "Cinco de Mayo does indeed mark a

Mexican military victory over the invading French army on May 5, 1862, but it's celebrated more in the United States because in 1862, U.S. Latinos of Mexican heritage parlayed the victory as a rallying cry that the Union could also win the Civil War."[1]

Looking at Mexican newspapers in California from 1862, Hayes-Bautista discovered that, for Mexican Americans on the West Coast, the American Civil War and Mexico's war against the French were "basically look[ed] at [as] one war with two fronts, one against the Confederacy in the east and the other against the French in the south." Mexicans were squarely against the French goal of returning their country, which had been under democratic rule for more than four decades, to a monarchy. He added,

> In California and Oregon, the news [of the victory in Puebla] was interpreted as finally . . . the army of freedom and democracy [had] won a big one against the army of slavery and elitism. And the fact that those two armies had to meet in Mexico was immaterial because they were fighting for the same issues—defending freedom and democracy. Latinos were joining the Union army, Union cavalry, and Union navy.[2]

Mexicans in Los Angeles were closely following the events of the invasion of France, taking place more than two thousand miles away. If news was slow coming from Mexico, it was further delayed in reaching Los Angeles, as most of the Spanish-language newspapers were published in San Francisco and were delivered by stagecoach—four days after being printed in the Bay Area. Hayes-Bautista describes this scene: as the stagecoach arrived on May 25 and the bundles of newspapers were thrown down to the anxious crowd, where they were ripped open and passed around. The crowd began to cheer as they read the combat reports published in *La Voz de Mejico*[3]:

> *Retirada de los Franceses. Viva Mejico! Viva la independencia! Vivan los valientes soldados Mejicanos!* (The French retreat. Long live Mexico! Long live independence! Long live the brave Mexican soldiers!)[4]

Filled with the excitement of the unlikely victory, Mexicans in Los Angeles decided to hold a local celebration to recognize their heroes and the triumph of freedom and democracy. The Los Angeles *Junta Patriotica Mejicana* (Mexican Patriotic Assembly) sponsored the first official celebration of Cinco de Mayo that very night, as over four hundred people came together on a hill behind what was then just a town (the gathering occurred just about where the Music Center is located today). The Mexican militia fired their rifles into the air and a giant bonfire (*fogata*) illuminated portraits of President Juarez and General Zaragoza.

The Cinco de Mayo victory continued to be memorialized for months afterward through a network of *juntas patrioticas Mejicanas* (patriotic Mexican meetings or groups), mostly in California but also in Oregon, Nevada, and Arizona. These were celebrated with monthly parades, speeches, dances, banquets, and bull fights as a morale builder for Abraham Lincoln and Mexican president Benito Juarez, who, despite the Cinco de Mayo victory, was subsequently engaged in a five-year struggle against French occupation until 1867. "From 1862 to 1867, the public memory of Cinco de Mayo was forged in the American West,"[5] Hayes-Bautista noted.

A David versus Goliath Victory and the Commercialization of Cinco de Mayo

Since then, the meaning of the holiday has shifted, specifically as Mexican immigrants flooded into the American Southwest following the Mexican Revolution. The connection to the American Civil War became lost as the day came to signify a David versus Goliath story really only known to Mexican immigrants. Later, Cinco de Mayo was used to political advantage to promote U.S.-Mexico unity during World War II and, in the 1960s and 1970s, by the Chicano Power movement. More recently, a sort of fake holiday has been reinvented by beverage companies, who see a big commercial opportunity to penetrate the Latino market. "But if you ask people why they are celebrating, no one knows. And then you get some people who say it shouldn't be celebrated at all because it's a foreign holiday—and yet it's as American a holiday as the Fourth of July,"[6] concludes Hayes-Bautista.

CHEESE FONDUE WITH MUSHROOMS / QUESO FUNDIDO CON HONGOS

(SERVES 4)

1 tablespoon butter

1 tablespoon canola or vegetable oil

⅓ Spanish white onion, sliced finely

2 cups fresh mushrooms, sliced

Salt and pepper to taste

10 ounces Mexican Asadero or Manchego cheese, grated

4 ounces chorizo (optional, store bought or see recipe, p. 131)

Parsley to garnish

Salsa of your choice (see pp. 17–24)

MENU 15.1: CINCO DE MAYO PARTY

In keeping with the spirit of this predominantly Mexican American holiday, here is a menu of Mexican favorites.

Appetizer / *Botana*
Cheese Fondue with Mushrooms
/ *Queso Fundido con Hongos*

Entrée / *Plato Fuerte*
Chilaquiles with Chicken /
Chilaquiles con Pollo

Dessert / *Postre*
Horchata Gelatin / *Gelatina de Horchata*

Beverage / *Bebida*
Brain Freeze Margarita / *Margarita Congela Cerebros*

Cheese Fondue with Mushrooms / *Queso Fundido con Hongos.*
Photo by Adriana Almazán Lahl.

IN a cast-iron pan, warm ½ teaspoon butter and oil, sauté onions, add mushrooms, and cook until lightly brown; season with salt and pepper. In a clay pot, add ½ teaspoon butter and melt in low heat. Add shredded cheese and let it melt slowly. Add mushrooms and onions and mix gently; serve with warm tortillas. Optional: You may want to place the pan under the broiler to finish it off, browning for just a few minutes. You can make this *Queso Fundido* with chorizo as well. Brown chorizo well, drain on a paper towel to remove extra oil, and add to cheese mixture. Garnish Queso Fundido with chopped parsley. Serve warm with salsa of your choice and tortillas. 🪶

CHILAQUILES WITH CHICKEN / CHILAQUILES CON POLLO

12 tortillas, day old (or good-quality store-bought chips)
3 cups water
3 tomatoes
4 tomatillos, remove husks and clean tomatillos well
1 garlic clove
½ onion
3 serrano chiles, seeded
1 ancho chile, seeded
1 epazote sprig
Pinch of oregano

Chilaquiles.
Photo by Adriana Almazán Lahl.

1 cup corn oil

Salt and pepper to taste

2 cups shredded chicken breast (see "Basic Recipes for Mexican Cooking," p. 11)

1 cup Mexican sour cream

½ raw onion thinly sliced (garnish)

7 ounces Monterrey jack cheese

¼ cup chopped fresh cilantro

CUT tortillas in four quarters the day before and let them dry. The next day, fry them in hot corn oil until crispy. Drain on paper towels to absorb excess oil or use good-quality, store-bought chips.

For the sauce, bring water to a boil and cook tomatoes, oregano, tomatillos, garlic, onion, chiles, and epazote sprig for 12 minutes. Remove epazote and blend these ingredients with two cups of the hot water used for cooking. Season with salt and pepper.

Add 2 tablespoons of the remaining corn oil to a casserole and cook salsa over medium to medium-high heat for 15 minutes (be careful as you add salsa to hot oil as it tends to splatter). Add one cup of water and bring to a boil again and drench tortilla chips in the sauce; mix in shredded chicken, allow to rest for 3 minutes, and serve on a hot plate. Drizzle with sour cream, raw onions, and cheese; sprinkle with chopped fresh cilantro.

You can omit chicken and top with two sunny-side eggs per serving for a breakfast option. ❧

HORCHATA GELATIN DESSERT / GELATINA DE HORCHATA

1 cup rice
2 cups water
1 (5-ounce) can condensed milk
1 cinnamon stick
1 envelope gelatin

SOAK rice overnight in the water. In the morning, place rice and water in blender, liquefy, and pass through a sieve, straining liquid well. Mix condensed milk and cinnamon stick. Hydrate gelatin for 5 minutes in ¼ cup of water, then add to a pan and bring to a boil. Add rice water to the pot and mix well. Bring to a boil and simmer for 5 minutes; turn off and remove cinnamon stick. Place in gelatin molds and refrigerate for 4 hours or overnight. To unmold, dip mold halfway into hot water for 5 seconds, flip over a serving plate. To serve, sprinkle with a dash of cinnamon and slices of fresh mango. 🐗

BRAIN FREEZE MARGARITA / MARGARITA CONGELA CEREBROS

(MAKES 1 DRINK)

8 ounces ice
1½ ounces tequila (*Blanco*, 100 percent agave)
2½ tablespoons sugar
1 ounce freshly squeezed lime juice
½ ounce orange liquor (Cointreau)
Chile-Salt Mix for rimming the glass (A) (optional)

IN a blender place ice tequila, sugar, lime juice, and Cointreau; blend until smooth. Serve immediately. 🐗

A. Chile-Salt Mix

4 tablespoons sea salt
4 tablespoons ancho chile powder

MIX equal quantities of salt and chile powder. Place in a shallow dish. Moisten all around the rim of a Margarita glass with lemon wedge, then dip in salt mix. 🐗

GRİLLED STEAKS / CARNE ASADA I

NOTHING SAYS BBQ LIKE A GREAT *CARNE ASADA*. BARBECUE FLAVOR IS DETERMINED BY MARINADE (ADOBO), THE SAUCE (SALSA), AND THE CHARCOAL OVER WHICH YOUR STEAK IS COOKED. FOR REAL MEXICAN WOOD-SMOKED FLAVOR, USE MESQUITE OR OAK CHARCOAL.

(SERVES 4–6)

¼ cup Worchestershire Sauce
2 tablespoons Maggi Seasoning
Juice of 3 lemons
2 sprigs chopped cilantro
2 garlic cloves
¼ piece of white onion
8 ounces beer
2 pounds flank steak

MENU 15.2: CLASSIC MEXICAN BBQ PARTY
Entrée / *Plato Fuerte*
Grilled Steaks / *Carne Asada*
Sides / *Guarniciones*
Guacamole
Cowboy Beans / *Frijoles Charros*
Salsa of choice
(see recipe pp. 17–24)
Salad / *Ensalada*
Classic Baja Caesar Salad /
Ensalada Cesar Clásica
Beverage / *Bebida*
Tamarind Water /
Agua de Tamarindo
Dessert / *Postre*
Peanut Marzipan /
Mazapanes de Cacahuate

COMBINE all ingredients but the meat in a blender and mix until smooth. Place meat in a glass bowl, pour mixture over the meat, and drench every steak in the sauce. Cover with plastic wrap and let it rest in refrigerator for 3 hours or overnight. Place steaks on a hot griddle or grill and cook for 3 minutes on each side, adjust cooking time for doneness. 🐦

GRİLLED STEAKS / CARNE ASADA II

(SERVES 4–6)

2 pounds flank steak
½ cup lard
Coarse salt

MIX steaks with lard, covering each steak completely; add coarse salt before you place on grill and cook for 3 minutes each side, adjust cookng time for doneness. 🐦

GRILLED STEAKS / CARNE ASADA III

MARINATE meat with adobo sauce (see "Basic Recipes for Mexican Cooking," p. 10) overnight if possible; if not, at least 2 hours. Cook steaks over hot charcoal on grill for 2–3 minutes per side, adjusting time for doneness. 🐝

GUACAMOLE

THE name comes from two Aztec Nahuatl words: *ahuacatl* (avocado) and *molli* (sauce). Be sure to pick avocados that are perfectly ripe. It is best if you buy these a day or two before you plan to use them. Be sure that the avocados are not overripe, in which case the texture of your "mole" will be mushy and the taste can even be a bit bitter (remove and discard any brown areas you find inside your avocado), or, if the avocados are underripe, they will be too hard to get out of their skins and cut into chunks.

GUACAMOLE

(SERVES 4–6)

5 large avocados
Juice of 2 Mexican limes
¾ teaspoon salt
1 medium tomato, chopped
½ onion, chopped
5 sprigs cilantro
2 serrano chiles, seeded, deveined, and chopped

IN a bowl, partially mash avocados with a fork; add lime juice and salt. Once mashed, add tomato, onion, chopped cilantro, and chiles and fold gently. Leave a couple of avocado pits in your guacamole to help maintain green color. Refrigerate 1 hour for best flavor or serve immediately with tortilla chips. 🐝

COWBOY BEANS / FRİJOLES CHARROS

(SERVES 6–8)

4 cups boiling water
2 pounds black beans
1 small onion
2 garlic cloves
Bunch of epazote
4 pig's feet
1 dark Mexican beer (Negra Modelo)
1 chorizo link, cooked in slices (see p. 131 for recipe, or use store bought)
1 small Spanish white onion, cut in half
½ pound bacon, cut in squares
4 serrano chiles, seeded and deveined
1 small onion, small-chopped
1 cup of chopped cilantro
Salt to taste

BRING water to a boil in a large pot. Add beans with 1 small onion cut in half, garlic, epazote, pig's feet, and beer. Cook for 2 hours or until beans become tender (note: if you increase the quantity of beans, the cooking time may be significantly longer); remove pig's feet, epazote, garlic, and onion. Fry chorizo slices in a sauté pan; set aside. Meanwhile, in another frying pan, sauté the remaining onion, bacon, and chiles; incorporate chorizo and add the sautée mix to the beans. Once the beans are cooked, add ½ cup of chopped cilantro to the beans; allow to cook an additional 15 minutes. Salt to taste and serve in a small bowl as a side dish, garnished with chopped onions and fresh cilantro. 🐗

CAESAR SALAD

CAESAR Cardini, an Italian immigrant who operated restaurants in Mexico and the United States, is credited with creating the Caesar salad. According to an account by Cardini's daughter, Rosa, her father invented the dish when on July 4, 1924, a rush unexpectedly depleted the kitchen's pantry. Chef Cardini had to create meals with whatever he had on hand, adding the table-side tossing "by the chef" for dramatic flair. Julia Child reported that she had eaten a Caesar salad at Cardini's restaurant as a child. The earliest contemporary documentation of Caesar salad is from the Garden Room at the Town House restaurant in Los Angeles, on a menu dated October 8, 1946.

CLASSIC BAJA CAESAR SALAD / ENSALADA CESAR CLÁSICA

(SERVES 6–8)

½ cup olive oil
½ day-old baguette, cut in cubes
Salt and pepper to taste
1 small garlic clove, puréed
3 anchovy fillets, mashed well with a fork
1 teaspoon Dijon mustard
1 egg yolk, pasteurized (see "Common Mexican Cooking Tools and Techniques," p. 335)
    or store bought
2 tablespoons white vinegar
2 tablespoons freshly squeezed lemon juice
1 tablespoon Worcestershire sauce
1 head romaine lettuce, leaves washed and dried
½ cup Parmesan cheese, grated

IN a frying pan, heat ⅛ cup olive oil and sauté the bread until nicely browned; place on paper towels to drain excess oil. 🐖

FOR THE DRESSING:

Add salt and pepper to a salad bowl. Using a small whisk, incorporate garlic purée with salt and pepper, combine with anchovy paste, and mix well. Add Dijon mustard and continue mixing. Add pasteurized egg yolk and mix in white vinegar. Finally, add lemon juice, remaining olive oil, and Worcestershire sauce. Mix well every time you incorporate an ingredient; adjust salt and pepper to taste.

Toss romaine lettuce leaves in the dressing and serve over a plate with croutons and fresh Parmesan cheese on top. 🐖

TAMARIND WATER / AGUA DE TAMARINDO

(SERVES 6–8)

6–8 tamarind pods, peeled
3 cups water to boil tamarind
8 cups water
¾ cup sugar or to your taste
Ice

IN a saucepan, boil the tamarind pods in 3 cups of water on a low heat for about 20 minutes. Remove from heat and let steep for about 2 hours. Place tamarind pods in a cheesecloth and knead the tamarind pods in the water until all the seeds and pulp separate from the shells. Pour the mixture into a strainer and push the pulp through. Strain a couple of times to be sure no shells get into the water. Pour mixture into a pitcher. Add 8 cups of water, sugar to taste, and ice; stir and serve. 🦂

PEANUT MARZIPAN / MAZAPANES DE CACAHUATE

(MAKES 12 PIECES)

2 cups peeled, toasted, unsalted peanuts
    (or cashews)
1½ cups confectioner's sugar
10–15 drops sesame oil or peanut oil

IN a food processor add peanuts and grind them; add sugar and mix well, then add sesame oil. Pulse food processor, scraping the sides three or four times during this process to ensure that all ingredients are incorporated and finely ground and a paste has formed. To test the consistency of the paste, grab with your fingers and press. If the paste holds together, the paste is ready; if it is still too crumbly, add a few more drops of sesame oil and pulse until paste holds together.

MARZIPAN

Marzipan, as it is known in Europe, is a sweet treat made of almonds ground with sugar. It has been around since medieval times. It is believed to have its origins either in Persia or possibly Spain. Called *"mazapán"* by the Spanish, today it is Toledo's (Spain) most famous confection, where it is especially popular at Christmastime. When this dessert migrated to Mexico, the almonds were replaced with peanuts. A perennial Mexican favorite, you'll find little discs wrapped in wax paper imprinted with a rose everywhere.

Marzipan.
Photo by Adriana
Almazán Lahl.

Scrape the paste out onto a flat surface Using a 1½-inch round cookie or biscuit cutter, add paste inside the mold and press firmly with your hands until paste is well compacted. Push paste off the ring carefully and wrap in tissue paper. Refrigerate in an air tight container for up to 2 months. 🕊️

La Comida Afrancesada: The Culinary
Legacy of the French Intervention

The culinary contributions of the brief occupation of Mexico by France, from 1861 to 1867, are significant. Perhaps the most lasting impression of that period in Mexican history is what is called *La Comida Afrancesada*, French cooking techniques combined with Mexican ingredients and Mexican staples like squash blossoms, and avocados, which were well suited to French mousses, crepes, and soups. Some

Traditional Mexican kitchen of the colonial era.
Photo by Adriana Almazán Lahl.

lasting examples are flan; *bolovanes* or *volovanes*, which are pastry shells that can be filled with *mole con pollo* or seafood; *quiche de calebaza* (recipes follow); and *crepes de hongos* (mushroom crepes).

CHICKEN MOLE OR SHRIMP VOL-AU-VENTS (IN PUFF PASTRY SHELLS) / VOLOVANES DE MOLE O VOLOVANES DE CAMARÓN

(SERVES 20)

Vol-au-Vents (Puff Pastry Shells) (A)
Shrimp Filling, with Tarragon Sauce (B/C)
Chicken Filling with Mole (D)

A. Vol-au-Vents (Puff Pastry Shells)

Puff Pastry Dough, well chilled (E)
Egg wash (1 egg or yolk beaten with a small
    amount of water)

LINE a baking sheet with parchment and set aside. Using a knife, divide your chilled puff pastry dough into three equal pieces. While working with one piece of dough, leave the rest wrapped and chilled.

On a floured surface, roll the piece of dough into a rectangle about ⅛ to ¼ inch thick. Transfer it to the baking sheet and refrigerate for about 10 minutes before proceeding to cut. Use 2 different sizes of circular cookie/biscuit cutters to form the walls as well as the bottoms of your vol-au-vents. Using the larger pastry ring (about 2½ inches) cut rounds. You will end up with approximately 24 rounds. With the smaller pasty ring (about 1 inch), cut the centers from 12 of the rounds, creating a doughnut shaped ring. The result will be 12 large doughnut-shaped rings of pastry. These rings will become the sides, or walls, of the vol-au-vents. The remaining twelve 2½-inch solid disks will be the bottoms.

Use egg wash to brush around the edges of the 2½-inch solid dough rounds and place the 2½-inch doughnut-like rings on top. Cover with egg wash and repeat action until you get a full tray (12 pieces). Place in the refrigerator for about 1 hour.

Preheat oven to 400° and place vol-au-vents in oven for 10–15 minutes and reduce heat to 350°. Bake for another 15–20 minutes or until golden brown. Remove from oven, using a fork to carefully remove the dough that fluffed inside the center of the vol-au-vents while baking. Fill with stuffing of your choice.

> **MENU 15.3:**
> **FRENCH-MEX / *COMIDA AFRANCESADA***
>
> Entrées / *Platos Fuertes*
> Shrimp Vol-au–Vents /
> *Volovanes de Camarón*
> Chicken Mole Vol-au-Vents /
> *Volovanes de Pollo con Mole*
> Side / *Guarnición*
> Poblano, Corn, and Zucchini
> Quiche / *Quiche de Calabaza
> con Chiles Poblanos y Elote*
> Dessert / *Postre*
> Dulce de Leche Crepes /
> *Crepas de Cajeta*

Shrimp Vol-au-Vents / *Volvones de Camaron.*
Photo by Adriana Almazán Lahl.

B. Shrimp Filling, with Tarragon Sauce

Tarragon Sauce (C)
2 cups small cooked shrimp
Pinch cayenne pepper
Salt and pepper to taste

PREPARE Tarragon Sauce according to these directions. Bring to a boil and add shrimp, cayenne, and salt and pepper to taste. Stuff vol-au-vents with the shrimp and garnish each with a fresh tarragon leaf. 🦐

C. Tarragon Sauce

½ cup butter
2 tablespoons shallots, finely chopped
½ cup flour
1 cup milk
1 tablespoon tarragon, finely chopped

IN a saucepan, melt butter and add shallots; cook for 3–4 minutes until translucent. Add flour and cook for 5 minutes over medium-low heat, stirring constantly with a wooden spoon; do not allow to brown. Add milk and tarragon. 🐦

D. Mole Stuffing

1 cup mole paste (see recipe p. 306)
1 large chicken breast, boiled and shredded (see "Basic Recipes for Mexican Cooking,"
      p. 11)
½ cup white sesame seeds

RECONSTITUTE mole sauce (see "Basic Recipes for Mexican Cooking," p. 13), add shredded chicken, and heat thoroughly. Fill vol-au-vents. Top with sesame seeds. 🐦

E. Rough Puff Pastry Dough

1¼ cups all-purpose flour
¼ teaspoon salt
1 stick (½ cup) plus 5 tablespoons unsalted butter, frozen and cut in small cubes
5–6 tablespoons ice water

SIFT together flour and salt in a chilled large metal bowl. Set a grater in flour mixture and grate frozen butter cubes into flour; mix and toss. Drizzle 5 tablespoons of ice water evenly over flour mixture and stir with a fork until incorporated.

Test mixture for readiness by gently squeezing a small handful: When it has the proper texture, it will hold together without crumbling apart. If necessary, add another tablespoon of water and repeat test. Gather mixture together and form into a 5-inch square; wrap in plastic wrap and chill until firm, about 20 minutes.

Roll out dough on a floured surface with a floured rolling pin into a 15-by-8-inch rectangle. To chill dough properly, you will need to arrange dough as follows: With a short side nearest you, fold dough into thirds like a letter—bottom third up and top third down over dough. Rewrap dough and chill in refrigerator until firm, about 20 minutes.

After 20 minutes, remove dough from refrigerator; repeat rolling out, folding, and chilling 3 or 4 more times. Brush off any excess flour, then wrap dough in plastic wrap and chill at least 1 hour. 🐦

POBLANO, CORN, AND ZUCCHINI QUICHE / QUICHE DE CALABAZA CON POBLANOS Y ELOTE

(SERVES 6)

Pie crust (see recipe, p. 91)
½ Spanish white onion, finely sliced
2 tablespoons olive oil
4 poblano chiles, prepared in strips (rajas, see "Common Mexican Cooking Tools and Techniques," p. 334)
2 cups fresh corn niblets
1 Mexican zucchini, chopped
2 eggs
Salt and pepper to taste
½ cup Mexican sour cream
½ cup milk
2 cups Mexican Manchego cheese, shredded
1 cup Parmesan cheese, shredded

COVER a pie pan or quiche tin (preferred) with pie crust dough and pinch with a fork all around the crust; bake for 20 minutes at 350° and allow to cool. Keep oven warm. Add olive oil to a hot skillet and sauté onion for 4–5 minutes. Add the poblano strips, corn, and zucchini and sauté for 5 additional minutes. Set aside.

In a large bowl, crack eggs and whisk them, season with salt and pepper, add Mexican sour cream and milk, and mix well. Distribute sautéed vegetables evenly over prebaked quiche crust. Add Manchego cheese and egg mix and cover with shredded Parmesan cheese.

Bake for 30 minutes at 350°. Turn off oven and allow quiche to rest inside the oven for 10 more minutes. 🌶

Dulce de Leche Crepes / *Crepas de Cajeta*.
Photo by Adriana Almazán Lahl.

DULCE DE LECHE CREPES / CREPAS DE CAJETA

(SERVES 6)

1 cup milk
1 egg
1 cup all-purpose flour
1 tablespoon orange rind
Dash of nutmeg
1 cup Dulce de Leche (A) or Cajeta Envinada
1 tablespoon sherry wine
1 (5-ounce) can evaporated milk (such as Carnation)
3 ounces pecans, chopped
Butter to grease pan

IN a blender add milk, egg, and flour; mix well. Place mix in a bowl and add orange rind and a dash of ground nutmeg. Mix and reserve covered with plastic wrap in the refrigerator for at least 3 hours or overnight. When ready to cook, grease a flat pan with butter and place on stove over medium heat. Once hot, pour a ladle full of mix, and extend in circle to form a thin crepe. Once crepe acquires a white uniform color (45 seconds to 1 minute), flip and finish cooking (30 seconds). In a saucepan, warm Dulce de Leche or Cajeta Envinada and add sherry wine and ¼ cup of evaporated milk to desired consistency. It should resemble honey or a thick caramel; mix well and set aside. Then, fold crepes in a fan shape, place two crepes on a plate and drizzle generously with the Dulce de Leche sauce. Garnish with chopped pecans. 🐦

A. Dulce de Leche

1 (5-ounce) can sweetened condensed milk
3 cups boiling water

REMOVE the label from the condensed milk can. Put the can into a pot, and fill up the pot with enough water to cover half the can. Put the pot on the stove and let the can simmer gently for 3 hours to get a solid dulce de leche. Add more hot water every half hour or as necessary, and flip the can every half hour. After 3 hours, remove and allow to cool. Carefully open up the can completely. The final product should be colored tan or brown and have the consistency of a thick sauce. 🐦

MOTHER'S DAY /
DÍA DE LA MADRE
(MAY 10)

DÍA DE LA MADRE is celebrated every year in Mexico on May 10. There are festivals at schools where children perform, present artwork, and participate in other activities, all dedicated to their mothers. Although it is not an official national holiday, most offices are closed or give their employees a half-day off. Some mothers start their special day with a serenata at midnight. The Virgin of Guadalupe, mother of all Mexicans, is also honored on this day.

Mazahua mother dresses her daughter in traditional clothing. Many of the Mazahuas are farmers, subsisting on small plots of land, growing the crop that sustains them—corn from which tortillas are made. Widespread unemployment has resulted in migration from their pueblos to Mexico's cities, to northern border areas, or to the United States. The Mazahua people are known for their hospitality. Photo by Jorge Ontiveros.

There is not a special menu typically served on Mother's Day in Mexico; we have selected a floral theme for ours.

STUFFED SQUASH BLOSSOMS / FLORES DE CALABAZA RELLENAS

YOU CAN SERVE THIS AS AN APPETIZER OR AS A SIDE DISH WITH SALSA OR TOMATO STOCK (SEE "BASIC RECIPES FOR MEXICAN COOKING," P. 14). IT IS BEST TO USE A MILD-FLAVORED CHEESE SO AS TO ENHANCE THE DELICATE FLAVOR OF THESE BLOSSOMS. YOU CAN ALSO PICK A CHEESE WITH A LOW FAT CONTENT.
(SERVES 4 AS A SIDE DISH, 8 AS AN APPETIZER)

16 squash blossoms (pistil removed)
2 eggs, whites and yolks separated
½ cup flour
1 cup panela cheese or a mild cheese like queso fresco or ricotta
2 cups vegetable or corn oil
Salt to taste

MENU 16.1: MOTHER'S DAY

Appetizer / *Antojitos*
Stuffed Squash Blossoms / *Flores de Calabaza Rellenas*
Soup / *Caldo*
Squash Blossom Soup / *Sopa de Flor de Calabaza*
Entrée / *Plato Fuerte*
Chicken Breast Rolls in Rose and Hibiscus Sauce / *Rollos de Pollo con Salsa de Rosas y Jamaica*
Side / *Guarnición*
Tortillas with Pressed Flowers / *Tortillas con Flores Prensadas*
Dessert / *Postre*
Lavender Almond Custard / *Flan de Lavanda y Almendra*
Beverage / *Bebida*
Hibiscus Flower Water / *Agua de Jamaica* (see recipe, p. 156)

RINSE blossoms gently and trim the stems; gently remove pistil and open blossoms butterfly style. Extend blossoms on a paper towel, cover with another paper towel, and roll paper towel with blossoms gently to absorb moisture; unroll and set aside. In a bowl, add egg whites and whisk until soft peaks form. Add egg yolks and slowly mix into egg whites with a fork.

In another bowl, add flour. Cut cheese about ⅛ inch thick by 1 inch long; place cheese in the cavity of the blossom and close. Repeat with every blossom.

In a cast-iron pan or other thick-bottomed frying pan, heat oil to 350°. Take a stuffed blossom and dredge in flour bowl. Then, drench the blossom with the egg mixture until completely covered. Place blossom in the hot oil over medium flame, and fry until brown, flip blossom once until it gets a nice crisp brown color (2–3 minutes each side). Place on paper towels to absorb excess oil. Salt to taste. Repeat with all the blossoms.

Stuffed Squash Blossoms / *Flores de Calabaza Rellenas.*
Photo by Adriana Almazán Lahl.

SQUASH BLOSSOM SOUP / SOPA DE FLOR DE CALABAZA

(SERVES 6)

30 squash blossoms
7 ounces tomatoes
1 onion
1 garlic clove, finely chopped
7 ounces prepared masa (Maseca for tortillas, see "Basic Recipes for Mexican Cooking," p. 14)
3 tablespoons vegetable oil
8 cups chicken stock (see "Basic Recipes for Mexican Cooking," p. 11)
2 epazote sprigs (or cilantro)
Salt and pepper to taste

WASH blossoms, remove pistil, and chop blossoms roughly. In a blender, combine tomatoes, ¼ onion, and garlic and mix until smooth; pass through a sieve and set aside.

Make ¼-inch balls with the prepared masa and pinch balls in the center to make a hollow; set aside.

In a soup pot, warm oil over medium-high heat, purée tomato mix, and cook for 12 minutes. Once cooked, add chicken stock and bring to a boil. Lower heat to

Squash Blossom Soup / *Sopa de Flor de Calabaza.*
Photo by Adriana Almazán Lahl.

medium-high and add masa balls and epazote sprig and cook for 10–12 minutes more. Turn off stove and add squash blossoms to broth. Season broth with salt and pepper and allow to rest, covered, for 5 minutes. Serve hot. 🐟

CHICKEN BREAST ROLLS IN ROSE AND HIBISCUS SAUCE / ROLLOS DE POLLO CON SALSA DE ROSAS Y JAMAICA

(SERVES 6)

3 whole boneless chicken breasts, skin on (ask your butcher to remove bones)
Salt and pepper to taste
1 cup goat cheese
1 cup roasted pine nuts
2 tablespoons tarragon leaves, minced
4 white or red organic roses or Rose Petal Marmalade (A)
½ cup prepared Herb Butter (B)
Rose and Hibiscus Sauce (C)
Bunch of tarragon leaves

TO BUTTERFLY THE CHICKEN BREASTS:

SEPARATE each breast into 2 halves so you get 6 large pieces. Remove skin and reserve. Place your hand flat, on top of the breast half, and using a very sharp knife carefully cut into the thickest part of the breast lengthwise, creating a pocket. Continue slicing through until breast half opens completely, as if opening up a book. Once butterflied, place each breast in between two layers of plastic wrap or inside a large plastic bag; pound with a meat hammer until it is ¼ inch thick.

Sprinkle flattened chicken breasts with salt and pepper. Combine goat cheese with ½ cup of roasted pine nuts and 1 teaspoon tarragon in a small mixing bowl. Place cheese mixture toward the bottom third of each chicken breast, closest to its narrowest point, adding a couple of fresh rose petals or rose petal marmalade if you prefer. Roll the breast around the stuffing, tucking in the ends as you roll, burrito style.

Lay the reserved chicken skins out, pat them dry, and divide the prepared herb butter, spreading the butter in the center of the skins. Place the rolled breast directly on top of the butter and then wrap the skin around the chicken; secure the skin with a toothpick.

Preheat oven to 350°. In a large cast-iron skillet, add 2 tablespoons oil and sauté rolls over medium heat until all chicken is seared (3–4 minutes per side).

Chicken Breast Rolls in Rose and Hibiscus Sauce.
Photo by Adriana Almazán Lahl.

Transfer the pan to the oven and bake until breasts reach an inside temperature of 165° (check with meat thermometer, about 10–15 minutes). Remove from oven and allow chicken to rest and drain on paper towels for 7 minutes. Remove skin and toothpicks; cut by the center diagonally.

Add Rose and Hibiscus Sauce to pan and warm sauce, deglazing the pan and mixing sauce with chicken juices. Place warm sauce in the center of a plate, place chicken breast standing up and garnish with fresh rose petals, fresh tarragon leaves, and roasted pine nuts. 🐝

A. Rose Petal Marmalade / Mermelada de Rosas

2 ounces organic rose petals (red or white)
2½ cups sugar
1 cup sweet red wine
1 teaspoon lemon juice
2 ounces pectin

WASH and dry rose petals. Cut their white pits close to the stem with a knife. Working with your hands, crush the rose petals into 1 cup of sugar in a bowl until well bruised. Cover with plastic wrap and allow to rest for 3 to 5 hours. Then, place rose petals and sugar in a saucepan with wine and bring to a boil. Add lemon juice and pectin; cook for five minutes. Store in a clean, sterilized jar. 🐝

B. Herb Butter

½ cup butter room temperature
½ teaspoon salt
Pepper to taste
½ tablespoon finely chopped tarragon

MIX all ingredients until completely combined. Use as is or refrigerate until ready to use. 🐝

C. Rose and Hibiscus Sauce

2½ cups water
¼ cup hibiscus flowers (dehydrated)
½ cup sugar
1 cinnamon stick
1 tablespoon ground cinnamon
5 cups organic rose petals, red or white
¾ cup white wine
¼ cup rose water
Salt and pepper to taste
1 tablespoon butter
2 tablespoons shallots, minced
1 tablespoon flour

BRING 1 cup of water to a boil in a medium saucepan. First, make hibiscus water by adding hibiscus flowers, ¼ cup sugar, and a cinnamon stick and simmer for 15 minutes on high. Remove from flame, pass through a sieve, and allow to cool. Next, wash rose petals, cutting their white tips close to stem with a sharp knife. Add the petals to 1½ cups water and ¼ cup rose water; pass through a sieve and set the petals aside, saving 1 cup of the liquid in a large saucepan. Add 1 teaspoon ground cinnamon, 1 tablespoon sugar, and ¼ cup white wine. Allow to simmer for 2 minutes. Once ingredients cool down add ½ cup of hibiscus and rose water in a blender and mix until smooth; season with salt and pepper. In another saucepan, add 1 tablespoons butter and on low heat cook minced shallots for 4 minutes. Add 1 tablespoons flour, cook for 2 minutes, stirring all the time. Add rose/hibiscus blended sauce, bring to a simmer, and cook for 5 minutes more until it thickens; set aside. 🐗

Tortillas with Squash Blossoms.
Photo by Adriana Almazán Lahl.

TORTILLAS

TORTILLAS are ubiquitous in Mexico—at once eating utensils, comestibles, and even a dinner bell. Tortillas left quite an impression on the Spanish colonizers in Mexico, as noted by a lady of the Spanish aristocracy in her letters home:

> Those who are rather particular, roll up two tortillas, and use them as a knife and fork, which, I can assure you from experience, is a great deal better than nothing, when you have learnt how to use them.
>
> They first cook the grain in water with a little lime, and when it is soft peel off the skin; then grind it on a large block of stone, the *metate*, or, as the Indians (who know best) call it, the *metatl*. For the purpose of grinding it, they use a sort of stone roller, with which it is crushed, and rolled into a bowl placed below the stone. They then take some of this paste, and clap it between their hands till they form it into light round cakes, which are afterward toasted on a smooth plate, called the *comalli* (*comal* they call it in Mexico), and which ought to be eaten as hot as possible[1]

Tortillas, in order to be served up hot off the comal, are the very last item prepared when making a Mexican meal. When they say, *"calentando las tortillas"* (I'm heating the tortillas), it is the equivalent of "dinner is served." Only enough tortillas are heated and placed in the warmer (*chiquihuitle*) for the "first round." Someone always gets up and heats more in the middle of the meal, maybe even a couple of times. Dinner is over when everyone at the table has said they have had enough tortillas.

Nahua woman preparing tortillas in a *tequihl*, an outdoor Mexican kitchen. *Photo be Jorge Ontiveros.*

TORTILLAS WITH PRESSED FLOWERS / TORTILLAS CON FLORES PRENSADAS

(MAKES 14 TORTILLAS)

7 squash blossoms, or any edible flower (optional)
1 pound prepared masa for tortillas (see "Basic Recipes for Mexican Cooking," p. 14)
5 epazote or cilantro sprigs (optional, leaves only)

OPEN squash blossoms and remove pistil, cut in half and reserve.
Make balls the size of golf balls with the masa. You will need two 4-inch square plastic sheets, which are easy to make by cutting a sandwich baggie into 2 equal sheets. Place squash blossoms on top of one of the 4-inch plastic squares. Carefully place a dough ball on top and flatten the dough gently, then finish flattening tortillas with tortilla press or rolling pin to make a 3-inch disc (see complete directions and diagrams for using a tortilla press to make tortillas on p. 236). Remove plastic from top and place tortilla in your hand. Remove the second plastic carefully so you don't break the tortilla. Place tortilla on a hot, dry grill or comal, with flower facing down first. Cook for 1 minute each side; tortillas should puff when done.

NOTES FROM THE ALMAZÁN KITCHEN

FOR tortillas pressed with squash blossoms and herbs, rinse blossoms gently and trim the stems; remove the pistil carefully. Open blossoms butterfly style. Extend blossoms on a paper towel, cover with another paper towel, and roll gently to absorb moisture. Unroll paper towels and cut blossoms in half lengthwise; set aside. Rinse and pat dry epazote or cilantro sprigs, separate leaves, and set aside.

Place squash blossom petal (or any edible flower) and 2 cilantro or epazote leaves in the middle of the lower surface of the tortilla and press. Place masa ball on top and press gently. Cover with the plastic and close tortilla; press carefully. Proceed to press the tortilla and follow instructions as before, adding 30 seconds of cooking time on the flower side.

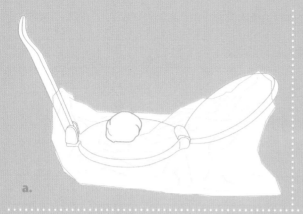

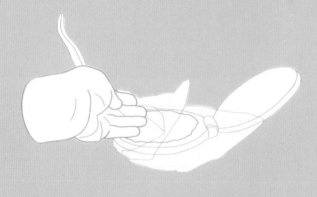

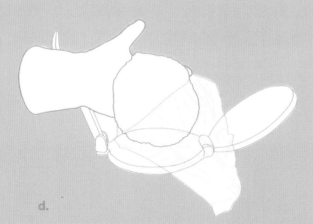

Making tortillas. **A.** Place masa ball between two 4-by-4-inch plastic sheets, which are easy to make by cutting a sandwich baggie into two equal sheets. **B.** Flatten tortillas with tortilla press or rolling pin to make a 3-inch disc. **C.** Remove plastic from top and place tortilla in your hand. **D.** Remove the second plastic carefully so that you don't break the tortilla.
Figure by Verticalarray, Inc.

LAVENDER ALMOND CUSTARD/
FLAN DE LAVANDA Y ALMENDRAS

(SERVES 6–8)

1½ cups sugar for caramel
4 cups milk
1 tablespoon lavender buds
1 vanilla pod
1 tablespoon almond essence
5 egg yolks
1 pound sugar
1 tablespoon shaved toasted almonds

IN a saucepan, add 1½ cups of sugar and cook, stirring constantly until you get a dark caramel. Add caramel to a 9-inch round, glass, ovenproof pan, thoroughly covering the bottom of the pan.

In another saucepan, heat milk and lavender over medium heat. Split open vanilla pod and scrape seeds. Add vanilla pod seeds to milk with the almond essence. Let mixture simmer for 5 minutes without allowing to boil. Remove from heat, wait 5 more minutes, and pass through a sieve.

Lightly beat egg yolks and add sugar; slowly incorporate milk mixture, stirring constantly. Pass through a sieve again and pour on top of caramel in the round glass pan. Cover with foil. Place in the oven over Baño Maria (see "Common Mexican Cooking Tools and Techniques," p. 333) for 50 minutes at 350°. Allow to cool completely before unmolding over a large serving platter; garnish with shaved toasted almonds. 🐛

CORPUS CHRISTI DAY / DÍA DEL CORPUS CHRISTI [SIXTY DAYS AFTER EASTER SUNDAY]

CORPUS CHRISTI DAY, also known as the Day of the Holy Eucharist, is a moveable feast hosted sixty days after Easter Sunday, celebrated since 1246 in commemoration of the Last Supper on the day before Jesus's crucifixion. Many Christians around the world receive Communion on this day.

History and Turmoil

The history of Corpus Christi Day in Mexico is a study in colonial Mexican politics, one that gives rare insight into how the Spanish officials looked to major festivals as an opportunity to assert social control. Celebrations in Mexico started in 1526, and by 1618 Corpus Christi was the largest and most ostentatious annual festival in Mexico City,[1] the seat of power of New Spain.[2] It was also unique in that the elite of Nueva España's capital participated alongside Mexico's ethnic groups, the mestizos or *criollos* (terms used during the Colonial era to refer to people of mixed heritage, usually of Spanish and indigenous blood),[3] as well as the Aztecs, with the location of each group in the procession a reflection of their place in the social order. Representatives of the Spanish Crown recognized the potential of the Corpus Christi festival to advance political goals, and it was used to advantage, bringing together the country's disparate population with the goal of creating a consistent colonial identity.

The authorities sponsoring the event believed that by losing themselves in the spectacle and sounds of the moment, the participants would unite in support of Church and Crown. Much like carnivals today, the Corpus Christi processions included floats, *cabezudos* (people in costume with big heads), and *gigantes* (giant figures made of wood, paper, and fur and complete with clothing and wigs) representing individuals, as well as *tarasca* or dragons symbolizing the power of the Holy Spirit to overcome sin. Indigenous groups, even from far regions of the country, were paid generously to perform music and dance and to create the various floats, gigantes, and costumes, and theatrical performances and fireworks were added to the festivities. The event grew and reached its peak at the turn of the eighteenth century. Historians have noted over eighty-five participating guilds or fraternities and a procession that was three-quarters of a mile in length. Streets were cleaned, altars were erected, and buildings decorated with luxurious fabrics and tapestries.

However, after civil disturbances in the capital in the first two decades of the seventeenth century, a widespread revolt in 1692, and another in 1701, vestiges of Indian contributions began to be eliminated by the Bourbon viceroy as he sought to control the indigenous population. The Corpus Christi celebrations became a prime battleground in the struggle for control over common spaces and festival days, defining where the vestiges of power lay in Mexico. By 1777, there were no native dancers and the budget for the event was just 6 percent of what it had been in 1618. In 1790 a decree was issued banning the dragons, big heads, and giants, and in 1866, the last citywide procession took place in Mexico City.

Modern Celebrations

In Mexico today on Día del Corpus Christi, small altars (*reposiares*) are lovingly decorated with flowers and candles are placed along the route of subdued religious processions that are now common. Children dressed in traditional indigenous costumes gather outside the cathedral in Mexico City to have their baskets of fruits and vegetables blessed.

In a custom that migrated from Spain, where traditional reenactments complete with costumes, bands, horses, and banners continue to be observed, some parts of Mexico celebrate Corpus Christi with symbolic battles between the Moors and the Christians, especially in the Sierras of Puebla and Veracruz.

Day of the Donkey

In Mexico, Corpus Christi Day is also *Día de las Mulas*, or Day of the Donkey. On this day, which coincided with the spring equinox, the Aztecs brought their mules carrying all kinds of produce in a procession to offer to thanks to God for a bountiful harvest. The legend is that an *Indio* named Ignacio spoke out, saying, "If God exists, even the mules will kneel," and at that precise moment, a mule kneeled. Ever since, it has been customary to give little mule toys made out of cornhusk decorated with miniature clay pots filled with food as a symbol of plenty. It is traditional to assemble a salad with an abundance of produce, as a symbol of the blessings of Jesus that nurture both the soul and the stomach—the *Ensalada de Corpus Christi*.

Danza de los Voladores

Another spectacle that takes place on this day is an ancient Mesoamerican ceremony that still occurs in some areas, performed by various indigenous people including the Nahua, the Otomi, and the Totonacs. The *Danza de los Voladores*, or Flying Pole Dance, was named an Intangible Cultural Heritage by UNESCO in 2009. It is believed that in pre-Hispanic times, the participants impersonated birds representing the gods of the earth, air, fire, and water and may have dressed as parrots, macaws, quetzals, and eagles. By the sixteenth century, the ritual was strongly associated with solar ceremonies, such as the spring equinox, which would explain its coincidental timing with Día de las Mulas.

In the most traditional and lengthy version, the tree selection and cutting ritual is called the *tsakáe kiki*, and includes requesting a pardon from mountain god Quihuicolo for taking the tree. As part of the ceremony, before erecting the pole made from the tree whose branches have been stripped, offerings of flowers, incense (*copal*), alcohol, candles, and even a live turkey are placed in a deep hole, into which the tree pole is to be placed. When the heavy pole is elevated, the contents of the hole are crushed, adding to the fertility of the earth. This very tall post (thirty meters), sunk deep into the ground, represents a connecting point between the sky, the surface world, and the underworld.

With forests so scarce in Mexico today, the more typical ceremony uses a permanent steel pole. Five participants, almost always men, represent the four cardinal directions as well as the four elements: earth, air, fire, and water. The fifth man, called a *caporal*, represents the fifth sun of the Aztecs. He does not descend or fly, but stays at the top of the pole playing a flute and drum, while the four *voladores* wind the ropes around the pole and tie themselves to the ends by one foot. The four ropes are each wound thirteen times for a total of fifty-two, the number of years in a Mesoamerican great year. The men then drop, "flying" and causing the ropes to unwind.

Although the ritual did not originate with the Totonacs, today it is often associated with these indigenous people of the Papantla area in the state of Veracruz. According to myth, over 450 years ago there was a severe drought created by the gods because the people had neglected them. The Danza de los Voladores was a

Flying pole dancers.
Photo by Graeme Churchard.

way to appease the gods and bring back the rains. Diego Durán noted in his history and culture of the Aztecs, based on firsthand observations in the early 1600s, a rite where an Aztec prince, Ezhuahuacatl, sacrificed himself by diving from a pole twenty *"brazas"*[4] high.

While there is no particular menu associated with this festival, there is a traditional, colorful Corpus Christi salad presented in the menu below as an introduction to the repast, and we have chosen to present a meal focused on fruits and vegetables that reflect the bounty of a rich harvest.

CORPUS CHRISTI SALAD / ENSALADA DE CORPUS CHRISTI

(SERVES 6–8)

1 cup fresh corn kernels

1 cup fresh peas

1 cup zucchini, small diced

1 small cucumber, seeded and finely diced

1 pear, peeled and finely diced

1 firm, sweet peach, peeled and finely diced

2 small avocados peeled, finely diced

Seeds of 1 pomegranate (1 cup)

¼ cup plus 3 tablespoons olive oil

1 teaspoon white vinegar

Juice of 2 Mexican limes

1 teaspoon salt

Pepper to taste

1 teaspoon sugar to taste

MENU 17.1: CORPUS CHRISTI DAY

Salad / *Ensalada*
Corpus Christi Salad /
Ensalada de Corpus Christi
Entrées / *Platos Fuertes*
Stuffed Zucchini /
Calabacitas Rellenas
Green Beans Scramble in
Tomato Sauce / *Ejotes con
Huevo en Salsa de Tomate*
Side / *Guarnición*
Chayote au Gratin /
Chayotes con Queso y Crema
Dessert / *Postre*
Peaches and Guava in Syrup /
Duraznos y Guayaba en Almibar
Beverage / *Bebida*
Strawberry Shake /
Licuado de Fresa

IN a medium saucepan, steam corn, peas, and zucchini for 5–7 minutes. Once cooked, set aside to cool down and immerse in cold water with ice so cooking stops. Combine all the diced fruits and vegetables including pomegranate seeds

Corpus
Christi Salad /
*Ensalada de
Corpus Christi.*
Photo by
Adriana
Almazán Lahl.

in large salad bowl (or you may choose to arrange the ingredients as in the photo on p. 243). In a small bowl, whisk together olive oil, vinegar, and lime juice with salt, pepper, and sugar. Pour dressing over salad; if comgining ingredients, toss until thoroughly mixed. 🗦

ZUCCHINI

SQUASH is one of the earliest crops for which we have records, dating back to 7500 BC in the valley of central Mexico. Originally cultivated for use as storage receptacles for food, seed, and water, they quickly became a staple of the Mesoamerican diet. Mexican (white) differs from yellow or dark green zucchini; it is a pale-green squash, found in Mexican markets in a size (and shape) somewhere between a tennis and golf ball and has a firm texture and sweet flavor. Although we think of zucchini as a vegetable, botanically, zucchini is an immature fruit, actually the swollen ovary of the female zucchini flower.

STUFFED ZUCCHINI / CALABACITAS RELLENAS

(SERVES 6)

12 medium Mexican zucchini (or chayote)
2 tablespoons oil
1 onion, chopped small
3 tomatoes, seeded and chopped
3 ounces ham, finely chopped (for a vegetarian version, omit ham)
2 cups Mexican Manchego or Oaxacan cheese
1 egg
Tomato stock (see "Basic Recipes for Mexican Cooking," p. 14)

CUT zucchini in half (lengthwise; if you get round zucchini, trim the top) and steam for 6–7 minutes (if substituting chayotes, longer steaming time may be required). The vegetable should be medium firm, not soft. Meanwhile, add oil to a stir-fry pan and sauté onions, tomatoes, and ham. Once zucchini is cooked, seed the zucchini with a spoon and add seeds to the pan with the onions, tomatoes, and ham. Turn off stove and add 1 cup of cheese. Mix well. Set aside and cool for 10 minutes, then add beaten egg and mix well again. Place zucchini in a deep dish and stuff them with the vegetable/ham/cheese mixture and cover with cheese. Place in a preheated oven at 400° for 7 to 10 minutes or until cheese turns golden brown. Serve zucchini over tomato stock. 🗦

Stuffed Zucchini /
Calabacitas Rellenas.
Photo by Adriana Almazán Lahl.

GREEN BEAN SCRAMBLE ÍN TOMATO SAUCE / EJOTES CON HUEVO EN SALSA DE TOMATE

(SERVES 6)

1 large tomato
1 serrano chile
1 garlic clove
3 cups tender green beans, washed and trimmed into 1-inch pieces
2 tablespoons vegetable oil
¼ Spanish white onion, finely sliced
5 eggs
¼ cup chicken stock (see "Basic Recipes for Mexican Cooking," p. 11)
1 sprig cilantro, finely chopped
Salt and pepper to taste

IN a medium saucepan, boil tomato and serrano chile for 15 minutes; set aside, retain liquid, and let cool. Once cold, peel tomatoes and combine with chile, garlic, and

2 cups of liquid you used to boil the tomato; mix in blender until smooth. Reserve and set aside. In separate saucepan, heat one cup of water, green beans, and a pinch of salt. Cook for 10 minutes until tender but still firm. Once cooked, strain and set aside.

In a sauté pan, preheat oil and add onion, cook for 1 minute. Add eggs and green beans and scramble. Add tomato mixture from blender to scrambled eggs, incorporate chicken stock, and cilantro and let it simmer for 10 minutes or until sauce thickens. Add salt and pepper to taste. Serve with warm tortillas or as a side dish.

CHAYOTES AU GRATIN / CHAYOTES CON CREMA Y QUESO

(SERVES 6)

4–6 chayotes, diced into ¼-inch squares
3 cups water
1 tablespoon butter
1 cup Mexican sour cream
Pinch of nutmeg
½ tablespoon salt or to taste
1 cup Oaxaca or Mexican Manchego cheese, shredded
½ cup cilantro, chopped

IN a saucepan cook chayote for 15–20 minutes in 3 cups of boiling water until fork tender. (Alternatively, chayote cooks beautifully in a microwavable glass bowl in

Chayotes au Gratin / *Chayotes con Crema y Queso.*
Photo by Adriana Almazán Lahl.

just about 1 inch of water, covered with plastic wrap for about 5 minutes. Be sure to add salt to the water and punch a few holes in the plastic wrap before putting into the microwave on high). Drain chayotes. Melt butter in a saucepan. Add sour cream, nutmeg, and salt; mix well to create a sauce.

Place chayotes in an ovenproof pan with the sauce on top and cover with cheese. Place under broiler in oven for 7 minutes or until cheese melts and starts browning. Sprinkle with chopped cilantro before serving. 🐦

PEACHES OR GUAVA IN SYRUP / DURAZNOS O GUAYABA EN ALMÍBAR

(SERVES 6)

6 ripe firm peaches or guava
4 cups of water
1 cup sugar
1 vanilla pod, split open, or ½ tablespoon vanilla essence
1½ cups whipped cream

WASH fruit and place in a large saucepan with 4 cups of water, sugar, and vanilla and cook for 20 minutes. Remove fruit from pot and allow to cool a few minutes while the syrup continues to cook on medium heat so it reduces. Peel fruit, cut in half, and remove pits. Add skin and pits into the syrup and keep cooking until you get a medium-thick syrup. It should be the consistency of a maple syrup. Remove skins and pits from syrup.

Place peach or guava halves in sterilized glass jars and add hot syrup to top; be careful, as syrup will be extremely hot. Close and flip jar upside down; let it rest for a few hours until it cools down. Place in refrigerator for a few hours before serving. Serve 2 halves in a small bowl topped with whipped cream or vanilla ice cream. 🐦

LICUADOS

LICUADOS, which you'll find in pueblos throughout Mexico sold by street vendors, are Mexico's answer to the smoothie, made with milk, fruit, and ice. They differ from the American-style smoothie in that licuados use a milk base rather than fruit juice. This actually makes them lower in calories and higher in protein than the typical smoothie. Some licuado recipes call for added nuts.

STRAWBERRY SHAKE / LICUADO DE FRESA

(SERVES 4)

½ pound clean strawberries, quartered and with stems removed
8 tablespoons sugar
4 cups milk
½ tablespoon vanilla essence
Large pinch of cinnamon
6 ice cubes

PLACE all ingredients in a blender, mix until smooth, and serve in a tall glass. Garnish with a strawberry wedge on the rim of the glass.

You can substitute any fruit you like, such as mango, banana, mamey, or papaya, or use 8 tablespoons of cocoa powder for a chocolate licuado. You can also add walnuts or pecans. Feel free to adjust sugar to your liking. 🐾

INDEPENDENCE DAY / DÍA DEL GRITO
(SEPTEMBER 15–16)

18
CHAPTER

SEPTEMBER 15 begins the days of celebration known as *fiestas patrias*, or Independence celebrations, with *"El Grito de Independencia"* (Cry of Independence), commemorating the battle cry of the Mexican War of Independence. This is Mexico's most important civic holiday and the occasion of one of her most widely celebrated fiesta periods. Schools, banks, and all businesses close for several days.

The Original "Secret" Grito

At the heart of the celebration is the story of a special Mexican hero, Miguel Hidalgo y Costilla, a Roman Catholic priest from the small town of Dolores (now known as Dolores Hidalgo), near Guanajuato. Hidalgo and his loyal criollos (a term used to refer to people of mixed heritage during the colonial era, usually of Spanish and indigenous blood) planned a revolt against the Spanish colonial government, which considered Mexico its own, even naming it Nueva España (New Spain).

It was on September 16, 1810, that Hidalgo ordered the church bells to be rung and gathered his congregation, encouraging them to revolt with what Hidalgo and his group of insurgents referred to as "el grito," a call to sedition which they had been secretly planning for some time: the initiation of their plot to reclaim Mexico. The other principal actors in the rebellion that night were Captain Ignacio Allende, a soldier, and Juan Aldama, councilman of the village of San Miguel el Grande, thus forming a triumvirate of the key powers in New Spain: clergy, militia, and local government. Authorities were soon to put a price of 10,000 pesos on each of their heads. It is widely held throughout Mexico that these are the famous words, uttered just before midnight on September 15, 1810, sparking the revolution: "Long live our Lady of Guadalupe! Death to bad government! Death to the gachupines!" (*gachupines*, a derogatory term, is what they called the native Spaniards).

Some historians note more specific references to religion and an interesting use of the concept of "America," recording the battle cry as including, "Long live religion," or perhaps, "Long live the Catholic religion," adding "Long live America," or, some suggest, "May our holy patroness, the Holy Virgin of Guadalupe, live and reign forever in this American continent!" In fact, the insurgents were soon to carry a banner of the Virgin of Guadalupe as the emblem of their fight.

The Long Fight for Mexican Independence

Sometime in the afternoon of September 16, 1810, Hidalgo and his insurgents left Dolores with a fighting force made up of Mexican-born Spaniards, indigenous people, and mestizos (people of mixed Spanish and indigenous lineage) armed with sticks and machetes. This battle was just the beginning; as they marched across Mexico, Hidalgo's army grew to nearly ninety thousand, attracting poor farmers and other Mexican civilians long frustrated with Spanish rule. The end would come, after eleven years of bloody and often politically complicated struggle, with Mexico's independence from Spain on September 27, 1821, when General Agustin de Iturbide rode victorious into Mexico City. For just a few years, this was the official date of Independence Day celebrations. However, Iturbide proved to be an unpopular leader, and in 1823 the date of the anniversary of the birth of the nation was changed to September 16, acknowledging Hidalgo as "the father of the Independence of Mexico."

Porfírio Díaz and the One-Hundred-Year Anniversary of El Grito

September 15 or 16

Like so many Mexican holidays, the ceremony surrounding Día del Grito has been reinvented to create "the illusion of continuity between the present and the founding of the country."[1] In reality, prior to 1910, only Mexico's elite participated in Día de la Independencia events, which included cockfights and fireworks on September 16. President Porfírio Díaz (Díaz's "presidency" lasted from 1876–1911, and he is commonly considered by historians to have been a dictator) saw the opportunity to insert himself into the "pantheon of national heroes"[2] by staging a much larger and more egalitarian celebration, which, not coincidentally, fell on his birthday.

Thus, the tradition of gathering in *el Zócalo* (the plaza in front of the National Palace in Mexico City) and repeating "El Grito" was born, a celebration to which all Mexico was invited. But, Díaz manipulated the dates to begin festivities on September 15, so Independence Day could be celebrated jointly with his eightieth birthday (September 16, 1910). At presidential birthday parties, it was common to host the most powerful of Mexican "politicos" and high society and to invite political figures from Argentina, Italy, France, Spain, Colombia, and Japan, among others. Díaz saw an opportunity to show off the progress he had made during his period of power in "acculturating" Mexico along European lines, and particularly his esteem for French culture. Thus, a tradition that Mexicans now take for granted as rooted in the original celebration was, at least partially, born not so much of patriotism as of egoism and political expediency.

Banquets and Bravado

The exuberant tastes of the era were reflected in the festivities of the one-hundred-year anniversary of Mexican independence hosted by Díaz. A journalist assigned to report on the festivities for the French newspaper *Figaro* reported that the city was

> decorated at every intersection with commemorative arcs made of flowers and foliage. . . . Between the arcs were massive facades entirely covered with fresh vegetables. Needless to say, this drew the admiration of the Indian onlookers. . . . Everywhere one could see statues and portraits of Father [Miguel] Hidalgo—liberator and hero of the National Independence that we are celebrating. At night, we saw a thrilling light show. . . . As soon as the sun had set, thousands of lights appeared in elegant lanterns in vivid colors and of endless varieties. These lanterns were fastened to windows, balconies, tress and shop fronts . . . the white rays of which illuminated every last nook and cranny.[3]

He goes on to describe a parade lasting five hours, with twenty thousand armed soldiers and floats representing "all the arts, trades and industries known to man."[4]

Over twenty banquets were given during the month of September 1910, providing suitable pretext for a show of presidential abundance. Far from demonstrating Mexican patriotism with pre-Columbian cuisine, Díaz's menus spoke more to his admiration for the French and their gastronomy, in an ironic contradiction to what should have been the true spirit of Mexican Independence.

Given the political climate of the day (a growing discontent, which gave birth just a few months later to the Zapatistas and what would become known as the Mexican Revolution [see chapter 19]), this display of wealth and kowtowing to French culture was not popular with many outside the Mexican upper class. Ironically, and perhaps impervious to the atmosphere inside Mexico, the *New York Times* wrote of the occasion, "Mexico, in these days of festivity, has been glorifying in its past, and there is much in that past to glorify. But the political and material significance of the centennial relates to a new Mexico, a Mexico of awakened industry, a country that is striving to take its rightful place among the nations of the world."[5]

The main celebration hosted ten thousand people at the National Palace in Mexico's capital, which required a new set of china to be printed with the colors of the Mexican flag and the eagle representative of the Porfirio Díaz era, as well as his monogram, complete with a fourteen-karat gold rim. Adding insult to injury, the exorbitant expenditure for this china produced the only patriotic symbol of the entire feast.

Twelve dishes were served, in a menu carefully crafted by Díaz's personal chef, Sylvain Daumonty, and the first lady, Carmen Romero Rubio (known as Doña Carmelita). The culinary delicacies could easily have transported any guest directly to Paris. They served foie gras from Strasburg, Bordeaux wines including el Mouton Rothchild 1889, fine sherry wines, and G. G. Mumm & Co. Cordon Rouge champagne. The menu was written in perfect French, which dinner guests where expected to be able to read, and an after-dinner dance featured Austrian waltz music played by an orchestra located at the center of the main patio. Red roses and gladiolas adorned the tables, and palm trees surrounded the main patio. Electricity was a new commodity and a novelty; the use of lights to decorate the banquet halls exemplifies the extravagant nature of these parties.

Although the Porfírio Díaz one-hundredth-anniversary menu has been widely published, recipes associated with the menu have disappeared. So, for this book, Adriana has re-created recipes for the dishes that were served at this event.

CHILLED CANTALOUPE DRIZZLED WITH PINK CHAMPAGNE / MELON GLACÉ AU CLICQUOT ROSÉ

(SERVES 8)

1 large cantaloupe
1 bottle of pink champagne
1 tablespoon mint, finely chopped
1 tablespoon confectioner's sugar

CUT cantaloupe in half and remove seeds. Using a melon baller, carve balls and place them back into the empty canteloupe half, place into refrigerator for at least 1 hour. To serve, place cantaloupe balls in martini glasses, add cold pink champagne, sprinkle with minced mint leaves and a pinch of confectioner's sugar. ❧

> ### MENU 18.1: ORIGINAL MENU AS SERVED BY PORFÍRIO DÍAZ IN 1910
>
> Chilled Cantaloupe Drizzled with Pink Champagne /
> *Melon Glacé au Clicquot Rosé*
> Christopher Columbus Cream Soup / *Potage Christophe Colomb*
> Rhine River Grilled Salmon in St. Malo Sauce / *Saumon du Rhin sautée à la St. Malo*
> Scarlet Young Chicken / *Poularde a L'écarlate*

CHRISTOPHER COLUMBUS SOUP / POTAGE CHRISTOPHE COLOMB

(SERVES 8–10)

3 tablespoons olive oil
1 large ancho chile, seeded and sliced in strips
4 Spanish white onions, thinly sliced
3 bay leaves
8 cups beef stock (see "Basic Recipes for Mexican Cooking," p. 11)
3 tablespoons piloncillo, shredded (see "Common Mexican Cooking Tools and Techniques,"
    p. 336)
Salt to taste
¼ cup sherry wine
2 bolillos or French baguette, sliced and toasted
1 cup Grana Padano or quality Parmesan cheese

ADD olive oil to a large soup pot and sautée ancho chile. Drain chile over paper towel and crumble; set aside. In the same oil, sautée onions until caramelized and tender, 25–30 minutes over a medium-low flame. Add, bay leaves, beef stock, and piloncillo; allow simmering for 20 minutes, adding salt to taste. Add sherry wine and bring to a fast boil. Serve hot with a piece of sliced toasted bread and a generous amount of cheese on top, sprinkle with ancho chile strips. 🐦

RHINE RIVER GRILLED SALMON IN ST. MALO SAUCE / SAUMON DU RHIN SAUTÉE À LA ST. MALO

(SERVES 6)

½ tablespoon olive oil
6 salmon fillets
Salt and pepper to taste
St. Malo Sauce (A)

HEAT a large nonstick or a cast-iron skillet, add ½ tablespoon oil, and bring to medium-high heat. Season salmon with salt and pepper on both sides. Add fish to pan; cook 5 minutes or until crisp. Turn fish and cook for 5 more minutes or until fish flakes easily when tested with a fork; only turn once. In a large plate serve sauce and place fish on top, serve with a nice green salad on the side. 🐦

A. St. Malo Sauce

1 Spanish white onion, finely diced
1 tablespoon olive oil
3 tablespoons flour
5 canned anchovy filets
1 cup dry white wine
2 tablespoons prepared mustard
2 cups fish stock (see "Basic Recipes for Mexican Cooking," p. 12)
1 tablespoon potato starch
3 tablespoons water

SAUTÉ the onion in the oil for 4–5 minutes over medium heat until the onion is translucent.

Stir in the flour and cook 3 more minutes until it sticks to the onion. Purée the anchovies, blending with half of the wine. Over medium heat, blend the anchovy mix and the mustard with the onions. Mix in the rest of the wine and the fish stock. Bring to a boil.

Mix the potato starch with 3 tablespoons of water. Add this mix to the sauce while stirring. Boil for 2 more minutes. 🐟

SCARLETT CHICKEN / POULARDE À L'ÉCARLATE

(SERVES 6)

1 cup fresh raspberries, washed, plus ½ cup for garnish
6 chicken breasts, boneless with skin on
Salt and pepper to taste
2 tablespoons butter
2 small shallots, minced
1 canned chipotle chile, minced
¼ cup sherry wine
¼ cup heavy cream

PURÉE and strain the raspberries, save for later. Season the chicken breasts with salt and pepper.

Heat the butter in a sauté pan over high heat; add the breasts skin side down, cook until golden, and turn them over and continue cooking for an additional 5–7 minutes until well done; remove from heat. Lower heat to medium and in the same pan, add the minced shallots, sautée 2 minutes, and add chipotle chile and the sherry wine. Cook until the shallots are soft, about 3 minutes. Mix in the raspberry

Poularde à L'écarlate.
Photo by Adriana Almazán Lahl.

purée and keep cooking for another 5 minutes. Stir in the cream, remove from heat, and plate the sauce, remove skin from chicken breast and place on top. Drizzle more sauce on top of breast. Garnish with a few raspberries.

El Grito in Modern Mexico

Each year on the night of September 15 at 11 p.m., the president of Mexico steps onto the balcony of the National Palace in Mexico City, overlooking the Zócalo, and rings the parish bell (which was transported to El Distrito Federal from Dolores, Guanajuato, in 1896), just as Hidalgo rang the bell over two centuries ago. He repeats the words, known as *El Grito Mexicano* of Padre Hidalgo, in an event that draws up to half a million spectators and is broadcast over radio and television to all Mexico. One observer describes it thus: "The echoes of the *grito* have barley died down, when, suddenly, an ear-splitting racket fills the air. Armed with noisemakers, whistles, horns and firecrackers, the multitude marks the transition between the official ceremony and the beginning of the popular fiesta itself."[6]

Shooting pistols in the air is common, in spite of laws dating as far back as 1825 to the contrary. In cities and towns all over Mexico, El Grito is celebrated with parades, wearing of traditional costumes, and local festivals. Of course, there is the singing of popular rancheros (folk songs) recounting the bravery of the soldiers, sung into the wee hours of the morning, accompanied by drinking and dancing. In many of Mexico's pueblos the local government provides free atole and tamales, even ponche. In Mexico City, in the early morning hours on September 16, a national military parade marks Mexican Independence Day.

TORTILLA SOUP / SOPA DE TORTILLA

(SERVES 8)

1 cup corn oil
12 tortillas, cut in strips
½ Spanish white onion, finely chopped
¾ cup tomato purée (see "Basic Recipes for
     Mexican Cooking," p. 15)
1 garlic clove
1 epazote sprig or ¼ tablespoon
     dry epazote
1 chipotle chile in adobo sauce,
     finely chopped
8 cups chicken stock (see "Basic Recipes for
     Mexican Cooking," p. 11)
Salt and pepper to taste
1 cup of pulled chicken (see "Basic Recipes for Mexican Cooking," p. 11)
1 avocado, cubed
½ cup Cotija or shredded Oaxaca cheese
4 dry pasilla chiles, seeded and dry-roasted on a comal
Mexican sour cream
1 Mexican lime, cut in wedges

> **MENU 18.2: MEXICAN INDEPENDENCE DAY**
>
> Soup / *Sopa*
> Tortilla Soup / *Sopa de Tortilla*
> Entrée / *Plato Fuerte*
> Stuffed Peppers in Walnut Sauce /
> *Chiles en Nogada*
> Side / *Guarnición*
> Mexican Rice with Peas and
> Carrots / *Arroz a la Mexicana con
> Chicharos y Zanahorias*
> Dessert / *Postre*
> *Chongos Zamoranos*

IN a deep pot, warm oil to 350° and fry tortillas strips. Once golden brown, place on paper towels to drain excess oil. Set aside. In a separate pot, heat 2 tablespoons oil, add onion, and sautée until lightly brown, add tomato purée, finely chopped garlic, epazote sprig, and chipotle chile. Let ingredients simmer for 10 minutes on medium-high, stirring occasionally. Add chicken stock and bring to a boil, allow to cook for 5 more minutes. Add salt and pepper to taste.

To serve, place tortilla strips in individual soup bowls, ladle 1 cup of tomato-chicken stock and top with shredded chicken, avocado, cheese, pasilla chile pieces, and a dollop of sour cream. Serve warm with a wedge of lime. 🌶

THE CUISINE OF PUEBLA AND *CHILES EN NOGADA*

THE city of Puebla was an important center in New Spain, a crossroads situated between the busy port of Vera Cruz and Mexico City. Along with its rapid development came the advent of Puebla's convents and the birth of the cuisine for which these are now famous. Besides rompope (see p. 94), mole, tinga de pollo (see p. 133), and a vast array of sweets, legend credits the sisters of Puebla with the original recipe for *chiles en nogada*.

This story is of a special meal for Agustin de Iturbide, a military commander who fought in Mexico's War of Independence, and later proclaimed himself Emperor of Mexico (from 1822 to 1823). In August of 1821, he signed what was to be the most important document in the country's history, the Treaty of Cordoba, which granted Mexico its independence from Spain. After signing the treaty in Veracruz, Iturbide traveled to Mexico City, stopping on the way in the town of Puebla. There, the locals decided to hold a feast to celebrate the country's independence and to honor Iturbide. The Augustinian nuns of the convent of Santa Monica prepared a special dish, *chiles en nogada*, using local, seasonal ingredients.

The original recipe is made with a fruit and nut stuffing consisting of apples, pears, peaches, raisins, olives, almonds, pine nuts, plantains, and acitron (caramelized cactus leaves). The modern version combines meat or chicken with the fruit. This is a seasonal dish and either recipe is delicious. It is a tradition to serve chiles en nogada in the months of August and September when the ingredients are in season, coinciding with the Independence Day celebration. Both versions of this dish are finished off with pomegranate seeds and walnuts (the nuts are rumored to represent the politicos of the day) in dish that is as beautiful to look at as it is delicious to consume, a virtual Mexican flag on a plate.

STUFFED PEPPERS IN WALNUT SAUCE /
CHILES EN NOGADA

(SERVES 6)

6 poblano chiles, prepared (see "Common Mexican Cooking Tools and Techniques," p. 334)
Picadillo (ground meat filling) (A)
Nogada (Walnut Sauce) (B)
½ cup pomegranate seeds
2 tablespoons parsley leaves, coarsely chopped

Chiles en Nogada, a virtual Mexican flag on a plate.
Photo by Adriana Almazán Lahl.

PREPARE the chiles as directed (see "Basic Recipes for Mexican Cooking," p. 334). Carefully stuff the picadillo meat mixture into the peppers through the slit, taking care not to rip the peppers. Transfer the stuffed peppers to a serving platter. Cover with cold nogada and garnish with pomegranate seeds and parsley, mimicking the Mexican flag. 🦂

A. Picadillo

(FILLING FOR 6 PEPPERS)

1 pound pork shoulder or chicken breast (or omit for original, vegetarian version)
2 cups water
2 bay leaves
5 medium ripe tomatoes, finely chopped
½ cup white onion, finely chopped
2 garlic cloves, plus 2 cloves of garlic, coarsely chopped
1 tablespoon olive oil
1 tablespoon freshly minced cilantro leaves
2 cups apples, finely diced
2 cups pears, finely diced
2 cups diced apricot
1 ripe plantain, finely diced
2 tablespoons dried black currants or raisins

2 tablespoons sliced blanched almonds, toasted

2 tablespoons white vinegar

1 tablespoon white sugar

¼ teaspoon ground cinnamon

⅛ teaspoon ground cloves

Pinch of cumin

Salt to taste

½ teaspoon freshly ground black pepper

COOK the meat in medium saucepan with 2 cups of water and 1 bay leaf. Once cooked, let it rest and shred; set aside. Put all the tomatoes, ¼ cup of onion, and 2 cloves of garlic in a blender, purée until smooth. Add 1 teaspoon of oil to a saucepan and add the remaining ¼ cup onion and chopped garlic. Sauté 2–3 minutes and pass the tomato mixture purée through a sieve and into the saucepan with 1 teaspoon of olive oil; cook uncovered on medium-high heat for 10 minutes.

Add shredded meat, fruit, spices, bay leaf, and all remaining ingredients to the saucepan and let simmer for 20 minutes. Set aside to cool. Place saucepan over a sink full of ice to stop cooking process, stir mixture frequently to allow the center of the pan to cool as well. Place in the refrigerator once cooled. 🐦

B. Nogada (Walnut Sauce)

(SERVES 6)

½ cup Mexican sour cream

½ cup goat cheese

1 cup walnuts, blanched (see "Common Mexican Cooking Tools and Techniques," p. 334)

1 cup white bread, small diced

1½ cups milk

¼ cup sugar

2 tablespoons port or sherry wine

½ teaspoon salt

MIX together all the ingredients in a blender until puréed into a smooth sauce (the consistency should be a little thicker than a gravy). Keep in refrigerator until ready to serve. 🐦

MEXICAN RICE WITH PEAS AND CARROTS / ARROZ A LA MEXICANA CON CHICHAROS Y ZANAHORIAS

(SERVES 6)

1 teaspoon olive oil
¼ onion, finely chopped
1 cup white rice
4 tablespoons tomato purée (see "Basic Recipes for Mexican Cooking," p. 15)
2 cups chicken stock (see "Basic Recipes for Mexican Cooking," p. 11)
2 sprigs fresh cilantro
1 garlic clove
½ teaspoon salt
½ cup peas
¾ cup carrots, finely diced

IN a hot skillet add oil and sauté onion and rice for 2 minutes over medium-high heat; stir frequently. Add tomato purée and cook another minute. Add chicken stock and remaining ingredients except peas and carrots, bring to a boil, then reduce heat to medium-low and cover. Cook for 20 minutes. Add peas and carrots and cook for an additional 5 minutes or until rice is done and vegetables are al dente. Fluff with a fork before serving. 🐦

CHONGOS ZAMORANOS

8 cups whole milk
1 rennet tablet
Juice of 2 lemons
4 cinnamon sticks
1 cup sugar
1 tablespoon fresh orange zest

WARM milk slowly, meanwhile dissolve rennet tablet in a little bit of hot milk and add to the warm milk and mix well. Cook for ½ hour and add the lemon juice; mix well. Once milk curdles, add cinnamon sticks; add sugar without stirring. Keep cooking on low heat for 2 hours; remove from heat when most liquid has been reduced (milk should never come to a boil), watch it closely as the liquid can become a thick caramel and burn easily. Let it cool down and refrigerate. Serve cold with fresh orange zest sprinkle on top. 🐦

ZUCCHINI CORN SOUP / SOPA DE CALABACITAS CON ELOTE

(SERVES 8)

2 tablespoons vegetable oil

3 cups fresh corn kernels

4 cups zucchini, diced

1 medium Spanish white onion, finely chopped

1 cup tomato purée (see "Basic Recipes for Mexican Cooking," p. 15)

7 cups chicken stock (see "Basic Recipes for Mexican Cooking," p. 11)

12 cilantro sprigs

Salt to taste

MENU 18.3:
INDEPENDENCE DAY

Soup / *Sopa*
Zucchini Corn Soup / *Sopa de Calabacitas con Elote*
Entrée / *Plato Fuerte*
Cold Beef Salad / *Salpicón de Res*
Side / *Sopa Seca*
Mexican-Style Pasta with Chorizo / *Fideo Seco con Chorizo*
Dessert / *Postre*
Three-Color Gelatin Dessert / *Gelatina de Tres Colores*

HEAT vegetable oil in a large soup pot; once hot, add corn kernels and cook for 5 minutes over medium heat. Add diced zucchini and onion; cook for additional 5 minutes, stirring occasionally. Add tomato purée and cook together for 7 minutes. Add chicken stock, cilantro sprigs, and salt to taste. Bring to a boil and cook for 3 minutes. Serve hot removing cilantro sprigs. 🦐

Zucchini Corn Soup / *Sopa de Calabacitas con Elote*.
Photo by Adriana Almazán Lahl.

Cold Beef Salad / *Salpicón de Res*.
Photo by Adriana Almazán Lahl.

COLD BEEF SALAD / SALPICÓN DE RES

(SERVES 8–10)

2 pounds skirt steak

2 cups water

2 bay leaves

5 carrots, peeled, cooked, and cut in small cubes

4 potatoes, peeled, cooked, and cut in small cubes

2 tablespoons cilantro, chopped

1 chipotle chile (canned)

4 medium tomatoes

8 tablespoons fine olive oil

4 tablespoons white vinegar

Salt and pepper to taste

1 tablespoon sugar

1 medium onion, finely sliced

2 large avocados

IN a large saucepan, cook meat in 2 cups of water with bay leaves for 30 minutes or until tender; allow to cool and shred. Meanwhile, in a large salad bowl, add carrots, potatoes, cilantro, and half of a very finely chopped chipotle chile. Mix well and set aside. Bring some water to a boil and add tomatoes for a few seconds. Remove from water and peel the skin off, quarter them, and remove seeds; set aside. Combine olive oil, vinegar, salt, pepper, and sugar; mix well. Add the meat and mix well; refrigerate for 1 hour before serving.

Place onions in a small bowl and add some vinegar and water, let rest until ready to serve. To serve: take meat out of the fridge and mix with vegetables, tomatoes, onions, chopped cilantro and sliced avocado; serve with tostadas (toasted tortillas, see recipe on p. 80). ❧

MEXICAN-STYLE PASTA WITH CHORIZO / FIDEOS CON CHORIZO

(SERVES 4–6)

8 ounces fresh Mexican chorizo, casings removed (see recipe p. 130, or store bought)
8 ounces dried fideo noodles or angel hair, broken into smaller pieces
¾ cup tomato purée (see "Basic Recipes for Mexican Cooking," p. 15)
2 cups chicken broth (see "Basic Recipes for Mexican Cooking," p. 11)
2 bay leaves
1–2 tablespoons adobo sauce from chipotle chiles (canned)
1 whole (canned) chipotle chile (optional)
¾ teaspoon salt
¼ teaspoon ground black pepper
4–6 ounces queso fresco
¼ cup Mexican sour cream or sour cream
¼ cup milk
1 ripe avocado peeled and cut into slices
Chopped cilantro to garnish

IN a large sauté pan, cook chorizo over medium-high heat for 8 to 10 minutes, until crisped; be sure to break chorizo into small pieces as it cooks. When cooked, place chorizo in a colander to drain the remaining oil, reserving oil. In the same pan, add 3 tablespoons of the reserved oil from the chorizo. Add the fideos or angel hair pasta and cook over medium-high heat for a few minutes, stirring often, until the pasta changes color and starts to brown. Watch carefully as it can easily burn, strain extra oil.

Pour the cooked tomato purée over the pasta. Cook for about 2 minutes over medium heat, stirring often but carefully, taking care not to break up the fideos further or create a mushy consistency by over-stirring. Add the chicken broth, bay leaves, and adobo sauce from the chipotle chiles; if desired, add the whole chipotle chile, this will add additional heat. Salt to taste.

Mix well and, cook uncovered for 8 minutes, stirring gently but often to prevent pasta from sticking. The pasta should be dry at this point. Add the chorizo and stir gently to incorporate; serve hot, topped with crumbled cheese, fresh sour cream thinned with ¼ cup of milk, avocado slices, and chopped cilantro. ❧

THREE-COLOR GELATIN DESSERT / GELATINA DE TRES COLORES

(SERVES 8–10)

6 cups water, divided
1 envelope lime or green apple gelatin or lemon
1 envelope unflavored gelatin
1 envelope strawberry gelatin
1 cup milk
1 (5-ounce) can condensed milk
1 cinnamon stick

IN a medium saucepan add 2½ cups of water and make green apple gelatin according to instructions, add to 9-inch gelatin mold (mold should be about ⅓ full) and place in the refrigerator for 2–3 hours until it sets.

To make the milk gelatin, hydrate unflavored gelatin in ¼ cup milk, and warm over Baño Maria (see "Common Mexican Cooking Tools and Techniques," p. 333). In a small pot over medium heat, add milk and condensed milk; mix well and bring to a boil. Add 1 cup of water, bring back to a boil, and add hydrated gelatin; mix well. Lower heat to a simmer and cook for 5 minutes. Remove from heat and allow to cool for 20 minutes.

Pour this milk gelatin mixture over green gelatin carefully with a ladle (making sure first that the green gelatin has set well, now the mold should be about ⅔ full) and refrigerate until milk gelatin layer sets (this will probably will take 2 or 3 hours).

In a medium saucepan add 2½ cups of water and make strawberry gelatin according to instructions; allow to rest for 25 minutes and ladle gelatin on top of well-set milk gelatin layer (mold will now be full). Refrigerate again for at least 4 hours or overnight.

To unmold, place gelatin container in a large bowl of hot water for 10 seconds, taking care that none of the hot water enters the mold, and flip over onto a large serving plate. ❧

DAY OF THE DEAD / DÍA DE LOS MUERTOS (OCTOBER 30 TO NOVEMBER 2)

DAY OF THE DEAD, which is actually not a day at all, but a festival that is spread over several days from October 30 to November 2, is the oldest and one of the most famous Mexican celebrations and draws visitors from around the world.

While the holiday falls almost concurrently with Halloween, and the customs surrounding both events include sweets, skeletons, and spirits, that is where the similarity ends. Until recently, there was no dressing in costumes or asking for candy in Mexico (this is something that recently "emigrated" and only occurs in parts of the country). *Día de los Muertos* is neither scary nor somber; it is joyous. The skeletons are not morbid; they are gaily dressed and lively. The spirits are not ghostly phantoms but rather those of the deceased, who are thought to return to visit their eagerly awaiting families on these special days.

Although the seasonal smells and colors of Los Muertos are in evidence everywhere, from the largest city to the most remote rancho, this is a private, family fiesta, a time of reunion and reunification of the living with the dead. There are some regional differences in dates, but generally October 31 or November 1 is Day of the Innocents (*Día de los Santos Inocentes*), reserved for spirits of children who have passed, with a special day on October 30 in some locales for children who died before baptism (*los niños en el limbo*). November 1 or 2 is Day of the Dead (sometimes called *Día de los Difuntos*), a day to spend with the spirits of deceased adults.

European or Pre-Columbian Roots?

Mexico's Day of the Dead festival is a living example of what the Church sought to avoid when All Souls Day was established in thirteenth-century Europe: persistent adherence to pre-Christian rituals and attitudes. The Spanish may have introduced the custom of food offerings to Mexico. Spaniards, in spite of the Church's efforts to eradicate the tradition, enjoyed feasting with their dead. However, the similarities between pre- and post-Hispanic traditions in Meso-America make it difficult to trace the origins of specific aspects of the festivities honoring the dead.

Día de los Muertos is the only modern Mexican festival for which there is conclusive evidence of pre-Hispanic roots. During the month of Xocotlhuetzi, which fell in July and/or August, the Aztecs marked the Great Feast of the Dead. It was the conquering Spaniards who "relocated" the festival to coincide with All Hallows Eve. The Aztec celebration coincided with the harvest of beans, chickpeas, rice, corn, and pumpkin. These foods were part of the offering that was placed at the altar of the goddess Mictecacihuatl, ruler of the afterlife along with her husband, Mictlantecuhtli.

Researchers think that these traditions eventually became conflated with others, which included burying personal objects of the deceased, along with food and offerings. These newer rituals likely grew out of the Aztec belief that when people died, they traveled through the region of Mictlan on their way to Tlalocan (Aztec heaven), and on that long journey, the deceased needed food, water, and even candles to light their way. (For more on Aztec beliefs about death, see chapter 25.) The belief, still held in Mexico today, that the souls of the departed come back to visit every year, can be traced back to these ancient beliefs.

Day of the Dead Rituals in Modern Mexico

As Mexican families prepare for the festivities, houses are cleaned and furniture moved so as to have space to build a colorful altar. These altars (*altares*) are the fruit of a complicated family project, which may begin days, even weeks, prior and in which everyone in the family has a role. During Días de Los Muertos, almost everyone goes to the cemetery (*pantheon*), and in some areas of Mexico, people even spend the entire night visiting with the spirits of their loved ones, beside their graves. It is not uncommon to picnic at the gravesite. Family members clean up and decorate graves, which attracts vendors to the cemeteries selling flowers and decorations. Others play music to entertain the deceased and their families, hoping to earn a few pesos.

To allow time to prepare for Day of the Dead, in the final days of October, market stalls (*puestos*) line the streets, selling sweets, the most famous of which are the intricately decorated sugar skulls (*alfeñiques*) and Day of the Dead bread (*pan de muertos*).

A Guide to Elements of the Modern Altar

Far removed from their origins in rituals dedicated to Aztec deities, altars today usually have three levels, which represent the Father, the Son, and the Holy Spirit. On these, offerings (*ofrendas*) are placed to honor and nourish the dead.

On the first level are photographs of the deceased, seven candles representing the seven capital sins, and four *veladoras* (blessed candles) to guide the departed souls on their journey, their light symbolic of eternal love. Here, too, are the marigolds (*cempazuchil*), the traditional Day of the Dead flowers, their bright orange-yellow color representing the brightness of the sun, and their aroma attracting the souls of the dead to the altars prepared in their honor.

Día de Muertos Totonaco at Huehuetla, Puebla. The Totonaca language was spoken by 230,930 persons, according to data from 2005. The two states with the largest populations of Totonaca speakers are Veracruz (50.3 percent) and Puebla (42.0 percent). While most Totonacs are Roman Catholic, they practice a form of folk Catholicism, with vestiges remaining of pre-Conquest practices. Totonacs of Papantla, Veracruz, are perhaps best known for performing the "voladores" ritual (see p. 241). Photo be Jorge Ontiveros.a

Oranges and fruits are found on the second level. On this level are the papel picado banners, intricate hand-cut colored papers that represent the freedom that death brings, each color having a specific meaning: purple for Christian mourning, orange for Aztec mourning, white for purity, and pink for celebration.

On the last level, a tray with a pitcher of water called an *aguamanil* is placed along with a piece of soap, a towel, even a mirror, so the deceased can wash up before they eat. Here, treasured items of the deceased are located: perhaps an article of clothing, as well as their favorite foods (often mole, tamales, and atole), toys and sweets for the returning souls of children, and for the adults, even tequila and cigarettes. It is not expected that the departed will actually consume the offerings, but rather that they will "absorb" them. Afterward, the living usually partake of the food and drink that is left on the altars, sometimes wearing a favorite article of clothing that had been worn by the deceased. A cross made of ash is also created on the last level as way to purify the spirits of the dead. Incense (*copal*) is there to scare away evil spirits. Pan de Muertos and alfeñiques are also found on this level.

The Sweet Tradition of Skeletons and Sugar Skulls

Mexico's tradition of humorous, almost irreverent skeleton art (*calaveras*) is unique in all of Latin America, embodying an attitude toward death thought by many, erroneously, to have its roots in Aztec beliefs. The idea that the brave Aztec warrior embraced rather than feared meeting his end has no clear historical basis, nor is there any proven correlation to the merriment of Day of the Dead celebrations. Rather, the mood and corresponding traditions of Día de los Muertos are a combination of joy at the pending return of dead relatives, if only for a day, with some interesting satirical art forms that explain the proliferation of delightful skeletons and colorful skulls. Contrary to popular belief, there is no connection between these and any particular Mexican morbidity.

Calaveras are lively skeletal figurines that take the form of marionettes, giant puppets, and sweets. The most ubiquitous of these are Mexico's sugar skulls or alfeñiques. The word *alfeñique* has its root in the Arabic word *alfainid*, which refers to the preparation of a sweets made from sugar cane juice, which is stretched into very thin layers. The migration of the word, most likely first to Spain with the Moors and then to Mexico, echoes the migration of many spices and even recipes, especially those used in baking and the making of sweets. Boiled sugar is poured into ceramic molds in the shape of a coffin, a dove, or lamb, but the most traditional is the shape of a skull. Honoring the dead, the name of a loved one is written across the forehead and the skulls are decorated with colorful sugar icing. The alfeñiques are then placed on the family's altar.

The origin of skulls as a symbol associated with Day of the Dead is both interesting and controversial. While there is strong evidence of skulls displayed

Catrina.
Photo by Adriana Almazán Lahl.

for ceremonial purposes in pre-Columbian Mesoamerica, some anthropologists conclude that the appearance of skulls more likely stems from colonial imagery, harkening to the skull as a symbol of death in Christianity.

One school of thought is that the alfeñiques have their origins in the *tzompantli*, a wooden rack used in several Mesoamerican civilizations for the public presentation of human skulls. Rather than a frightening or morbid custom, these displays coincided with the Aztec belief that death was the conclusion of one phase of this life, and that life extended past death to another level. Accordingly, it was common practice to keep the skulls of the deceased and show them during those rituals that symbolized the end of a cycle (at the end of the calendar year, for example).

With the arrival of the Spaniards, the Catholic Church forbade the rituals using human skulls, but the Mexicas resisted the elimination of traditions so deeply held. Historians who trace the origins of sugar skulls to pre-Columbian times believe that the Aztecs were eventually persuaded to substitute sugar skulls for real ones. Other anthropologists argue that the icon of the skull and cross bones, as well as appearance of skeletons, was well documented in early European and Church history, and that the sugar skulls came across the seas with the Spanish.

Catrinas

During 1920s *Catrinas*, female skeletons fashionably attired with wide-brimmed hats, became popular as Mexico's Renaissance created a vogue for all things Aztec. Satirizing the Mexican upper class of the Porfirio Díaz era (Mexican president 1876–1880 and 1884–1911; see chapter 18), with their preference for European rather than indigenous culture and cuisine, Catrinas were just part of this movement led by artists like Frida Kahlo and Diego Rivera, as Mexico's artistic/intellectual community sought to reconnect with their indigenous roots. The first Catrina was created by graphic artist Jose Guadalupe Posadas between 1910 and 1913. The word *catrín* meant an elegant and well-dressed gentleman, usually accompanied by a lady with the same characteristics. Today, Catrinas are one of Mexico's most widely sought collectibles.

Origins of Day of the Dead Bread

Pan de Muertos (Day of the Dead bread) is as fascinating in its folklore as it is in its variety of shape and style. Undoubtedly a European import (after all, it's not cornbread de muertos or tortilla de muertos) the basic ingredients—butter, cane sugar, and wheat flour—were not known in Mesoamerica prior to the conquest. However, the animal forms (these breads often resemble turtles, rabbits, and crocodiles) are suggestive of Aztec traditions, in which anthropomorphic figures were formed from amaranth seed dough and eaten (for more on amaranth, see p. 195). Pan de Muertos dates back to the conquest years, when the Spaniards first arrived

Bread of the Dead /
Pan de Muertos.
Photo by Adriana
Almazán Lahl.

in Mesoamerica and were terrorized by their discovery of Aztec rituals of human sacrifice. In one ceremony, they sacrificed a virgin by taking her heart and burying it in a clay pot full of amaranth. The leader of the ceremony would then bite the heart. In an attempt to eliminate this ritual, the Spaniards created bread with a heart shape and coated with red sugar simulating the blood. Their acceptance of this substitute marked the first time the Aztecs gave bread divine attributes, and the beginning of a slow transition to Catholicism.

Many studies have sought to define the symbolic meaning of the configuration of Pan de Muertos. Some show that, in an effort to keep with indigenous roots, the four lines usually found atop the bread simulate the four cardinal points of the Aztec calendar, each of which, in turn, relates to one of their four principal deities. Another interpretation of the four lines, more in keeping with the teachings of the Catholic Church, is that they represent the bones of those who have passed away, and the center represents the heart or skull.

PUMPKIN MOLE / MOLE DE CALABAZA

(SERVES 25. YOU CAN RESERVE AND FREEZE SOME OF THE PASTE.)

8 puya chiles
4 mulato chiles
1 cup boiling water
¼ pound toasted pumpkin seeds, hulled
7 prunes, pitted
2 large tomatoes
1 bar of Mexican chocolate (Abuelita or Ibarra brand)
1 bolillo or ¼ French baguette, stale
2 tortillas, stale
3 cups cooked pumpkin or pumpkin purée
½ tablespoon cinnamon, ground
⅛ tablespoon cloves, ground
½ piloncillo
1½ cup chicken stock (see "Basic Recipes for Mexican Cooking," p. 11)
1 tablespoon salt
½ onion
3 garlic cloves

> **MENU 19.1: DAY OF THE DEAD**
>
> Entrée / *Plato Fuerte*
> Pumpkin Mole /
> *Mole de Calabaza*
> Sides / *Guarniciones*
> Mexican "Red" Rice / *Arroz a la Mexicana* (see recipe p. 145)
> Refried Beans / *Frijoles Refritos* (see recipe p. 152)
> Dessert / *Postre*
> Day of the Dead Cookies /
> *Galletas de Día de Muertos*

HYDRATE chiles in boiling water for ½ hour. In a blender, mix all ingredients except onion and garlic. Add 3 tablespoons of oil to a large saucepan with chopped

BREAD OF THE DEAD / PAN DE MUERTOS

THIS BREAD IS SHAPED INTO ROUND LOAVES WITH STRIPS OF DOUGH ROLLED OUT AND ATTACHED TO RESEMBLE BONES.
(MAKES 2 LOAVES FOR 8 PEOPLE)

½ cup butter
½ cup milk
½ cup water
5–5½ cups flour
2 packages dry yeast
1 teaspoon salt
Rind of 1 large orange
1 tablespoon whole anise seed
½ cup sugar
4 eggs

IN a saucepan over medium flame, heat the butter, milk and water until very warm but not boiling. Meanwhile, take 1½ cups flour and set the rest to the side. In a large mixing bowl, combine the 1½ cups flour, yeast, salt, orange rind, anise seed, and sugar. Beat in the warm liquid until well combined. Add the eggs and mix in 1 more cup of flour. Continue mixing in more flour until dough is soft and not sticky at all. Knead over floured surface for 10 minutes until smooth and elastic (you can use your mixer with the dough attachment).

Place dough in a lightly greased bowl, cover with plastic wrap, and let rise in a warm place until doubled in size (1½ hours). Punch the dough down and shape into round loaves, making long strips of dough to create bone-shaped figures, and place them around the loaves to decorate. Make a round golf ball–size dough ball to adorn the top of the bread (to represent the head). Let these loaves rise covered with some kitchen towels for 1 hour. Bake in a preheated 350° oven for 40 minutes. Remove from oven and sprinkle with or dunk into a bowl of sugar immediately (if they cool down, sugar will not stick to the bread). Serve with Mexican Hot Chocolate (see p. 104).

onion and garlic. Cook for 4 minutes, or until onion browns a little. Then add mixture from blender and cook over medium-low heat for 1 hour covered, but stirring constantly to avoid burning or sticking. Place in the oven for another 1½ hours at 350°. Add ½ cup of hot chicken stock every half hour during the entire cooking process, stirring as you do so. Adjust salt to taste and serve over chicken, turkey, or pork. Serve with rice and beans. 🪲

DAY OF THE DEAD COOKIES / GALLETAS DE DÍA DE MUERTOS

(MAKES 35)

¾ cup butter or butter-flavored shortening, brought to room temperature
1 cup white sugar
2 eggs
1 tablespoon milk
1 teaspoon vanilla extract
2½ cups all-purpose flour
1 teaspoon baking powder
1 teaspoon salt
Cookie Icing (A)

IN a large bowl, cream together the butter or shortening and white sugar until smooth. Beat in the eggs one at a time, then stir in the milk and 1 teaspoon vanilla. Combine the flour, baking powder, and salt; stir into the creamed mixture. Cover dough and chill for at least 1 hour.

Preheat the oven to 400°. Lightly grease cookie sheets or line with parchment paper. On a lightly floured surface, roll out the dough to ¼-inch thickness. Cut into desired shapes with cookie cutters. Place cookies 1½ inches apart on cookie sheets.

Bake for 6 to 8 minutes in the preheated oven. Remove cookies from baking sheets to cool on wire racks. Cool completely before frosting. 🪲

Day of the Dead Cookies /
Galletas de Día de Muerto.
Photo by Adriana Almazán Lahl.

A. Cookie Icing

1 cup confectioner's sugar
2 teaspoons milk
2 teaspoons light corn syrup
¼ teaspoon almond extract
Assorted food coloring

IN a small bowl, stir together confectioner's sugar and milk until smooth. Beat in corn syrup and almond extract until icing is smooth and glossy. If icing is too thick, add more corn syrup. Divide into separate bowls, and add food colorings to each to desired intensity. Dip cookies or paint them with a brush. Once frosting dries, you can decorate with additional colored frosting, or you can use edible markers to draw a design on your cookies.

MARIGOLD PATTIES IN TOMATO STEW / TORTITAS DE CEMPAZÚCHITL EN CALDILLO

(SERVES 6–8)

1 pound chicken breast, cooked and shredded (see "Basic Recipes for Mexican Cooking," p. 11)

1 egg white

10 *cempazuchitl* flowers, petals only (edible marigolds, should be organic)

½ cup Mexican sour cream

1 sprig epazote

½ tablespoon Mexican oregano

Salt to taste

White pepper to taste

2 cups of tomato stock (see "Basic Recipes for Mexican Cooking," p. 14)

2–6 tablespoons oil

MENU 19.2: DAY OF THE DEAD

Entrée / *Plato Fuerte*
Marigold Patties in Tomato Stew / *Tortitas de Cempazúchitl en Caldillo*
Sides / *Guarniciones*
White Rice Mexican-Style with Peas / *Arroz Blanco a la Mexicana con Chicharos*
(see recipe p. 151)
"Clay Pot" Beans / *Frijoles de Olla*
(see recipe p. 146)
Dessert / *Postre*
Candied Pumpkin / *Calabaza en Tacha*

MIX shredded chicken with egg whites and the petals of 4 flowers, finely chopped. Add sour cream, epazote, oregano, salt, and pepper; mix well. Form 2-inch patties. Chop the remaining flower petals and cover patties with the petals. Prepare tomato stock.

Add oil to a sauté pan and fry patties (you will need to continue adding oil, 2 tablespoons at a time, as you remove cooked patties and add new ones to the sauté pan). Cook 2 minutes on each side. Drain well on a paper towel and add to tomato stock. Serve with rice, beans, and warm tortillas.

CANDIED PUMPKIN / CALABAZA EN TACHA

PUMPKIN HAS BEEN AN ESSENTIAL PART OF THE DAY OF THE DEAD OFRENDAS SINCE AZTECS TIMES, WHEN THEY USED THE SAP OF A MAGUEY PLANT AS A SWEETENER FOR *CALABAZA* (PUMPKIN). THE ARRIVAL OF THE SPANISH BROUGHT SUGAR CANE, FIRST INTRODUCED IN VERACRUZ AS EARLY AS 1524, WHICH CHANGED THE WAY THE SWEETENED PUMPKIN WAS PREPARED. COOKS BEGAN TO CANDY THE PUMPKIN BY PLACING IT INTO CALDRONS CALLED *TACHAS* THAT WERE USED FOR MAKING SUGAR. IT SIMMERED ALONG WITH OTHER SPICES AND FRUITS, RESULTING IN THE *CALABAZA EN TACHA* WE KNOW TODAY.
(SERVES 8)

5 cups water

7 piloncillo cones

4 cinnamon sticks

2 oranges (juice and rind)

½ teaspoon anise seeds

½ teaspoon ground cloves

1 large orange pumpkin (8–10 pounds)

2 tablespoons cal (calcium carbonate)

BRING water to a boil, add piloncillo, cinnamon, orange juice, and rind. Wrap anise seeds and cloves in cheese cloth, close tightly and add to the pot. Cover pot and cook for 3 hours over low flame, stirring occasionally, until a medium light syrup forms.

Meanwhile, cut pumpkin into large chunks (3- to 4-inch pieces), place in a large pot and cover them with water and calcium carbonate and let rest for 3 hours. After 3 hours, drain and wash thoroughly.

Clear debris from spices from the syrup, combine pumpkin with syrup, and cook over low heat until pumpkin is tender, about 1½ to 2 hours. Allow to cool for 15 minutes before serving or refrigerate overnight and serve cold.

NOTES FROM THE ALMAZÁN KITCHEN

CERTAIN fruits like the pumpkin are naturally high in pectin, and in the presence of water and heat, they tend to gel. We add calcium (cal or calcium carbonate) to strengthen the structure of the pectin and prevent the heat from dissolving the fruit during the cooking process, keeping the fruit firm, even after cooking. You can find cal in any Mexican market, as it is a common ingredient to add to tortillas.

Candied Pumpkin / *Calabaza en Tacha*.
Photo by Adriana Almazán Lahl.

DAY OF THE MEXICAN REVOLUTION / DÍA DE LA REVOLUCIÓN (NOVEMBER 20)

20
CHAPTER

NOVEMBER 20 commemorates the Mexican Revolution, which began in 1910 and lasted until 1920. By some estimates, as many as two million Mexicans lost their lives in the struggle.[1]

Historical Background

In the era before *la Revolución*, there was a wide social chasm between the classes in Mexico. Although Porfírio Díaz brought progress and modernization to the country during his thirty-four-year rule, he also permitted foreign investors to exploit the nation's natural resources and labor force. These same investors ran businesses that frequently paid next to nothing to Mexican laborers. The conditions on Mexico's large estates were even worse, where workers and their families were literally prisoners of the haciendas on which they lived and labored, indebted to their *patrones* (*los hacendados* or hacienda owners) for basics such as rent and food, the cost of which often exceeded their wages.

At the same time, Porfírio Díaz, enchanted by the European lifestyle, was leading the country in a direction that threatened Mexico's rich traditions and culture, which was widely unpopular. Removing Díaz from power became a uniting force across various factions in Mexico.

Emiliano Zapata was one of many heroes of the Mexican Revolution. He organized La Bola, the Revolutionary fighting force, and led the struggle that would eventually result in a nation where the possibility of equality and hope existed for every Mexican, claiming, *"La tierra es de quien la trabaja"* (the land belongs to those who work it). His famous army became known as the Zapatistas. Other well-known revolutionary figures include Francisco "Pancho" Villa, Álvaro Obregón, Victoriano Huerta, and Francisco Madero.

Las Soldaderas

Adelitas or *soldaderas* are considered by many to be the silent heroes of the Revolution. These women fought alongside the troops and came along with La Bola to feed them and nurse their wounds, brave as any soldier and loyal to their men and their cause. Remarkable women who, along with their rifles, carried their cooking utensils, food, and sometimes even their children. No doubt it was a special kind of creativity that they put to work to develop recipes utilizing ingredients found on the road so that the soldiers were well fed and nurtured during their fight for freedom.

> These women soldiers not only carried their children with them on their backs, but also hung pots, pans and griddles around their waists, performing the same chores they did at home, but now in rebel camps, barracks or the patios of the haciendas taken over by the revolutionaries. In the breaks between the din of flying bullets and explosions were the reassuring sounds of tortillas being slapped from palm to palm or of chiles being ground for salsas.[2]

Parades and Kermesse

Nowadays, Mexico celebrates the national holiday with parades—the Army shows off their troops and artillery—followed by *kermeses* (street fairs), where traditional songs from the revolutionary era, called *corridos*, fill the air. At school, children are taught these corridos and present plays that recall the bravery of their heroes and recount Mexican folklore.

ADRIANA'S MEMORIES

FOR my family, El Día de la Revolución is a chance to remember our most famous relative, my grandfather's cousin, General Juan Andreu Almazán, who fought in *La Revolucion Mexicana* and went on to win a presidential election. According to his own account, his mother, María Almazán Nava, was a descendant of Moctezuma I.

At the age of nineteen, in December 1910, his unsuccessful attempt to raise funds, buy arms, and gather a fighting force to join the rebellion against the Porfírio Díaz government forced him into exile in San Antonio, Texas. The following year, he was able to return to Mexico, and on May 5, 1911, he was appointed brigadier general, to be known thereafter as *"El General Niño"* ("The Child General") due to his youth when receiving this title. In August 1914, he joined forces with Zapata. Complex as Mexican politics are, a few years afterward they parted ways, and Zapata ordered General Almazán's (unsuccessful) assassination. In 1939 he was granted retirement from the army, and on July 25, 1939, he announced his candidacy for president. Almazán unofficially won the 1940 presidential election and the legitimate congress of the nation recognized his triumph. However, the opposition party leader, Lázaro Cardenas, controlled the election board and through electoral fraud and manipulation was able to claim victory. My Grandpa and his cousin El General Almazán had grown up together, and always stayed in touch. He died in 1965, a successful and respected businessman.

AL PASTOR

AL *pastor* is an important example of how Mexican cuisine continued to evolve, subsequent to the arrival of the Spanish and, later on, the French. Tacos al Pastor has become a signature Mexican favorite. Throughout modern Mexico you will see street stands with meat for these "shepherd's" tacos roasting on vertical spits, topped with a pineapple, which is thinly sliced and served in the tacos. This method of cooking meat for the spit-roasted lamb, known as *shawarma*, was first introduced by Lebanese shepherds who immigrated to Puebla in the 1930s. The technique was copied by the Mexican *taqueros* (taco masters), who substituted pork for lamb. The original al pastor stand still exists in Puebla today, where vertical spits of pork continue to revolve in front of its huge wood-burning hearth.

RABBIT OR PORK AL PASTOR / CONEJO O PUERCO AL PASTOR

THE *TAQUITOS CON SALSA VERDE* AND THE *ATOLE DE PIÑA* PRESENTED HERE ARE REPORTED TO BE PART OF THE FARE AT THE VICTORY FEAST (PERHAPS EATEN ON MAY 25, 1911, THE DATE WHEN PRESIDENT PORFÍRIO DÍAZ RESIGNED AFTER HOLDING OFFICE FOR THIRTY-FIVE YEARS). ONE CAN EASILY IMAGINE THE SOLDADERAS PREPARING *CONEJO* (RABBIT) IN ONE OF THE REBEL CAMPS.

(SERVES 6–8)

½ cup white vinegar

10 pasilla chiles, stem removed

10 guajillo chiles, stem removed

2 garlic cloves

¼ tablespoon ground cumin

1 tablespoon oregano

5 cloves

Salt to taste

2 tablespoons oil

2 pounds pork steaks, thinly sliced, or 4 rabbits

Pineapple, sliced (fresh preferred)

3 Spanish white onions, thickly sliced

> ### MENU 20.1: DAY OF THE MEXICAN REVOLUTION
>
> Entrée / *Plato Fuerte*
> Rabbit or Pork al Pastor /
> *Conejo o Puerco al Pastor*
> Casserole / *Cazuela*
> Potato-Stuffed Taquitos
> in Green Sauce / *Taquitos de
> Papas en Salsa Verde*
> Side / *Guarnicón*
> Guacamole (see recipe p. 215)
> Beverage / *Bebida*
> Pineapple Atole / *Atole de Piña*

IN a medium saucepan, bring vinegar to a simmer; add chiles and cook for 5 minutes. Allow to cool for 5 minutes. Purée in a blender with garlic, cumin, oregano, cloves, and salt and until smooth. Add oil to saucepan and add purée from blender; bring to a boil and cook for 8 more minutes, stirring frequently.

Allow mixture to cool completely. Cut rabbits in half, lengthwise through backbone, place in glass container (or place meat in a glass bowl) with purée mixture, and cover with plastic wrap. Allow meat to marinate in the refrigerator for 3 hours or overnight for best results

Grill on open fire, place a foil-covered brick or a cast-iron skillet on top of rabbit and allow to cook for 10 minutes; remove brick, flip rabbit, and place brick back on top. Cook for another 10–15 minutes until well done. Remove rabbit meat from the bone and cut into small pieces. If you use pork chops to re-create the tacos al pastor recipe, just use thinly cut chops. Grill over open fire for 2 minutes each side or until well done. Cut meat into small pieces.

Place diced rabbit or meat into a pan with 1 tablespoon of oil, and 1 tablespoon of marinade and let cook for 4 minutes to let it caramelize. Serve with a piece of grilled pineapple over warm tortillas and garnish with diced onions, cilantro, a wedge of lime, and your favorite salsa (see "Salsa Recipes," pp. 17–24). ❧

Al pastor meat on a spit.
Photo by Adriana Almazán Lahl.

STİRRED BEANS / FRİJOLES MANEADOS

(SERVES 4–6)

3½ ounces chorizo (store bought or see recipe, p. 131)
2 tablespoons ancho chile powder
3½ ounces butter
9 ounces cooked beans (pinto or black)
3½ ounces Monterey jack cheese, shredded
3½ ounces queso Oaxaca, shredded, or substitute mozzarella

COOK chorizo and drain fat. Fry ancho chile powder in the butter. Smash beans or use hand mixer to blend beans, then stir in chorizo, ground chiles, and butter mix and add cheese at the very end prior to serving. Keep stirring beans until serving. Garnish with tortilla chips.

Rarámuri woman preparing atole. The Tarahumara people call themselves the Rarámuri, meaning "foot-runner" or "he who walks well," and, as the name implies, are extraordinary distance runners. They have lived in northern Mexico's Sierra Madre Occidental since escaping the Spaniards at the time of the Conquest. By the most recent government count, 106,000 Tarahumara live in Mexico, making them one of the largest indigenous groups in North America. The Rarámuri are retiring and private by nature and tend to live long distances from each other in small adobe or wood houses, even in caves. During fiestas, they drink an alcoholic beverage they brew from corn, passed in and consumed from a hollowed gourd. The Tarahumara practice a combination of Catholicism and an ancient faith that has survived since pre-Columbian times. Traditional Tarahumara dress is headbands and loincloths for men and multicolored head scarves and long, flowery skirts for the women.
Photo by Jorge Ontiveros.

POTATO-STUFFED TAQUITOS IN GREEN SAUCE / TAQUITOS DE PAPAS EN SALSA VERDE

(SERVES 6)

12 tortillas
4 ounces mashed potatoes
½ cup corn oil
Basic Green Salsa II, Cooked (see "Salsas Recipes," p. 18)
½ cup Mexican sour cream
Ranchero cheese or Parmesan cheese
½ cup Cotija cheese
½ onion, chopped

STUFF the tortillas with the mashed potatoes and roll tacos. Place a toothpick in the center of each and fry in hot oil until brown and crispy; allow to rest 10 minutes. Reheat salsa and add tacos to salsa (removing toothpicks), dipping the tacos into the salsa for a just few seconds. Remove and place tacos on serving platter. Pour some additional salsa over tacos and drizzle with cream, sprinkle with cheese, and add raw onions. You may also make taquitos with refried beans in place of mashed potatoes. 🐟

ATOLE

AS early as 1651, the process by which atole was made was noted by botanist Francisco Hernandez in a report on the use of plants in Nueva España: *Atolli* was eight parts water and six parts maize, plus lime, cooked until soft.[3] The maize was then ground and cooked again until it thickened. This description of Mexican atoles by Englishwoman Fanny Chambers Gooch, written in 1887, gives us some interesting insight into the varieties of the time:

> I found plain atole much the same in appearance as gruel of Indian meal, but much better in taste, having the slight flavor of the lime in which the corn is soaked, and the advantage of being ground on the metate, which preserves a substance lost in grinding in a mill. . . . Atole de leche (milk), by adding chocolate takes the name of champurrado [see recipe chapter 7]; if the bark of cacao is added, it becomes atole de cascara; if red chile—chile atole. If, instead, any of these agua miel, sweet water of the maguey is added, it is called atole de agua miel; if piloncillo, the native brown sugar, again the name is modified to atole de pinole.[4]

PINEAPPLE ATOLE / ATOLE DE PIÑA

(SERVES 6–8)

5 ounces masa harina (tortilla flour)
5 cups water
16 ounces chopped fresh pineapple
6 ounces piloncillo or sugar (for working with piloncillo, see "Common Mexican Cooking
    Tools and Techniques," p. 336)
Dash of cinnamon

WHISK together masa harina and 2 cups of water in a 4-quart heavy saucepan. Purée pineapple with grated piloncillo or sugar, cinnamon, and 3 cups of water; blend until smooth and pass through a sieve into flour-water mixture. Stir with a wooden spoon and heat over a medium-low flame until atole simmers; maintain simmer, stirring constantly for 20 to 25 minutes. (You can substitute strawberries or 6 tablespoons of unsweetened cocoa for the pineapple).

PART II

RITES OF PASSAGE, FAMILY CELEBRATIONS, AND EVENTS

FAMILY LIFE events and associated rituals are paramount to cultural, social, and religious life in Mexico. It is no coincidence that the local church is usually in the center of town—the masses celebrated for baptisms, confirmations, weddings, and quinceañeras are also very much the center of family life. These events not only bring folklore and Catholicism, friends and family together, they create opportunities for lifelong extended kinships.

Emergence of Modern Folk Religious Practices

They were many similarities between the belief system of the indigenous peoples of Mexico in the precolonial era and those of Christianity: both believed in an afterlife (the difference between Aztec beliefs and those of Christianity was that the Mexicas had no concept of hell), the cross was a sacred symbol for both, although for the Aztecs it symbolized the cardinal points of direction. Religious affairs and rites were seen to by a priest in both religious systems. Like Jesus, Huitzilopochtli, all-important deity of war, sun, human sacrifice, and patron god of the Mexicas, was born of a virgin goddess, Coatlicue (his father was a ball of feathers: according Aztec mythology, Coatlicue was sweeping the temple when a ball of feathers fell on the floor and impregnated her). The Aztecs practiced rites similar to baptism, confession, communion, and, of course, marriage. They associated periods of abstinence with religious purification, not dissimilar to those of Lent.

The Spanish priests who arrived with Cortés learned about these parallels and used them to advantage in their effort to convert the Aztecs and support the Spanish Crown in its efforts to conquer in the name of the Cross. Deep-rooted traditions and some firmly held beliefs were never completely obliterated, and what eventually developed in Mexico was a form of folk Catholicism, which is reflected to varying degrees in rites of passage celebrations. (The celebration of the Mexican Day of the Dead is the best example of this blending of traditions; see chapter 19.)

The Compadrazgo, or Spiritual Kinship System

In Mexico today, there is a unique system for managing the responsibilities and costs involved in creating fiestas for important life events, which is known as the *compadrazgo* system. Lifelong ritual kinships are formed when a married couple is invited to and accepts the role of godparents for a

Women preparing chickens.
Photo by Jorge Ontiveros.

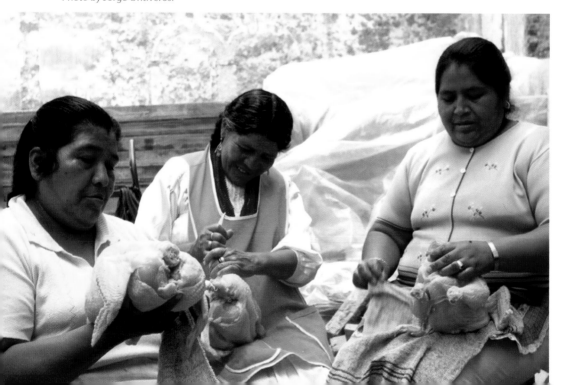

child to whom they are, usually, but not always, unrelated by blood. These events include baptisms, confirmations, quinceañeras, and weddings. The system is also in place for more minor events, such as graduations, even from kindergarten or primary school, although the associated fiestas are more low key. This not only fosters community building in a way that is unknown in the United States, it allows families of modest means to include everyone on their guests list, which often means three hundred to five hundred people.

While systems of spiritual sponsorship (initiated when an individual, usually as an infant, is accepted as a member of the religious community) also existed among European Catholics by the time of the Mexican occupation, the Aztecs and Mayas practiced a form of kinship relationships as well, with which elaborate ceremonies were associated.

Aside from Aztec customs, there is evidence of compadrazgo in Mexico as early as 1790. While the system, especially as it functioned between pueblos in the colonial era, may have begun as one of economic exchange, it has evolved into a system of long-lasting reciprocity on which people draw for support for a variety of things, not just the costs of special events, but also the preparations of food (usually the responsibility of the women), cleaning, and even painting of the houses and streets where the event host resides (this is typically done by the men). And after the event, the compadres count on each other for lifelong support through crisis and celebration.

Once invited to sponsor a lifestage ritual, etiquette dictates that the potential godparents must accept the honor being offered. Sometimes the commitment is minor (but potentially costly). One might, for example, be invited to be the *comadre* or *compadre* responsible for providing liquor for a wedding or paying for the rental *salon* (venue) for a quinceañera or even be responsible to provide a pretty dress and new shoes and a modest meal for a child graduating primary school. In other instances, it is more serious, as in being the godparents that present an infant or child at a baptismal mass, which brings the promise to watch over and guide that child as he or she grows.

Food Preparation and Reciprocity

As obligations are reciprocal and participation is, for all practical purposes, mandatory. Mexicans can count on being able to celebrate the important events in their children's lives in spite of having limited resources.

When it is time to prepare the food for these events, the women gather and the *mayordoma* (the hostess in charge) oversees the various tasks carried out by the group, as it is her reputation on the line. A successful meal brings honor, an unsuccessful one, shame. During the meal preparation, the hostess is expected to provide food for the busy prep chefs, as well as for any children that may be tagging along. Especially in Mexico's pueblos, arrangements can be fairly formal, as we see in this exchange:

> Petra . . . explains that she and her family are going to sponsor a posada, a three-day celebration involving several large meals and drinking when the statue of the Christ child is brought from the church to their home just before Christmas. She requests that [Gloria and her husband, Pedro] return the turkey she lent them two years ago when their youngest son was married. Pedro and Gloria pull out a small blue notebook and the entry recording the loan of Petra's turkey. They nod and agree to deliver a turkey of equal or greater weight one week before the Christmas posada.[1]

In all cases, the new members of the kinship community are henceforth greeted with their title, *"Hola, Comadre"* or *"Bienvenido, Compadre"* ("Hello, Godmother" or "Welcome, Godfather"), on all occasions, even when passing by each other in the street. More importantly, the kinships formed create a support network that will last a lifetime and is especially helpful in that it allows women to share responsibilities for labor-intensive food preparation and other chores. Consider the following description of Zapotec women preparing for a wedding:

> Soledad sits surrounded by the four oldest women at the wedding fiesta. Before them are the roasted carcasses of four pigs. The older women and Soledad work quickly to divide up the meat, putting large chunks into bowls to be served to the guests. They make sure the

largest portions are given to the most important people. This is the second meal of the day. A more elaborate meal will be served tomorrow to the two hundred men and women assembled in the courtyard. Outside, groups of younger women, some married with small children, are making tortillas."[2]

Lifestage Fiestas in Modern Mexico

While this was not always the case, in Mexico today a party with an eighty-person guest list is considered small, and typically upward of three hundred or even five hundred guests will be on hand for a major life event such as a baptism or wedding. Many such fiestas last from noon until the wee hours of the morning, even into the next day and all weekend. A *bautizo, confirmación, quinceañera*, or *boda* (wedding) is usually preceded by a Mass and ends with a *tornaboda* (chilaquiles or pozole served at the wee hours of the night), or a shared meal at which what was served the day or night before is reheated (*recalientado*). For the event, an entire pig, or several, might be slaughtered for carnitas, or goat for barbacoa. Mole is almost certain to be on the menu as well. No fiesta is complete without bottles of tequila on the tables. Creating an abundant and lively fiesta is a matter of pride for the host family.

Fireworks, Handcrafts, and Personal Invitations

Besides the elaborate and abundant preparation of food, fiestas in Mexico almost always include music, dancing, festive décor, and fireworks. Mexicans love their fireworks. For many, *"Si no lo llevan a la fiesta [cohetes], no es fiesta"* (If there are no fireworks at the fiesta, it's not a fiesta).[3] The production of fireworks or cohetes is a craft that is passed down through generations. With so many festivals, the successful *cohetero* will be busy year-round and never lack for work.

These celebrations also create a demand for fine hand-sewn and hand-embroidered items, known as *manualidades:* small, hand-sewn gifts or souvenirs for the guests known as *bolo*, baptism gowns, quinceañera dresses, tortilla napkins, and fancy aprons, a must for the hostess and various participating cooks. This creates an important year-round source of income for those in the pueblo who can produce these handcrafts. In an effort to support handcrafts and continue passing on precious traditions, the government pays *maestras* who teach embroidery to young girls and to women, sometimes even to young men.

Another aspect of rite-of-passage celebrations that is unique is the way the invitation to the event is delivered: in person and face-to-face. It is not unusual for a couple to travel to another city or even state if there are relatives living there who are to be invited to a wedding, for example. Written invitations may be used, but they are often delivered by hand. This custom is also true for invitations to less formal events, such as birthdays or graduation from primary school. In fact, a written invitation is taken as a sign that the guest is expected to bring a gift, and is often avoided so as not to cause embarrassment due to the financial circumstances of the invitee.

QUINCEAÑERAS

21
CHAPTER

IN LATIN AMERICAN cultures, quinceañeras mark the transformation from girlhood to womanhood. Although not considered a sacrament by the Catholic Church, local priests may require that the quinceañera (the girl who is turning fifteen) has been baptized and reached her First Communion, as well as being confirmed or that she is preparing for confirmation, perhaps even requiring participation in preparatory classes. This rite of passage is usually celebrated with a Mass, a big party, and all the pomp and circumstance, and even the price tag, of a wedding reception.

It is generally held that the quinceañera may have its origin in Aztec rites of passage celebrating fertility and coming of an age when the young woman was capable of giving birth, but there is no clear congruency from ancient times to modern. While modern quinceañera customs, which are similar to those of a debutant ball with the requisite waltzes, classical music, maids of honor, and *chambelanes*, or escorts (similar to the pages of European courts), are reminiscent of European traditions, there is no record of quinceañera fiestas before the 1940s. In Guadalajara, Mexico's second-largest city, "the first reports of the feast started to appear in the *Sociales* (social events) section of Guadalajara newspapers during the early 1940s."[1] And while middle-aged women interviewed there in 2010 recalled balls from their childhood, elderly women did not. Although the day has traditionally always begun with a Mass, the Catholic Church did not issue a formal ritual for the rites associated with the event until as recently as 2007.

Customs in Modern Mexico

The ceremony begins with a procession to the church in which parents accompany their daughter. During the ceremony, the girl prays to God in order to renew her baptismal commitment, to strengthen her faith, to ask for strength as she enters a new phase in life, to give thanks for arriving at the age of fifteen, and to honor her parents.

Nowadays, many Mexican families of varying income levels choose to have a quinceañera, with those from poorer families often participating in the compadrazgo system (see p. 288) to help manage costs, while some simply cannot afford the event and skip it altogether. Following are some of the traditional elements of a quinceañera celebration.

The Dress

In the past it was traditional to wear a pink dress. Nowadays girls prefer more sophisticated dresses, but usually they still wear a big puffy dress.

The Thanksgiving Mass

During the Mass, the quinceañera thanks God for all her blessings and asks for guidance in the new phase of her life and for the future. Most families belong to a church and have a family priest who has seen the child grow up, so he sends a nice personal message. Commonly the priest and a few nuns are invited to the reception.

The Reception

The family rents and decorates a party salon or a patio where, depending on the venue and resources of the family hosting the party, a traditional buffet-style or a plated dinner usually is served. A very important part of the celebration is the Mariachi band at the end of the evening.

The Changing and Gifting of Shoes

Prior to the first dance, the father of the quinceañera places a chair in the center of the dance floor. There he exchanges the sandals his daughter has been wearing for high heels.

The Waltz

Before turning fifteen a girl is not allowed to dance as a couple with a young man. At her celebration, the first dance is granted to the father of the quinceañera. Tradition

Quinceañeras in Chalco, State of Mexico.
Photo by Jorge Ontiveros.

is that this is followed by a routine dance (usually choreographed) performed by the young lady with her entourage (usually seven maids and their escorts). She will also have chosen a close male friend to perform a last waltz, and then they open the dance floor to all guests. It is also a tradition that the first fifteen men who dance with the quinceañera receive a red rose, in what is called "The Dance of the Roses" (*El Baile de las Rosas*).

The Gifts

Particularly in Mexico, there are some traditional gifts: a tiara given by the godparents (*padrinos*), symbolizing the closeness to God; earrings as a reminder to listen to God; a ring with wishes for a long and good life (usually given by the mother); and a cross and a Bible given by the priest. At the end of the evening, the father gives his little girl a last doll, as a symbol of love and as a sign that she will always be his little girl.

CHOSE a trip instead of having a traditional quinceañera; I had stage fright and I could not bear the idea of dancing in public, so the idea of traveling sounded more appealing than a party with three hundred people watching me dance. Fortunately I had many friends and family members who did choose to have quinceañera parties, so I enjoyed many *"quinces,"* as they are called, although I was never one of the maids.

I attended quinceañeras in the patio of some convents where they served delicious tamales and atole, in large patios with buffet style Mexican cazuelas, as well as a few in fancy salons at well-known hotels with decorated tables and exquisite food; some of these were more elegant venues than some weddings I have been to. At these, the dresses were handmade with intricate embroidery and the chambelanes wore tuxedos. Others were not as opulent but they were always a dress-up affair, with de riguer cocktail dresses for the ladies and suits and ties for the gentlemen.

MUSHROOM WALNUT SOUP / SOPA DE NUEZ CON CHAMPIÑONES

(SERVES 8–10)

3 tablespoons olive oil
1 teaspoon dried tarragon
1 large Spanish white onion, finely chopped
1 pound white mushrooms, cleaned and sliced
1 cup toasted walnuts
1 tablespoon flour
1 tablespoon butter
8 cups chicken stock (see "Basic Recipes for Mexican Cooking," p. 11)
½ cup milk
½ cup Mexican sour cream

MENU 21.1: QUINCEAÑERAS

Soup / *Sopa*
Mushroom Walnut Soup /
Sopa de Nuez con Champiñones
Entrée / *Plato Fuerte*
Pork Pipian Almazán Reyes /
Puerco en Pipián
Casa Almazán Reyes
Side / Guarnicíon
Fiesta Rice Casserole /
Cazuela de Arroz Fiesta
Dessert / *Postre*
Layered Fruit Gelatin Dessert
(see p. 193) / *Gelatina de Frutas*
Dulce de Leche Crepes
(see p. 225) / *Crepas de Cajeta*

IN a large pot, heat olive oil and add onions; sauté for 5 minutes. Add mushrooms and cook until they start to brown (10–15 minutes). Add walnuts, flour, and butter and cook for 3 minutes more. Add chicken stock and dried tarragon and bring to a boil; reduce heat and cook for 20 minutes over low flame. Remove from fire and add milk and cream. Purée mixture with an immersion blender or place ingredients in traditional blender and purée to a smooth sauce, bring back to the pot, heat thoroughly, and serve hot. 🐟

FIESTA RICE CASSEROLE / CAZUELA DE ARROZ FIESTA

(SERVES 8)

2 tablespoons butter plus butter to
    grease baking dish
1 cup Spanish white onion,
    finely sliced
1½ cups roma tomatoes, chopped
1 red bell pepper, finely diced
1 cup fresh corn kernels
½ cup Mexican sour cream or
    heavy cream
½ cup queso fresco or ricotta cheese
4 cups cooked white rice
1½ cups Monterey Jack or Mexican Manchego, shredded
Salt to taste
Black pepper

Walnut Soup / *Sopa de Nuez*.
Photo by Adriana Almazán Lahl.

PLACE the butter in a large skillet over medium heat. Sauté onions for 8 minutes, until soft. Increase the heat to medium-high, add tomatoes and bell pepper, and cook for 2 more minutes. Add the cream and queso fresco and continue cooking, stirring from time to time, until the mixture becomes thicker.

Preheat the oven to 375°. Butter a 9-inch baking dish. Layer half the rice and press it down gently. Pour half the tomatoes, corn, and bell peppers on top, then distribute the remaining rice evenly and add another layer of tomatoes, corn, and peppers. Cover with Monterey Jack or Manchego cheese. Bake for 20 minutes or until the cheese has melted and starts to brown. Let it rest for 10 minutes before serving. 🐟

PORK PIPIAN ALMAZÁN REYES / PUERCO EN PIPIÁN CASA ALMAZÁN REYES

(SERVES 8–12)

3 cups water
4 pounds pork shoulder, chopped in medium-size pieces
½ onion
1 garlic clove
Salt and pepper
2 bay leaves
Pipian (A)

BRING 3 cups of water to a boil. Add pork, onion, garlic clove, 1 tablespoon salt, pepper, and bay leaves. Cook for 1 hour on low heat. Set aside meat and reserve stock for a soup. Add meat to your sauce (*pipian*) just before serving. 🐟

A. Pipian

5 tomatillos, husks removed, clean tomatillos and boil until they turn color
7 ounces ground peeled pumpkin seeds
1–2 serrano chiles
4 lettuce leaves
⅛ cup epazote leaves or 1 teaspoon dry epazote
6 sprigs fresh cilantro
3 sprigs fresh parsley
4 leaves fresh root beer plant (*hoja santa*, Mexican pepperleaf)
½ cup onion, sliced
6 radish leaves
2 chard leaves
4 garlic cloves
2 cups chicken stock (see "Basic Recipes for Mexican Cooking," p. 11)
5 whole black peppers
2 cloves
Pinch of cumin
Salt to taste
2 tablespoons corn oil

(NOTE: These instructions allow you to prepare a pipian paste that can be stored for future use in the refrigerator for up to 3 months or 6 months frozen or used immediately.)

Blend together all ingredients except oil. Put 2 tablespoons oil in a large pan and once oil is really hot add blended mixture (be careful of splatter). If you want a paste that can be stored, stir constantly until it becomes such a thick paste that when stirred it tends to form a ball in middle. This requires constant stirring for 30–45 minutes in order to avoid burning or sticking. *Or for immediate use only*: add reserved pork stock as you stir to create a consistency of ketchup

To rehydrate stored pipian paste, add pork stock to paste (or you can use chicken stock), until you get the desired consistency; it should be a thick but runny sauce. Cook over low heat for 10 to 15 minutes or until well-heated throughout, stirring constantly to avoid sticking to the bottom of the pan. Add reserved meat and let simmer for 20 more minutes.

NOTES FROM THE ALMAZÁN KITCHEN

At home when we make mole or pipian, we usually make large quantities for future use. This is why we make a thick paste, for easy storage, packing the flavors. Because in our culture, guests often don't call in advance, it's best to have something special at hand that can easily become a festive meal. By adding pipian or mole to a roasted chicken or any meat, or simply using it to make enchiladas, the unexpected guests feel that they have been really well attended.

WEDDINGS /
BODAS

Courtship and Serenatas

MEXICANS ARE nothing if not romantic, and even today, the tradition of serenades is part of courtship customs. The evening begins as the boy typically gathers with a group of friends. They get together early and wait for the sun to go down. Then, in the town's plaza or park, he hires a mariachi band or a trio of singers with guitars and goes to his would-be girlfriend's house. There, on the street, in the middle of the night, in front of her window, they all start to sing the most romantic and heartfelt mariachi or trio traditional songs.

The purpose of the *serenata* is to wake up the young lady of interest, with songs that will touch her heart. The girl wakes up, but she is not supposed to respond immediately. She lets the musicians play two or three songs before looking out of her window, while her prospect nervously awaits for a positive response. If she likes the candidate in turn, the girl appears on her balcony, or window, which signifies that she approves, and is content with her boyfriend's serenade. Very few women can resist. More romantic songs will follow, and the boy, satisfied with his success, will even dare to sing while the musicians play. With the parents' permission, the boyfriend might even come into the house to chat for a little bit.

Not all the serenatas result in a happy ending, as some of the young ladies might not be impressed by the prospect, in which case they won't show their face or won't even turn on the light, so the poor prospect has to swallow his pride and walk home defeated.

In the meantime, the neighbors, who don't play any part in this party, try to go back to sleep, probably recalling that sometime a while ago, suitors tried to impress them or they tried to impress others in the same way.

A Glimpse at the Evolution of the Wedding Fiesta

Over the course of several interviews, anthropologist Lynn Stevens presents a view of the way a typical Mexican wedding feast has evolved since the early 1900s. One subject, Julia, in her seventies, recounts that her own wedding, in 1936 "was a very small *fiesta* . . . [that] only lasted one day . . . and about sixteen people came. Back then, only rich people got married [with music]."[1] Another woman, Maria, married in 1953 had a guest list of about fifty.

Triquis bride getting ready. The Triquis are an indigenous people who live in a mountainous region called "La Mixteca Baja" in the southwestern part of the state of Oaxaca, Mexico. They number around 23,000. One of the most notable and widely misunderstood customs of Triqui people is that of female dowries. During precolonial and colonial times, this practice was common among Native Americans in Mesoamerica and other groups, like the Mixtecs of Oaxaca, continue practicing a dowry-based marriage. It is typical in Triqui culture for a man to offer a bride's family money, food, and other products in exchange for the bride's hand in marriage. Generally, the husband and wife know each other before this arrangement, and there is no arrangement without consent. Photo by Jorge Ontiveros.

We killed one pig and about twenty turkeys. I think the party went on for one or two days. There was no music and no dancing. The presents I got included a trunk, two *metates*, and about five or six blouses. . . . In 1968 my oldest daughter got married. It was a big party. There were about 80 couples invited and there was a band and dancing. She got two trunks, a dresser, about eighteen different *metates* and some dishes. . . . My son was married in 1978. By then everyone had big weddings, not just the rich. . . . There was music for two days and they killed three pigs.[2]

Mexican Wedding Vows and Traditions

In 1859, Melchor Ocampo, a Mexican lawyer, scientist, and liberal politician, wrote a 537-word ode to marriage, which recommended that a husband should treat his wife with "generous benevolence that the strong should give to the weak" and that a wife should "avoid awakening the most brusque, irritable and hard part of (her husband's) character."[3] These "new" vows were to replace traditional religious bans as Mexican liberals sought to strip away the Catholic Church's control. Ocampo would be executed by firing squad for his views on the separation of church and state, but the amended vows became part of the new civil marriage law. They were reflective of a machismo that would permeate Mexican social norms until more recently.

Wedding customs today do not vary much from those of Nueva España (as Mexico was called during the time it was part of the Spanish Empire), as demonstrated in this period account:

> I witnessed a church wedding at "Santa Brigida," and the Mexican ceremony is a pretty one. The groom passed many coins through the hand of the bride, indicating that she is to handle and control the household funds. They knelt at the altar with lighted candles in their hands, emblematical of the Christian faith, and a silken scarf was placed around their shoulders, after which a silver cord was put around their necks, and the ceremony was complete.[4]

Thirteen Gold Coins

In Mexico today, similar traditions prevail. As a symbol of his confidence placed and signifying that he entrusts her with the responsibility of all material things, the groom gives the bride thirteen gold coins. These coins, called *arras*, also carry the promise that the groom will always support his bride. The groom places the coins into the bride's waiting cupped hands. Her acceptance symbolizes her love and dedication in looking after him and his possessions. Some believe the number thirteen represents Jesus and his twelve apostles, while others see the thirteen coins as representing the twelve months of year plus one to share with the poor.

Mexican Wedding Lazo

The wedding *lazo*, a ribbon, decorated cord, or large rosary, is first draped around the neck or shoulders of the groom and then of the bride, a symbolic affirmation of their union and their commitment. The couple wears the lazo throughout the service, after which it is removed and given to the bride as a keepsake. Many ceremonies incorporate the lazo in a symbolic binding ceremony wherein a figure eight is formed with two loops and one center, and draped loosely around the necks of the two partners. Padrinos or godparents selected for this honor slip the lazo over the heads of the bridal couple, who kneel at the altar to receive this blessing. This custom no doubt grew from the colonial-era tradition: "The ritual for finalizing the marriage involved the matchmaker tying the groom's cape to the bride's skirt, then the groom's mother would give the bride and groom each four mouthfuls of tamales. Four days of feasting followed the ceremony."[5]

Other Wedding Customs

The Money Dance is a popular tradition where male guests "pay" to dance with the bride. This is a practical way to collect funds to be used by the newlyweds as they set up their household. Other good-luck customs include tossing red beads at the couple as the leave the church and all the wedding guests forming a heart shape around the newly married couple as they have their first dance. Some couples choose to be entwined in orange blossoms, as this symbolizes fertility and happiness. A very important part of the celebration is the Mariachi band at the end of the event.

Madrinas and Padrinos

The compadrazgo system (see p. 288) allows for an extended family to be formed around the wedding ceremony, which provides ample opportunities for special assignments. There is a *madrina de copas* or *padrino de copas*, who carries a wine glass for the toast, and padrinos for the prayer book, the rosary, the guestbook, and an embroidered kneeling pillow. The bride can also choose a *madrina de velación* to guide her throughout her married life. The last person in the procession is *madrina de recuerdos (bolo)* who is in charge of carrying the wedding favors that are given out to guests. In some families, there are also godparents who promise to look after the couple financially and spiritually.

Traditional Mexican Wedding Banquets

While the entrées and sides may vary somewhat from wedding to wedding, some dishes are always served. The meal will usually begin with a consommé; sweet plantains are usually served as one of the side dishes over rice; and Mexican wedding cookies, candied almonds, and *café de olla con piquete* (spiked coffee prepared in a traditional clay pot) are traditional, as well as, of course, a wedding cake.

FIRST COURSE

CHICKEN CONSOMMÉ

(SERVES 10–12)

2 tablespoons oil
1 pound chicken breast with bones and skin
3 large carrots, 1 finely chopped
2 leeks, chopped
1 medium onion, cut in half
2 garlic cloves
2 bay leaves
12 cups water
1 celery stalk
4 egg whites
½ cup peas
1 shallot
1 parsley sprig
¼ cup sherry wine
Lemon wedges

IN a large casserole, add the oil and sauté chicken breast. Add 2 carrots, leeks, onion, garlic, bay leaves and celery, plus 10 cups of water; simmer on medium heat for 1 hour. Clear foam as it forms on top of stock.

Strain stock and pour back into pot, degrease with a spoon, and keep boiling. Meanwhile, whisk egg whites until you get soft peaks. Mix egg whites with chicken stock and stir constantly; simmer for 10 minutes.

Filter consommé though a fine sieve or through a clean cloth you have wet with cold water. Your stock should be clear as water. Add chopped carrots and peas and cook for 5 minutes. Serve in a soup bowl with chopped shallots, fresh parsley sprinkled on top, a splash of sherry wine and a wedge of lemon on the side.

CASA ALMAZÁN'S MOLE / MOLE CASA ALMAZÁN

(SERVES 25)

¾ cup vegetable oil plus 6 tablespoons

2 day-old tortillas, fried

1½ stale bolillos or baguette, fried

1 onion, sliced and fried

6 garlic cloves, fried

1 sweet plantain, sliced

1 pineapple slice

1½ pounds tomatillos, remove husk and
    clean tomatillos

1¼ quarts chicken stock (see "Basic Recipe for Mexican Cooking," p. 11)

5½ ounces ancho chile, ground

5½ ounces mulato chile, ground

3½ ounces pasilla chile, ground

3 ounces guajillo chile, ground

3½ ounces toasted peanuts, ground

3½ ounces sesame seeds, toasted and ground

3½ ounces peeled almonds, toasted and ground

Salt to taste

½ tablespoon ground black pepper

½ tablespoon ground cinnamon

½ tablespoon ground cloves

3 discs (90 grams each) Mexican chocolate bar (Abuelita or Ibarra brand)

1 piloncillo

8 whole chickens, poached, or 3 small turkeys (*guajolotes*), cut into pieces and poached (for
    instructions on cooking chicken or turkey, see "Basic Recipes for Mexican Cooking" on
    p. 11, complete all steps except *do not shred*)

½ cup white sesame seeds

MENU 22.1: WEDDING

Entrée / *Plato Fuerte*

Casa Almazán's Mole /
Mole Casa Almazán

Sides / *Guarniciónes*

Bean Tamales / *Tamales de Frijol*

Mexican "Red" Rice / *Arroz a la
Mexicana* (see recipe, p. 145)

Fried Sweet Plantains /
Plátanos Fritos (see recipe, p. 164)

TO prepare the paste, add oil to a large saucepan and sauté tortillas, bread, onion, garlic, plantains, and pineapple, one by one. In a separate pot, cook the peeled tomatillos in boiling water for 5 minutes.

Once all ingredients are fried, combine in blender with tomatillos and 4–5 cups chicken stock and blend until smooth. Place in a large pot and heat 6 tablespoons of vegetable oil; add all the blended ingredients (be careful of splatter). Then add the ground ingredients one by one, starting with the chiles, then the peanuts, sesame seeds, and almonds. Add chicken stock as needed so as to be able to stir it without difficulty; mole should have a thick but moist consistency at this

MOLE

THE word *mole* comes from the Nahuatl *molli*, which means concoction. This thick sauce is typically made from various chiles with any number of other ingredients, depending upon type (red, green, yellow, black, de Oaxaca, Poblano, etc.) and the particular family recipe. These can include almonds or other nuts, bread, tortillas ground up into something resembling breadcrumbs, raisins, plantains, chocolate, cloves, cinnamon, pepper (sweet and/or black), cumin, and other ingredients. There are over three hundred moles prepared in the various towns of Puebla alone, each with its special variation. It is considered the quintessential fiesta dish and typically served at weddings, quinceañeras, baptisms, and other important rites in central and southern Mexico. Recipes are closely held family secrets and passed down through the generations. It is not unusual for the *abuelitas* (grandmothers) to hide their mole recipes from the younger women, especially their daughters-in-law.

Various moles in a market in Mexico City.
Photo by Adriana Almazán Lahl.

Mole Almazán and *Tamal de Frijol*.
Photo by Adriana Almazán Lahl.

point. Add 1 teaspoon salt, pepper, cinnamon, and cloves and stir constantly with a wooden spoon to avoid burning and sticking at the bottom of the pan. After 20 minutes, add the chocolate and the piloncillo, both quartered, and stir until the mole becomes a thick paste and forms a ball. Mole should fall from the wooden spoon by itself; this should take about 1 hour.

Once the paste is ready, add chicken stock as required to achieve the desired consistency. Taste and season again if required. Once the sauce is runny and to your taste, add the poached turkey slices (if using turkey breast, it should be sliced) or poached chicken pieces.

Toast sesame in a comal or dry pan, taking care that they do not burn, which can happen very quickly. They will begin to jump when done. Top poultry in mole with toasted sesame seeds and serve with Mexican "Red" Rice (see menu), Fried Sweet Plantains, and Bean Tamalitos Wrapped in Hoja Santa.

Note: if you can't find ground almonds, peanuts, and pumpkin seeds (be sure they are hulled), you should fry the nuts and seeds in a little corn oil and blend these ingredients at the same time you blend the tomatillos.

BEAN TAMALES / TAMALES DE FRIJOL

(SERVES 25)

2 pounds prepared masa (see "Basic Recipes for Mexican Cooking," p. 13)
25 leaves of fresh root beer plant (*hoja santa*)
2 cups refried beans, room temperature (see recipe p. 152)
50 cornhusks, washed and patted dry

WORKING over a large sheet of plastic (20-inch square), spread masa with a rolling pin. Distribute masa evenly to create a ¼-inch-thick paste. Place hoja santa on top of masa, covering it completely. Flip and remove plastic, so the hoja santa is on the bottom. Gently, using your hands, spread the room-temperature refried beans, covering the surface completely. Cut with a sharp knife into 2-inch squares and fold them with the cornhusks. Cook over Baño Maria (see Common Mexican Cooking Tools and Techniques," p. 333) for 2 hours. Serve warm with mole dishes. 🐛

BRIDE'S MOLE / MOLE DE NOVIA

(SERVES 12)

4 fresh güero chiles (yellow chiles), seeded
½ sweet plantain
3 ounces butter
1 tortilla
1 slice of white bread
½ white Spanish onion
3 garlic cloves
3½ ounces sesame seeds
3½ ounces peeled peanuts
3½ ounces white pine nuts
3½ ounces yellow raisins
3½ ounces shredded coconut
1 cup coconut milk
1 cinnamon stick
3 cloves
½ tablespoon nutmeg
5 allspice berries
3½ ounces almonds
3½ ounces walnuts (blanched, see "Basic Recipes for Mexican Cooking," p. 334)
2 tablespoons oil
8 ounces white chocolate

> **MENU 22.2: WEDDING**
>
> Entrée / *Plato Fuerte*
> Bride's Mole / *Mole de Novia*
> Sides / *Guarniciónes*
> "Green" Rice / *Arroz Verde*
> (see recipe p. 163)
> Fried Sweet Plantains /
> *Plátanos Fritos* (see recipe, p. 164)

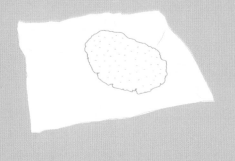

a.

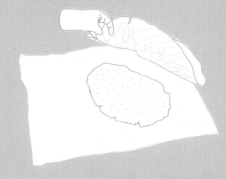

b.

c.

d.

e.

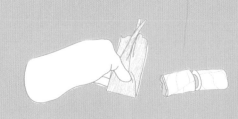

f.

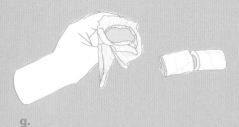

g.

Making a bean tamal. **A.** Working over a large sheet of plastic (20-inch square), spread masa with a rolling pin. Distribute masa evenly to create a ¼-inch-thick paste. **B.** Place hoja santa on top of masa, covering it completely. **C.** Flip and remove plastic, so the hoja santa is on the bottom. **D.** Gently, using your hands, spread the room-temperature refried beans, covering the surface completely. Then cut with a sharp knife into 2-inch squares, forming two rolls. **E.** Fold hoja santa in with the cornhusk. **F.** Roll tamal all the way to the right edge. **G.** Fold the husk over (think of an envelope) and lay tamal on the counter, fold facing down.
Figure by Verticalarray, Inc.

White pepper to taste

Sugar to taste

Salt to taste

2 cups chicken stock (see "Basic Recipes for Mexican Cooking," p. 11)

8 ounces Mexican cream

2 cups white wine

12-pound turkey or 6 whole chickens, poached (for instructions on cooking chicken or turkey, see "Basic Recipes for Mexican Cooking" on page 11, complete all steps except *do not shred*)

FRY seeded chiles and plantains with a little butter; set aside. Do the same with tortilla and bread; do not let it take any color. Fry onion and garlic. Lightly toast sesame seeds, peanuts, and pine nuts on the comal (see "Common Mexican Cooking Tools and Techniques," p. 335); do not allow them to brown. Boil raisins and coconut with a little coconut milk and set aside. Boil spices with a little coconut milk and strain; set aside. Blanch (see "Common Mexican Cooking Tools and Techniques," pp. 333–34) almonds and walnuts; set aside. Combine all ingredients including cream, and chicken stock in a blender and mix until smooth.

In a large saucepan, heat oil and add mixture (be careful of the splatter), let it cook, stirring constantly for up to an hour on medium-low heat with a wooden spoon. Take care that mole does not start to stick to the bottom of the pan. Incorporate white chocolate, white pepper, sugar, and salt to taste, and let it thicken. Remove from heat and add sherry wine, stir well and let it rest, covered for 10 minutes.

This mole sauce goes best with turkey, chicken, and fish. You can boil the poultry and incorporate into this sauce or blanch the fish and place sauce on top. Serve with green rice and sautéed vegetables.

CHICKEN IN ALMOND SAUCE / POLLO ALMENDRADO DE JOSEFINA

(SERVES 6–8)

6 pounds chicken breast, bone-in and with skin

1 teaspoon salt

1 onion

1 garlic clove

1 bay leaf

Almond Sauce (A)

> ### MENU 22.3: WEDDING
>
> Entrée / *Plato Fuerte*
> Chicken in Almond Sauce /
> *Pollo Almendrado de Josefina*
> Sides / *Guarniciónes*
> Cilantro Spaghetti / *Espagueti*
> *Gratinado al Cilantro*
> Chayotes au Gratin /
> *Chayotes con Crema y Queso*
> (see recipe p. 246)

WASH chicken and boil with salt, onion, garlic clove, and bay leaf for 20 minutes over medium-high heat; set aside. Once cold, remove bones and skin and set aside.

Bride's Mole.
Photo by Adriana Almazán Lahl.

A. Almond Sauce

2 tablespoons vegetable oil
7 ounces blanched almonds
1 cinnamon stick
4 cloves
3 slices white bread
½ Spanish white onion
2 garlic cloves
6 tomatoes, roughly chopped
Salt and pepper to taste
1 cup chicken stock (see "Basic Recipes for Mexican Cooking," p. 11)
¼ teaspoon nutmeg

IN a large pot, add oil and sauté almonds, once sautéed; set aside. Sauté cinnamon stick and cloves; set aside with almonds. Fry bread for 1 minute on each side until brown and set aside. Sauté onion and garlic, in the same pot add tomatoes, and season with salt and pepper; let them cook for 5 minutes over medium heat. Combine all ingredients and 1 cup of chicken stock. Let it simmer for 10 minutes; blend everything together until smooth

In a large casserole, add 2 tablespoons of oil and add blended Almond Sauce; allow to cook and season for 10 minutes. Add chicken stock if needed until you get the desired consistency (the sauce should be thick but still a little runny). Add cooked chicken breast and salt to taste and cook for another 10 minutes on low heat. ⁂

CILANTRO SPAGHETTI / ESPAGUETI GRATINADO AL CILANTRO

(SERVES 6–8)

1 package spaghetti
1 tablespoon olive oil
2 poblano peppers
1 garlic clove
1 bunch fresh cilantro
1½ cups Mexican sour cream
Salt to taste
½ cup chicken stock (see "Basic Recipes for Mexican Cooking," p. 11)
1 teaspoon black pepper
1½ cups Mexican Manchego cheese, shredded

COOK the spaghetti in salted boiling water for 8 minutes (it should not be al dente), drain, drizzle with 1 tablespoon of olive oil and toss; set aside. Seed and devein peppers (see "Common Mexican Cooking Tools and Techniques," p. 334). Peel the garlic clove. Wash and chop the cilantro. In a blender, combine cilantro, garlic, Mexican sour cream, peppers, salt, and ½ cup chicken stock and blend until smooth and creamy. Add pepper and adjust salt. Butter a glass baking dish and add spaghetti. Pour sauce over pasta and combine completely. Cover with Manchego cheese and bake at 350° for 30 minutes; serve warm. ⁂

MEXICAN WEDDING COOKIES / POLVORONES

(MAKES 36 COOKIES)

½ cup butter
½ cup vegetable shortening
½ cup sugar
2 large egg yolks
1 teaspoon almond essence
¼ cup orange juice
Peel of 2 oranges, grated
4 cups all-purpose flour
½ tablespoon baking soda
Powdered sugar to dust

SWEETS AND TREATS

Mexican Wedding Cookies /
Polvorones
Three-Milk Cake /
Pastel de Tres Leches
"Clay Pot" Coffee / *Café de Olla*
(see recipe p. 77)

PREHEAT the oven to 400°. Using a large mixing bowl, beat butter and shortening for 5 minutes until fluffy. Add sugar, 1 tablespoon at a time. When all is well mixed, add egg yolks, one at a time. Add almond essence, orange juice, and orange peel. Mix well with a spatula. Roll out the dough on a floured surface to a thickness of ¾ inch. Cut out 2½-inch circles and place on a pregreased baking sheet. Bake for 25 minutes until the cookies begin to brown lightly around the edges. Once cool, transfer to a plate and sprinkle with powdered sugar through a fine sieve.

THREE-MILK CAKE / PASTEL TRES LECHES

2 cups flour
2 tablespoons baking powder
6 eggs
1½ cups sugar
1 tablespoon vanilla extract
Milk Mix (A)
Frosting (B)

PREHEAT oven to 350°. Grease a 9-inch glass ovenproof baking pan. Combine flour and baking powder in a large mixing bowl. Using an electric mixer, in a separate mixing bowl, beat eggs and mix until they triple in size. Add sugar and vanilla to eggs and mix well until sugar completely dissolves. Add dry ingredients to egg mixture gently, in a folding motion. Place batter into the glass pan and bake for 30 minutes. Allow to rest for 30 minutes and stab with a fork all over. Pour Milk Mix over cake and refrigerate for at least an hour before serving. Cake can be served with or without frosting, depending on the occasion. 🐦

A. Milk Mix

1 (6-ounce) can condensed milk
1 (6-ounce) can evaporated milk
3 egg yolks, pasteurized (see "Common Mexican Cooking Tools and Techniques," p. 335)
¼ cup rum or brandy (optional)

BLEND the milks, rum, and pasteurized egg yolks; pour over cake. 🐦

B. Frosting

½ cup sugar
¼ cup water
3 egg whites (pasteurized)
1 peach, sliced, in syrup (see recipe, p. 247) or substitute canned

IN a saucepan, combine sugar and water over medium heat, dissolve sugar and cook until you get a stringy syrup; let it cool completely. Using an electric mixer, mix egg whites until stiff, add syrup and mix on high for 2 minutes. Frost the cake and decorate with peach slices. Cake should be served and maintained cold at all times. 🐦

BAPTISMS /
BAUTIZOS

Pre-Columbian and Modern
Mexican Baptism Rites

A FIRSTHAND account of baptism rituals among the Aztecs comes to us from Bernardino de Sahagún. The use of the word *baptism* to describe the ritual is Sahagún's. Given that the teachings of the Bible had not reached the Aztecs, the fact that their ceremony for acceptance of the newborn into the social group involved water is noteworthy:

> All the relations of the child were assembled, and the midwife, who was the person who performed the baptism, was summoned. At early dawn they met together in the court-yard of the house. When the sun had risen the midwife, taking the child in her arms, called for a little earthen vessel of water. . . . She placed herself with her face towards the west, and immediately began to go through certain ceremonies. . . . After this she sprinkled water on the head of the infant, saying: "O my child! Take and receive the water of the Lord of the world, which is our life. . . . It is to wash and to purify . . . and remove from you all the evil and sin . . . being all the children of Chalchiuhtlicue (the goddess of water)."[1]

Today, the religious ceremony is the most important aspect of *el Bautizo*, and the Catholic ritual of immersion or submersion of the infant is widely practiced in Mexico, with the ceremony typically taking place from three months to up to a year after birth, allowing the family time to save up and plan for this important event. The child wears a white baptismal garment called a *ropón*, the white color symbolizing purity in the newly baptized. The baptismal candle signifies that the child is now enlightened by Christ. Parents choose the padrinos (godparents) of the child very thoughtfully. In the compadrazgo (spiritual kinship system, for more on this see p. 288), this honor of being godparents for a baptism carries more responsibility. For a bautizo, there is a morning Mass, traditionally followed by almuerzo, which is more similar to our brunch. As is usual with rite-of-passage celebrations, the guest list will be large, typically from one hundred to three hundred people.

Naming, Birthdays, and Saint's Days

Although the tradition is no longer as strong in some parts of the country, it is a long-standing custom for a Mexican baby to be named after whatever saint was born on the same day as the child. So the priest, rather than the parents, actually gives the newborn its name. This practice may have its roots in the earliest conversions of Mexicas to Christianity. At the time of their baptism into their new faith, they took Christian names, which were most likely given to them by the priest conducting the ceremony.

When the parents do choose a given name that differs from that of the saint born on their child's birthday, the lucky boy or girl gets two different annual celebrations: one is the traditional birthday and the other the *día de su santo*, or the feast day for the saint who shares an actual birth date with the individual. When the given name is that of the saint born that same day, one will just as often hear people say that they are celebrating *"mi santo"* (meaning their saint's day) as their birthday.

MOTUL-STYLE EGGS (YUCATAN) / *HUEVOS MOTULEÑOS*

(SERVES 4)

4 tablespoons oil

4 corn tortillas

1 plantain, cut into ½ rounds

4–5 fresh tomatoes, diced

2 cloves garlic

1 bunch green onions, chopped

6 ounces ham, diced

1 cup fresh or frozen sweet peas (thawed)

4 tablespoons refried beans (see recipe, p. 152)

4 ounces Mexican Manchego cheese, thinly sliced

4 eggs

MENU 23.1: BAPTISM

Entrée / *Plato Fuerte*
Motul-Style Eggs (Yucatan) / *Huevos Motuleños*
Dessert / *Postre*
Royal Eggs / *Huevos Reales*
Beverages / *Bebidas*
Watermelon or Strawberry Water / *Agua de Sandia o Fresa* (see pp. 117–18)
"Clay Pot" Coffee / *Café de Olla* (see p. 77)

IN a frying pan, add 2 tablespoons oil and fry tortillas until crisp. Fry the plantain rounds, and once nicely browned on both sides, set aside and let them cool down. Heat 2 tablespoons of oil in a sauté pan and cook tomatoes, garlic, and onions for 10 minutes, until thickened, over medium-low heat; add half the ham and peas and cook for another 3 minutes.

Spread 1 tablespoon of warm refried beans on each tortilla and place on each plate, add cheese slices on top of beans. Cook eggs sunny side up to desired doneness (or you may make poached eggs). Place egg over tortilla with beans, cheese, and sauce and top with warm tomato sauce and Manchego cheese. Add more sauce and scatter the other half of ham and half of peas over each plate. Arrange 3 slices of fried plantain around the plate and serve immediately. 🐝

ROYAL EGGS / HUEVOS REALES

(SERVES 6–8)

10 egg yolks
2 teaspoons baking powder
1 teaspoon ground cinnamon
½ cup raisins
2 cups sugar
1 cup water
2 tablespoons dry sherry or port wine

PREHEAT oven to 275°. Beat egg yolks in medium bowl with wire whisk until thick and lemon colored. Add baking powder, cinnamon, and raisins; mix well. Pour into pregreased 8-inch square baking dish; cover with foil. Bake 45 minutes. Cool down 10 minutes.

Bring sugar and water to boil in small heavy saucepan, stirring constantly for 10 minutes or until mixture forms a light syrup. Remove from heat. Stir in sherry or port wine; pour over egg mixture. Sprinkle cinnamon if desired. Cut into 64 (1-inch) squares. Serve hot or cold. 🐝

FIRST COMMUNIONS AND CONFIRMATIONS / PRIMERA COMUNIÓNES Y CONFIRMACIONES

TWO EVENTS that mark the lives of children on the way to becoming adults in the eyes of the Catholic Church are First Communions and Confirmations; both involve study, ceremony, and fiestas.

Before children can take their First Communion, they are required to do a *doctrina* (two years of one-hour Saturday classes) where all the prayers related to the Catholic Mass are learned. Usually the First Communion ceremonies are in May. For this grand ceremony, the family invites two godparents (*padrinos*), who will pay for the little boy's suit or the young girl's big puffy white dress; *tiara*, or crown; and bracelet/necklace and usually a small party as well (which takes place after the ceremony). It is common for Catholic schools to have a group First Communion, where all the students in the third grade make their First Communion together.

Confirmation is more widely celebrated in Mexico. This act, usually taking place a few years after the First Communion, only requires that the child be older than eight, but it is common for Mexican children to study and pass a test in order to take their Confirmation, so it is usually given at the age of twelve or thirteen. The religious ceremony is a renewal and affirmation of the religious choice that the child's godparents made in the name of the child when he or she was baptized. In Mexico, as with almost all events that are celebrated with a Mass, it is traditional to have at least a shared family meal, if not a fiesta, after.

First Communion.
Photo by Jorge Ontiveros.

Making Carnitas

A specialty dish frequently served at rite-of-passage celebrations in Mexico is *car-nitas*. According to conquistador Bernal Díaz del Castillo, the first *tacos de carnitas* where prepared in Nueva España during the conquest era. Hernán Cortés offered his captains and soldiers a taquiza-style banquet in Coyoacán, where they butchered several pigs they had brought with them from the port of Cuba. While the "taco" was well known in the Valley of Mexico, where it was common to eat tacos of crayfish, minnows, and even grasshoppers, the Spanish were the first to fill a taco with prepared pork.[2]

Preparation of carnitas in Mexico's pueblos begins with the slaughter of a whole pig. Sometimes, this is ordered from *el carnicero*, but just as often, a male family member with this expertise is responsible for the butchering. In some regions, there is a formal ceremony for the sacrificed sow. In Mexico, every part of the pork is consumed, from the blood to make blood sausage (*Moronga*), to the skin (*Chich-arrón* or *Cueritos*). Nothing goes to waste—even the guts are used or consumed in some way. The hide always goes into a huge kettle of boiling water so that it can be scraped hairless and made into chicharron (pork cracklings). Making carnitas is a matter of pride for Mexican men, who are largely responsible for its preparation (this is also true of *Borrego*) and each have their preferred method. For some, boiling the meat in water instead of frying it in its own lard ruins it, while others swear by this method. One man in Xochimilco soaks the meat in tequila, oranges, pineapples, milk, and herbs before frying.[3]

Carnitas is the name of the final product once the pork has been butchered, cleaned, and marinated for hours with herbs, orange juice, water, salt, and other ingredients and fried in its own lard in a special large copper pot. There are names for all the different parts of the animal that are eaten. The boneless, skinless part is referred to as *maciza*; *bofe* is the lungs; *buche* is the stomach; then there are the *cachete* (cheek), *corazón* (heart), *criadilla* (testicles), *cuerito* (skin), *hígado* (liver), *tripa* (tripe or intestines), *lengua* (tongue), and *oreja* (ear). It is common to ask for a mix of the parts of pork, and each part has a flavor of its own, regardless of whether it has all been cooked in the same pot for the same amount of time and the same way.

Many states of the Mexican Republic claim to be the birthplace of this famous dish: Michoacán, Querétaro, Jalisco, Hidalgo, and even Mexico's capital. However, there are two regions that are generally acknowledged as having the best carnitas, the community of Quiroga, and Santa Clara del Cobre (because there they manufacture the copper pots that are used to fry carnitas).

Mazahua man making carnitas.
Photo by Jorge Ontiveros.

MY MOTHER'S CARNITAS / CARNITAS DE MI MAMA

(SERVES 14–16)

10 pounds pork leg or butt
2 pounds pork ribs
2 pounds pork shoulder
2 pounds any other pork of your liking
    (cheek, liver, nose)
¼ cup soy sauce
1 gallon vegetable oil
1 large white onion, thinly sliced
6 bay leaves
4 cups orange juice
1 cup vinegar
6 cups of water
2 cups cola-flavored soda
Salt and pepper to taste

> ## MENU 24.1: FIRST COMMUNION OR CONFIRMATION
>
> Entrée / *Plato Fuerte*
> My Mother's Carnitas / *Carnitas de Mi Mama*
> Sides / *Guarniciones*
> Guacamole (see p. 215)
> Cowboy Beans / *Frijoles Charros* (see p. 216)
> Dessert / *Postre*
> Mexican Rice Pudding / *Arro z con Leche*

PLACE pork in a large mixing bowl, add soy sauce, and pierce meat with a fork in several places to create holes to allow marinade to penetrate. Allow to rest for an hour. Meanwhile, warm oil in a 20-quart copper pot or other large pot, add onion and bay leaves, and heat oil to 365°. Allow onion and bay leaves to brown. Once they are dark, remove from oil.

Add meat to pot carefully so as not to splash oil and cook for 20 to 25 minutes, stirring frequently. After 20 minutes, carefully add orange juice, vinegar, and water and continue cooking, covered, for about 2 hours on medium-low heat, stirring frequently. Once liquid is almost gone add cola and cook until soda evaporates and carnitas acquire a nice golden color. Remove carnitas from pot and drain oil off; season with salt and pepper.

Serve with warm tortillas, chopped onion, cilantro, lime wedges, and your favorite salsas. See "Salsas and Salsa Pairings" (pp. 17–25) for suggestions.

Mexican Rice Pudding /
Arroz con Leche.
Photo by Adriana Almazán Lahl.

MEXICAN RICE PUDDING / ARROZ CON LECHE

(SERVES 8)

1 cup white rice
2½ cups of water
1 cinnamon stick plus 6 small cinnamon sticks to garnish
Vanilla pod, split open
4 cups whole milk
1 (5-ounce) can condensed milk
10 tablespoons sugar
3 tablespoons corn meal
1 egg yolk
¼ cup raisins
1 teaspoon ground cinnamon

PLACE rice in a colander and rinse well. In a deep saucepan, boil 2 cups of water, add rice and cinnamon stick and vanilla pod, cover, and cook on medium-low heat for 20 minutes.

In a different saucepan boil 2 cups of whole milk and the condensed milk; lower to medium-low heat, add sugar, and mix well. In a separate container, mix corn meal with ½ cup of lukewarm water and incorporate the egg yolk. Add a couple of tablespoons of hot milk into the mix, strain into the milk saucepan (this process will incorporate starch into the mix without adding the texture of the corn meal). Stir constantly to avoid burning milk, being careful not to allow the mixture to stick to the bottom of the saucepan. Cook for 3 minutes and incorporate rice and raisins. Cook rice pudding for 2 more minutes on low heat; cool it by placing saucepan over a sink full of ice to stop cooking process. Stir mixture frequently to allow the center of the pan to cool evenly. Once cool, place in the refrigerator.

Serve cold. Sprinkle ground cinnamon and garnish with cinnamon stick if desired. 🐦

FUNERALS / FUNERALES

25
CHAPTER

Ancient Beliefs

TO THE Nahua people, there was not an absolute distinction between life and death. In fact, life on Earth was considered a dream and it was in dying that one became truly awake, as reflected in these Nahautl poems:

> It is not true, it is not true
> That we come to live here
> We come only to sleep, only to dream.[1]
>
> It is true that on earth one lives
> Not forever on earth, only a little while
> Though jade it may be, it breaks;
> though gold it may be, it is crushed;
> though it be quetzal plumes, it shall not last.
> Not forever on earth, only a little while.[2]

To the Aztecs, death was not finality but part of one's journey, a stage in a continuing passage between this life and the next, and they practiced elaborate rites around it. Much of what we know on this subject comes to us from the study of what are known as Aztec codices, or pictorial manuscripts. Some depict cremations or burials. One shows a high-ranking Aztec official being buried with chocolate, corn, and other foodstuffs for the journey to the afterlife and even a metate to grind the corn. According to the writings of Dominican Friar Diego Durán in his work, *The History of the Indies of New Spain*, the Aztecs buried the deceased under houses or the yards behind them, in fields, and sometimes in special shrines in the woods, always dressed in their finest clothes.

The Aztecs' beliefs about death and the afterlife were quite distinct from those of Christianity, in that the way in which one died, rather than lived, determined where the departed soul would reside. Warriors who died in battle and sacrifice victims were assigned to the eastern paradise of the sun, called Ichan Tonatiuh Ilhuijacan, where they spent fours years, after which, in a resurrection of sorts, they returned to Earth as beautiful birds to spend the rest of their years among the flowers. This was also the fortunate destination for women who died in childbirth, who returned to Earth in the form of moths. Tlalocan was the destination for those who had died of disease or drowning or had been struck by lightning. It was also beautiful, a place where a perpetual summer existed. Some who died of natural causes spent eternity in Mictlan, the Aztec underworld. Children who died went to a beautiful garden paradise and were buried in front of maize beans, which signified the pleasant nature of their final destination.

The Aztecs practiced a death rite and feast called *Titilt*, which was celebrated in memory of the dead and repeated annually for four years after the individual had passed. It included creating a replica of the deceased upon which a mask and a headdress were placed, and music was played.

Colonial Practices

Fanny Gooch, in her work, *Face to Face with the Mexicans*, gives us this firsthand account of customs around funerals and mourning in Nueva España:

> The wearing of mourning is universal, not only for near relatives, but also for friends. A young lady dies, her companions don the somber garb for thirty days; if the father or mother of a girl should die, it is worn for fifteen days. During all this time they seclude themselves from society. . . . Ladies do not attend funerals, but visits of pesame (regret) are made immediately after death, and for nine days those who cannot call send letters or cards of condolences.[3]

Funerals in Mexico Today

Customs surrounding and attitudes toward death and dying in Mexico continue to reflect the pre-Columbian vision of life's continuum. Renowned Mexican poet Octavio Paz wrote that "death and life are opposites that complement each other. Both are halves of a sphere that we, subjects of time and space, can only glimpse. In the prenatal world, life and death are merged; in ours opposed; in the world beyond reunited again . . . as innocence regained."[4]

Today in Mexico, everyone gathers after a Mass, either at the home of the family of the deceased or at the funeral home (but this is less common), to exchange stories and memories. For at least twenty-four hours and up to two full days, family and friends, maintain *velorio*, or a prayer vigil. A reflection of the difference in views of death in Mexico as compared with those in the United States, children are present and become comfortable with these customs from a very young age. Often the coffin is painted with scenes of Our Lady of Guadalupe or The Last Supper to brighten it up.

An unusual custom is that of the *lloronas*, women who are hired to cry at the burial or the night before it, when visitors gather in the home of the mourning family. Food (often full meals) and drink are served to all who stop to pay their respects. Many guests stay the night, seated around the deceased, joined in prayer (rosarios). This gathering, at which the body is present, can be an all-day affair, even lasting into the night. The deceased are sometimes viewed on top of the coffin, rather than inside, dressed and with makeup, surrounded by flowers. The next day there is the procession to the *panteón*. The meal that occurs in honor of the deceased usually follows immediately after the funeral. Friends and relatives pray (a *novenario*) for nine days with the family of the deceased, after which the visitors are presented with a small gift from the family.

While there is there is not a specific menu traditionally served at funerals, it is usual to serve dishes that were the favorites of the deceased. The following menus are suitable for any occasion.

ADOBO DE JOCOQUE (AUNT CONI'S RECIPE)

(SERVES 8–10)

7 ancho chiles, seeded and split open
7 guajillo chiles, seeded and split open
4 tomatoes, dry-roasted (see "Common
    Mexican Cooking Tools and Techniques,"
    p. 337)
4 garlic cloves, dry-roasted
1 teaspoon black pepper
¾ teaspoon cloves ground
¾ teaspoon ground Mexican cinnamon
3 quarts Jocoque (A)
10 chicken pieces, legs, thighs, and breasts
Salt to taste

MENU 25.1: FUNERAL

Entrée / *Plato Fuerte*
Adobo de Jocoque
Sides / *Guarniciones*
"Clay Pot" Beans / *Frijoles de Olla*
(see recipe p. 146)
White Rice Mexican-Style
with Peas / *Arroz Blanco a la
Mexicana con Chicharos*
(see recipe p. 151)
Dessert / *Postre*
"Scribble Cookies" / *Garibaldis*
(see p. 134)
Beverage / *Bebida*
"Clay Pot" Coffee / *Café de Olla*
(see p. 77)

SEED and devein chiles and toast them on a dry comal or cast-iron grill; add the toasted chiles to a bowl filled with hot water to hydrate. Meanwhile dry-roast tomatoes and then garlic on the comal until they become soft. Peel and seed tomatoes; add tomatoes, chiles, and garlic to the blender and mix until smooth (this is your adobo).

In a large pot, add mixture from the blender, spices, seasonings, and Jocoque, mixing frequently. Add chicken pieces and cook on low heat for 30 minutes or until chicken is completely cooked; remove chicken and set aside. Keep reducing the sauce until it thickens and the fat starts releasing. Skim fat as it appears and continue until fat stops releasing; this will take some time (40–60 minutes). Salt to taste. Incorporate chicken pieces (skin removed) into the adobo and warm for 10 minutes. Serve with rice, warm tortillas, and beans.

A. Jocoque

1 teaspoon salt
2 quarts yogurt
¼ cup olive oil

LINE a large colander with cheesecloth. Stir salt into the yogurt and pour the yogurt into the cheesecloth. Set the colander in a bowl to catch the liquid that drains off. Cover with a cloth towel and let it drain in the refrigerator for 24 hours.

After draining for 24 hours, transfer the resulting cheese to a bowl. Stir in the olive oil. Store in a covered container in the refrigerator.

CHICKEN ENCHILADAS IN SALSA VERDE / ENCHILADAS DE POLLO CON SALSA VERDE

(SERVES 6)

½ cup corn oil plus 2 teaspoons
12 tortillas
9 ounces shredded chicken (see "Basic Recipes for Mexican Cooking," p. 11)
3 cups cooked Salsa Verde (see "Salsas and Salsa Pairings," pp. 17–25)
Salt and pepper to taste
Mexican sour cream
Oaxaca cheese (or mozzarella), shredded

TO prepare tortillas to make enchiladas, heat ½ cup corn oil in a pan and

MENU 25.2: FUNERAL

Entrée / *Plato Fuerte*
Salsa Verde Chicken Enchiladas / *Enchiladas de Pollo con Salsa Verde*
Sides / *Guarniciones*
Refried Beans / *Frijoles Refritos* (see recipe p. 152)
Mexican "Red" Rice / *Arroz a la Mexicana* (see recipe p. 145)
Dessert / *Postre*
Horchata Gelatin Dessert / *Gelatina de Horchata* (see recipe p. 213)
Beverage / *Bebida*
Guava Atole / *Atole de Guayaba* (see p. recipe 41)

Enchiladas Verdes.
Photo by Adriana Almazán Lahl.

dip tortillas briefly in oil to soften (*sofreir*, see "Common Cooking Techniques and Tools for Mexican Cooking," p. 337); remove almost immediately and drain on a paper towel. Next, stuff the tortilla with shredded chicken and roll a tight taco. Place a tooth pick in the center and fry them in hot oil until they get brown and crispy. Let them rest 10 minutes; remove toothpick. Proceed to make the taquitos as directed on page 285 for Taquitos de Papas.

To prepare the salsa, add 2 teaspoons oil to a saucepan and add salsa (being careful of splatter); cook for about 12–15 minutes, season with salt and pepper to taste, and set aside (the sauce should be runny, add water if necessary).

Place taquitos in an ovenproof pan and pour salsa on top with Mexican cream and shredded cheese. Place in oven preheated to 350° for 30 minutes. Serve hot with rice and beans. Garnish with raw onion and cilantro. 🐝

APPENDIX

COMMON MEXICAN COOKING TOOLS AND TECHNIQUES

BAÑO MARIA

A cooking technique that migrated to Mexico from France during the Intervention and is part of the lexicon of Comida Afrancesada (Mexican-French fusion food). In English, it is what would be referred to as using a double boiler or water bath. This method of cooking involves placing the pan with ingredients inside another pan that contains water. This second pot or pan is directly exposed to the source of heat. It has the advantage of heating ingredients gently and gradually to fixed temperatures.

Bains-marie, as they are called in French, were originally developed by alchemists who needed a way to heat materials slowly and gently. The name, literally translated, means Mary's bath and may have been taken from the originator of the technique, an Italian woman named Maria in sixteenth-century Florence.

BLANCHING ALMONDS

2 cups almonds

3 cups water

Place almonds in a pot covered with cold water. Bring water to boil. Immediately remove from heat and strain almonds and place them in a bowl with ice cold water. Dry over paper towels. To remove skins, pinch an almond between thumb and pointer finger, and the skin should come off with ease. Be careful, as almonds will be very slippery.

BLANCHING SPINACH

Bring a large pot of water to a boil over high heat. Wash spinach leaves, and pat them dry. Put ice cubes and water in a large bowl. Fill the bowl ¾ full with ice, and add cold water to reach the top of the ice. This needs to be ready after the spinach is boiled to shock the spinach. Put the spinach leaves in the boiling water, and allow them to boil for 30 seconds to 1 minute until you see a bright-green color. Drain the excess water from the spinach with a strainer. Put the spinach in the ice water. Leave the blanched spinach in the ice bath for a few minutes or until it is no longer warm. This will stop the cooking process, keep the spinach tender, and retain the nutrients. Squeeze the spinach with your hands to remove all excess water. Spinach is approximately 90 percent water, so no additional water is required to cook spinach. You can freeze the spinach for later use.

BLANCHING WALNUTS

2 cups walnuts
3 cups water

Place walnuts in a pot covered with cold water. Bring water to boil. Immediately remove from heat and strain walnuts. Place in a bowl of ice-cold water. Allow to dry on paper towels. To remove skins, grab walnuts and remove skin carefully scrapping skin off with the help of a pairing knife. This is a labor-intensive job, but you will eliminate all the bitterness in the skin with this method.

CAZUELA OR OLLA

One of the key ingredients in Mexican *frijoles de olla* is the clay pot, the *olla* (or in the case of a clay casserole, a *cazuela*), which imparts a flavor that is not found elsewhere when beans, coffee, or other ingredients are slow-cooked in it for hours. These hand-thrown, hand-decorated Mexican clay casseroles impart a subtle but perceptible flavor to foods. A well-made cazuela is one whose bottom is not too thin, so it cooks well without burning. These pots need to cured before use. Rub the reverse side of the bottom (the side that will be directly on the fire) with garlic and/or cook with milk in it until the milk scalds. Not for oven use.

CHILES, WORKING WITH AND PREPARING
(ALSO SEE "GUIDE TO MEXICO'S CHILES," P. 339)

To Remove Skin: Some recipes require the skin to be removed. This technique is most commonly used for poblano chiles, especially when preparing them to make chiles rellenos (stuffed chiles) or rajas (strips of chile). Prepare the peppers by heating on the comal until the skin is blackened and blistered on all sides, turning frequently with tongs. Remove chiles from the heat and immediately place them in a plastic bag and tie it closed, allowing the peppers to sweat for 5–10 minutes (don't leave them in the bag for longer as they will over cook). This cooking technique is known in Mexico as *sudar*. Remove the peppers from the bag and, using your fingers (wearing gloves), peel the blackened skin. Cut a small (2- to 3-inch) slit lengthwise, trying not to break the pepper and keeping the stem intact, then proceed to carefully take the seeds out without breaking the flesh. Place peppers in the fridge to cool down until ready to serve.

Another method is to cook as directed and immediately after blackened, grab a dry paper towel and carefully rub the skin off; this method will facilitate peeling the chile without overcooking (which can happen during the "sweating" stage in the method above), helping the chile to retain its shape without easily breaking.

To Devein and Remove Seed from Larger Dried Chiles: This technique is most commonly used when preparing chiles to make adobado. Soak in warm water until softened (some recipes will ask you to dry-roast first; in this case, follow instructions in recipe). When chiles become soft, usually takes about a half hour, pull stem from top gently. In many cases, veins will come out along with the stem. If not, break chile open and remove veins and seeds.

To Devein and Remove Seed from Dried Del Arbol Chiles: This is more easily done without presoaking these small chiles. Just break off stems, break open chiles, and separate seeds from chiles.

CHIQUIHUITE

Used to keep tortillas warm as they come off the comal, the *chiquihuite* (pronounced "cheeky-wheety") is traditionally made with palm leaves. It is best described as a basket with a lid (although some use a basket without a lid and count on a special kitchen towel to keep the tortillas warm). This basket is placed at the center of every Mexican table, lined with a beautifully hand-embroidered table linen made especially for this purpose.

COMAL

A griddle used to heat tortillas; dry-roast chiles, tomatillos, and red tomatoes; and also is great for dry-roasting garlic and spices (really enhances the flavor of, for example, cumin or sesame seeds before adding them to your dishes). The Aztecs used a *comalli*, which is basically a clay disc on three stones over a fire; you'll still find these in use in Mexico today. A comal is a round disc made of cast iron, about 12 inches in diameter, which is perfect for a family of four, or oval, which heats 6 tortillas at a time for a larger crowd. If you want to look like you know your way around a comal, learn to grab the tortillas with your fingertips to flip them and remove them from the fire.

EGG, PASTEURIZING

Add enough water in a saucepan to cover the eggs (do not put eggs in now, but do take them out of the refrigerator early to bring to room temperature), add 1 teaspoon salt, bring water to a boil, and add the eggs for 3 minutes. Keep water temperature at 140° and no more than 142° (you'll need to use a cooking thermometer); flip eggs once while cooking. After 3 minutes, drain and place eggs in cold water to stop cooking, use immediately or place in the refrigerator until you use them.

MOLCAJETE AND TEJOLOTE

The word *molcajete* (mortar) derives from Nahuatl *molli* (seasoning or sauce) and *caxitl* (bowl); *tejolote* (pestle) is also from Nahuatl: *tetl* (stone) and *xolotl* (doll). A mortar and pestle is usually made from porous volcanic rock. The best-quality molcajetes are made of basalt with the lowest possible sand content. To achieve coarser texture for grinding, the basalt is mixed with granite, feldspar, and quartz for a hard, rough surface. The molcajete and tejolete need to be cured: First rinse well with water, no soap; with the pestle grind small amounts of rice several times until the resulting gray sand and grit are ground away. Rinse again and allow to air dry. The method of using a mortar and pestle to grind releases more flavor from herbs and spices than when they are puréed in a blender.

MOLER (TO MILL OR POUND)

Usually the second step in creating a salsa using a blender, which is arguably the most indispensable tool in any Mexican kitchen, replacing, for most recipes, the molcajete. A molcajete and tejolote, or traditional Mexican mortar and pestle, is the implement used to *moler*, to pound anything from piloncillo (solid blocks of cane sugar) and Mexican chocolate to the ingredients for salsas. When preparing a blended base using a molcajete, garlic and salt should be ground together before adding the remaining ingredients.

PILONCILLO, WORKING WITH

This smoky, unrefined earthy sugar is commonly used in Mexico. For small amounts, it can be grated using a cheese grater or just stand the block straight up and "shave" small quantities off. If recipe calls for more piloncillo, pound with a meat hammer while it's still in its plastic baggie, or in Mexico, it is common to throw the plastic bag of piloncillo on the floor to break it up into usable pieces. To create a "sauce," place the piloncillo upright in a sauté pan with a small amount of water over a low flame. It will begin to melt. Watch carefully so it doesn't burn, add more water if needed. It can be used in moles and other sauces, as well as to simply sweeten coffee or top off a baked sweet potato (for a delicious flavor combination, mix with fresh Mexican lime juice and pour over sweet potato 10–15 minutes before completely baked) or in any recipe that calls for brown sugar.

PONER A SUDAR [TO SWEAT]

Refers to the method used to "sweat" usually chiles to remove the skin that was charred during the dry-roasting process. The poblano is Mexico's favorite chile, showing up in everything from chunky salsas to chiles rellenos. After you prepare the chiles by dry roasting, remove and place them immediately into a plastic bag, and tie the bag well so that the chiles can sweat. This will make it possible to remove their thin outer skin. To do this, take the chiles out of the plastic bag after about 10 minutes (do not sweat for longer as chiles will overcook) and run them briefly under cold water (do not use cold water for more than a few seconds as it will dilute the rich taste of the chiles). The skin should separate easily.

SOFREIR [TO SOFT FRY]

A method of sautéing so as to soften a tortilla, usually in salsa, as in preparation for enchiladas. Heating the tortilla this way, in a little very hot oil (just enough to cover your sauté pan but not enough to cover the tortilla—you'll want to flip it so as to "wet" both sides), "seals" it so it won't fall apart when dipped in the hot salsa. Take care to thoroughly heat the oil, so the tortilla doesn't soak it up and become greasy.

TORTILLA PRESS [*TORTILLADORA*]

Used to make tortillas by hand (see p. 236), available in cast-iron (best), aluminum, or wood (which is harder to use).

TOSTAR OR ASAR [TO DRY-ROAST]

Frequently this is the very first step in preparing a Mexican dish, utilizing the comal, over high heat. Oils were not introduced to Mexico until the arrival of the Europeans, so the Aztecs used this dry method of sealing flavor into, or getting the most flavor out of, chiles or tomatoes (red or green), primarily for salsas. Wash and dry chiles before roasting them on a very hot comal, and remove from heat quickly, before they begin to change color (unless recipes specifies otherwise), at which point the flavor can become bitter. For tomatoes, roast until their skins blister, turning frequently so all sides of the tomato are charred. Leaving the charred skin on adds a smoky, more intense flavor, often favored in salsas. Preroasting garlic (usually with the skin on) on a hot comal a little softens the garlic, just until it jumps, which makes the skin come off easily and makes a sweeter garlic flavor than raw garlic, desirable in some recipes. Some seeds such as cumin and sesame should be toasted on the comal before being ground in a molcajete or a spice mill (watch carefully as these tend to burn easily).

B
APPENDIX

GUIDE TO MEXICAN CHILES

CHILES DE MEXICO	BEST FOR	COLOR	INTENSITY	HEAT RATING IN SCOVILLE UNITS
Anaheim	Mostly used in United States to stuff chiles rellenos	Green	Mild to Medium	1,000–2,500
Anchos	Salsas, stews	Brownish Red	Mild	1,000–2,000
Bola	Salsas	Green to Red	Medium	3,000
Cascabel (dried Chile Bola)	Salsas, soups, and stews	Brownish Red	Medium	3,000
Cayenne pepper	Seasoning	Red	Hot	30,000–40,000
Chilaca	Similar to Anaheim chiles	Dark Green	Mild	500–1,000
Chipotle (dried or canned)	For cooking in stews, soups; to add a sweet smoky flavor	Brownish Red	Hot	10,000–50,000
Guajillos	Dehydrated, thin, smooth skin; good for salsas and stews	Red to Dark Red	Medium	5,000
Güeros	Stews, escabeches	Pale Yellow	Mild	0–500

CHILES DE MEXICO	BEST FOR	COLOR	INTENSITY	HEAT RATING IN SCOVILLE UNITS
Habaneros	Salsas, escabeches, and stews	Bright Yellow to Orange	Super Hot	100,000–350,000
Jalapeños or Cuaresmeño	Salsas, stuffed, stews, escabeche	Dark Green to Red	Medium	2,500–5,000
Mulatos	Often used as substitute for anchos	Dark Brown	Mild to Medium	1,000–5,000
Pasillas	Salsa	Dark Green	Medium hot	2,500–3,000
Piquin or Pequin	Used ground to garnish	Bright Red	Hot	50,000–75, 000
Poblanos	Used to stuff and make rajas	Dark Green	Mild to Medium	1,000–2,500
Rat's Tail Chile or Chile de Arbol	Garnish, salsas	Bright Red	Hot	15,000–30,000
Serranos	Salsas or canned in vinegar	Bright Green	Medium to Hot	7,000–25,000

C

APPENDIX

INGREDIENT AND COOKING WARE SOURCES ONLINE

Achiote paste	latinmerchant.com	mexgrocer.com	
Avocado leaves	latinmerchant.com	mexgrocer.com	
Amaranth	ranchogordo.com	mexgrocer.com	
Annato seeds	latinmerchant.com	mexgrocer.com	
Bacalao—salt cod	tienda.com	amazon.com	
Beans, heirloom, dried all varieties	ranchogordo.com		
Casings, for sausages and chorizo	sausagemaker.com	amazon.com	
Canela, Mexican cinnamon	ranchogordo.com		
Cajeta Envinada	mexgrocer.com	amazon.com	
Cazuelas, ollas—Mexican clay casseroles and pots	mexgrocer.com		
Cheeses, Mexican various	mexgrocer.com	mexgrocer.com	
Chiquihuite tortilla warmer	sears.com	thelatinproducts.com	
Chia seeds	nuts.com	getchia.com	
Chocolate, Mexican			
Comal	mexgrocer.com	thelatinproducts.com	
Corn husks	mexgrocer.com	thelatinproducts.com	
Cocoa butter	cocoasupply.com		
Dried chiles, various whole and ground	latinmerchant.com	mexgrocer.com	Ranchogordo.com
Dried hibiscus	culinarydistrict.com	mexgrocer.com	

Dried shrimp, whole or ground	latinmerchant.com	mexgrocer.com
Dulce de leche	latinmerchant.com	mexgrocer.com
Epazote, dried	latinmerchant.com	mexgrocer.com
Fava beans, dried	latinmerchant.com	mexgrocer.com
Hibiscus flowers	culinarydistrict.com	
Hoja santa or Mexican pepper leaf *(Piper auritum)*	generationfarms.com (*Note*: this is a source for the live plant)	
Hominy, white or gold	ranchogordo.com	latinmerchant.com
Larding needle	foodservicedirect.com	amazon.com
Lavender	latinmerchant.com	
Lecithin	pleasanthillgrain.com	
Maseca tamale flour	latinmerchant.com	
Maseca tortilla flour	latinmerchant.com	
Mexican chocolate— Abuelita, Ibarra brands or stoneground	mexigrocer.com	ranchogordo.com
Mexican cooking classes	tressenoritagourmet.com	saldevidagourmet.com
Mexican oregano	mexgrocer.com	ranchogordo.com
Molcajete and Tejolote	mexgrocer.com	thelatinproducts.com
Molinillo	mexgrocer.com	thelatinproducts.com
Nonpareils	ohnuts.com	
Olla	mexgrocer.com	thelatinproducts.com
Orange blossm water	amazon.com	
Pepitas molidas (ground pumpkin seeds)	nuts.com	
Piloncillo	latinmerchant.com	ranchogordo.com
Plantain leaves (banana leaves)	mexgrocer.com	
Quesos: Panela, Cotija, Oaxaca, and more	mexgrocer.com	
Rennet	amazon.com	
Rim salts	saldevidagourmet.com	
Rompope	amazon.com	
Rose petals	latinmerchant.com	
Rosette molds	casa.com	amazon.com
Sugar cane, canned	latinmerchant.com	
Tamarind	foodservicedirect.com	
Tejocotes	mexgrocer.com	
Tequesquite	mexgrocer.com	
Tortilla press—*Tortilladora*	mexgrocer.com	thelatinproducts.com

NOTES

Preface

1. French and Mexican cuisines were added November 16, 2009. UNESCO, Traditional Mexican Cuisine—Ancestral, Ongoing Community Culture, the Michoacán Paradigm, www.unesco.org/culture/ich/index.php?lg=en&pg=00011&RL=00400.

2. Octavio Paz, from *Labyrinth of Solitude*, trans. Lysander Kemp, quoted in Stanley Brandes, *Power and Persuasion: Fiestas and Social Control in Rural México* (Philadelphia: University of Pennsylvania Press, 1988), 2.

3. Maria Elisa Christie, *Kitchenspace: Women, Fiestas, and Everyday Life in Central Mexico* (Austin: University of Texas Press, 2008), 106.

4. Mexico's population breaks down as: Roman Catholic: 88 percent, Jehovah's Witnesses: 1.25 percent, Seventh Day Adventists: .58 percent, LDS (Mormons): .25 percent, Jewish: .05 percent, and no religion: 3.53 percent, according to the U.S. State Department's 2010 International Religious Freedom Report.

5. William Beezley, in a 1977 survey, counted 5,083 civil and religious occasions throughout the year, noting that no more than nine days go by without a fiesta somewhere in Mexico as cited in Maria Elisa Christie, *Kitchenspace: Women, Fiestas, and Everyday Life in Central Mexico* (Austin: University of Texas Press, 2008), 16.

About the Photos

1. Estimate by CDI CONAPO Comisión Nacional para el Desarrollo de los Pueblos Indígenas Consejo Nacional de Población, 2011. www.cdi.gob.mx/.

2. www.cdi.gob.mx/.

Introduction

1. Author's translation. Spanish version as cited by Juan R. Palomo in *Mole, Olé* www.northwestern.edu/magazine/northwestern/janfeb99/p22.htm.

2. Encarnacion Pinedo, *Encarnacion's Kitchen, Mexican Recipes from 19th-Century California*, ed. and trans. Dan Strehl (Berkeley: University of California Press, 2005), 15.

3. Mayer Brantz, *Mexico as It Was and Is* (Philadelphia: G. B. Zieber, 1847), 109.

4. Pinedo, *Encarncion's Kitchen*, 16.

5. Jeffrey M. Pilcher, *¡Que Vivan Los Tamales! Food and the Making of Mexican Identity* (Albuquerque: University of New Mexico Press, 1998), 240.

6. From 1862 to 1867 Archduke Ferdinand Maximilian of Austria ruled Mexico on behalf of France as Emperor Maximilian I of Mexico. He was captured and executed in 1867; he was just thirty-four years old. For more information, see chapter 15, on Cinco de Mayo.

7. Pilcher, *¡Que Vivan Los Tamales!*, 65

8. Karen Hursh Graber, "A Guide to Mexican Cheese: Los Quesos Mexicanos," *Mexconnect*, October 1, 2000.

9. Bernal Díaz del Castillo, as quoted in Coe, *America's First Cuisines*, 76.

10. Maria Elisa Christie, *Kitchenspace: Women, Fiestas, and Everyday Life in Central Mexico* (Austin: University of Texas Press, 2008), 15.

11. Christie, *Kitchenspace*, 15.

12. JJ Virgin, "7 Ways Eating Gluten Makes You Fat, Sick and Tired," *Huffpost Healthy Living*, September 21, 2012.

13. Manuel Aguilar-Moreno, *Handbook to Life in the Aztec World* (Oxford: Oxford University Press, 2007), 371.

Chapter 1

1. Don Antonio Valeriano, *Nican Mopohua*, an account of the events written in Nahuatl, circa 1560. See a rendering of the account in Jody B. Smith, *The Image of Guadalupe: Myth or Miracle?* (Macon, GA: Mercer University Press, 1994).

2. Altogether an estimated 1.5 million people living in Central Mexico, mostly in rural communities, more than any other indigenous tongue, speak these dialects today. It is recognized as part of what is called *lenguas nacionales* ("national languages") that have the same status as Spanish within their region. Over sixty-three indigenous languages are spoken throughout the country. During the canonization of Juan Diego, the Bible was read in Spanish and Nahuatl.

3. Don Antonio Valeriano, *Nican Mopohua*.

4. Construction of the original basilica was not finished until 1709. The bomb damaged the interior of the old basilica, which was also sinking as it had been built on the site of an ancient lake. The new basilica was commissioned in 1974 and finished in 1976.

5. "Las estrellas del manto de la Virgen de Guadalupe" (The Stars in Our Lady of Guadalupe's Tilma), in collaboration with the Astronomy Institute of UNAM (Universidad Nacional Autonoma de Mexico). See www.virgenperegrina.es/articulos/articulo.phtml?se=71&ca=113&te=%&id=220.

6. This triple reflection is known as the Samson-Purkinje effect.

7. The report states that the resulting images are located exactly as they should be, noting that the distortion of the images agrees with the curvature of the cornea in Smith, *The Image of Guadalupe*, 54

8. Bernardino de Sahagún, *A General History of the Things of New Spain*, as cited in Betty Fussell, *The Story of Corn* (Albuquerque: University of New Mexico Press, 2004), 20

9. Maria Elisa Christie, *Kitchenspace: Women, Fiestas, and Everyday Life in Central Mexico* (Austin: University of Texas Press, 2008), 147.

Chapter 2

1. St. Ignatius Loyola (1491–1556) proposed that a *novena* or special prayers be offered on each of the nine days before Christmas; St. John of the Cross (1542–1591) added a religious pageant to the event.

2. Stanley Brandes, *Power and Persuasion: Fiestas and Social Control in Rural México* (Philadelphia: University of Pennsylvania Press, 1988), 162.

3. Author's translation.

4. David Karp, "Tejocote Is No Longer Forbidden Fruit," *Los Angeles Times*, December 9, 2009.

5. Karp, "Tejocote Is No Longer Forbidden Fruit."

Chapter 3

1. World Book, Inc., ed. *Christmas in Mexico*, vol. 2 (Chicago: World Book, 1996).

Chapter 5

1. Ruperto de Nola, *Libro de guisados* (Spain, 1568). Modern recipe translation by Ken Albala.

Chapter 8

1. Maria Elisa Christie, *Kitchenspace: Women, Fiestas, and Everyday Life in Central Mexico* (Austin: University of Texas Press, 2008), 117.

Chapter 10

1. Juan Pedro Viqueira Alban, *Propriety and Permissiveness in Bourbon Mexico*, trans. Sonya Lipsett-Rivera and Sergio Rivera Ayala (Lanham, MD: Rowman & Littlefield, 2004), 104.

2. Maria Elisa Christie, *Kitchenspace: Women, Fiestas, and Everyday Life in Central Mexico* (Austin: University of Texas Press, 2008), 55.

3. Ricardo Urquijo posted in the blog *M!*, February 1, 2009.

4. A body of prophecies passed down and shared by all the thirty-three existing Maya tribes of Guatemala, as well as by the Maya of Oaxaca and Chiapas, as depicted on at least three stone monuments and one of the Maya codices.

Chapter 11

1. Mayer Brantz, *Mexico as It Was and Is* (Philadelphia: G. B. Zieber, 1847), 150.

2. Simony Varey, ed., *The Mexican Treasury: The Writings of Dr. Francisco Hernández* (Stanford, CA: Stanford University Press, 2000), 108.

Chapter 12

1. The London Religious Tract Society, *Mexico: The Country, History and People* (London: Warren Hall and Co., 1863), 203.

2. Passion plays depicting events during Jesus's last days, from the Farewell Discourse at the conclusion of the Last Supper to his arrest.

3. Fanny Chambers Gooch Iglehart, *Face to Face with the Mexicans* (New York: Fords, Howard and Hulbert, 1887), 274.

4. J. V. Amor, "Holy Week at Tasco, Mexico," *The Month: A Catholic Magazine and Review*, April 1885, 512–17.

Chapter 14

1. Fanny Chambers Gooch Iglehart, *Face to Face with the Mexicans* (New York: Fords, Howard and Hulbert, 1887), 74.

Chapter 15

1. Michael Martinez, "Cinco de Mayo a Mexican Import? No, It's as American as July 4, Prof says," CNN, May 5, 2012, available at www.cnn.com/2012/05/05/us/cinco-de-mayo-origins.

2. Martinez, "Cinco de Mayo a Mexican Import?"

3. David E. Hayes-Bautista, "Cinco de Mayo: The Real Story–Part 3," http://egpnews .com/2009/05/cinco-de-mayo-the-real-story-3/.

4. Quoted in David Hayes-Bautista, *El Cinco de Mayo: An American Tradition* (Berkeley: University of California Press, 2012), 61.

5. Martinez, "Cinco de Mayo a Mexican Import?"

6. Martinez, "Cinco de Mayo a Mexican Import?"

Chapter 16

1. Frances Calderon de la Barca [Frances Erskine Inglis], *Life in Mexico* (Boston: Charles C. Little and James Brown, 1843).

Chapter 17

1. According to records of city income and expenditures, in this year 21 percent of disposable income was allocated to Corpus Christi festivities. William H. Beezley, Cheryl English

Martin, and William E. French, eds., *Rituals of Rule, Rituals of Resistance: Public Celebrations and Popular* (Wilmington, DE: Scholarly Resources, 1994).

2. The Spanish viceroyalty of New Spain was established immediately after the conquest of the Aztecs in 1524 and extended well beyond what we now know as Mexico: north to the California border and including what is now New Mexico, Texas, and Arizona; south through Central America (excluding Panama) and South America; and much of the Caribbean including Cuba and the Dominican Republic. All of this was ruled from the seat of power in Mexico City.

3. Mestizos are people of mixed indigenous and Spanish heritage. In Mexico's total population of 108 million in 2007, they represented about 60 percent, while indigenous populations represent 30 percent and just 10 percent were of pure European decent.

4. Diego Duran, *The History of the Indies of New Spain*, translated and annotated by Doris Heyden (Norman: University of Oklahoma Press, 1994), 143.

Chapter 18

1. William H. Beezley, Cheryl English Martin, and William E. French, eds., *Rituals of Rule, Rituals of Resistance: Public Celebrations and Popular* (Wilmington, DE: Scholarly Resources, 1994), xviii.

2. Beezley, Martin, and French, *Rituals of Rule*, xviii.

3. Clement Bertie-Marriot, "Un Parisien au Mexique," in *Mexico Otherwise: Modern Mexico in the Eyes of Foreign Observers*, trans. Jürgen Buchenau (Albuquerque: University of New Mexico Press, 2005), 98. Originally published in Paris: E. Dentu, 1886.

4. Marriot, "Un Parisien au Mexique," 100.

5. Gustavo Arellano, "Notes from the Banana Republic: Santa Ana, Mexico Circa 1910, Miguel Pulido, Porfirio Diaz, and the Amazing Similarities," *OC Blog*, September 17, 2010, http://blogs.ocweekly.com/navelgazing/2010/09/santa_ana_mexico_circa_1910_mi.php.

6. William H. Beezley and David E. Lorey, *Viva Mexico! Viva Indepencia! Celebrations of September 16* (Wilmington, DE: Scholarly Resources, 2001), 4.

Chapter 20

1. Robert McCaa, *Missing Millions: The Human Cost of the Mexican Revolution* (Minneapolis: University of Minnesota Population Center, 2001).

2. Adela Fernandez, *La Traditional Cocina Mexicana y Sus Mejores Recetas*, trans. Ann-Marie Evans and Guillian Glas (Colonia San Rafael, Mexico DF: Panorama Editorial, 1985).

3. Francisco Hernandez, *Plantas y Animales de la Nueva Espana* (Morelia, Mexico: Imp. & Lit. En Escuela des Artes, a cargo de Jose Rosario Bravo, 1888).

4. Fanny Chambers Gooch Iglehart, *Face to Face with the Mexicans* (New York: Fords, Howard and Hulbert, 1887), 74.

Part II

1. Lynn Stephen, *Zapotec Women: Gender, Class, and Ethnicity in Globalized Oaxaca* (Durham, NC: Duke University Press, 2005), 2.

2. Stephen, *Zapotec Women*, 2.

3. Maria Elisa Christie, *Kitchenspace: Women, Fiestas, and Everyday Life in Central Mexico* (Austin: University of Texas Press, 2008).

Chapter 21

1. Ilan Stavans, ed., *Quinceanera* (Westport, CT: Greenwood Publishing, 2010), 50.

Chapter 22

1. Lynn Stephen, *Zapotec Women: Gender, Class, and Ethnicity in Globalized Oaxaca* (Durham, NC: Duke University Press, 2005), 250.

2. Stephen, *Zapotec Women*, 250.

3. Kara Andrade, "Wives Weak? Delicate? Mexicans Tossing Old, Macho Wedding Vows," *Seattle Times*, July 31, 2006.

4. Fanny Chambers Gooch Iglehart, *Face to Face with the Mexicans* (New York: Fords, Howard and Hulbert, 1887), 282.

5. Phillips, Charles, *The Complete Illustrated History: Aztec & Maya* (London: Hermes House, 2011), 351.

Chapter 23

1. Bernardino de Sahagún, as cited in William Prescott, *Nations of the World: Mexico and the Life of Fernanado Cortes* (New York: Peter Fenolon Collier, 1898), 390.

Chapter 24

1. From website www.elombligodelaluna.com.mx.

2. Maria Elisa Christie, *Kitchenspace: Women, Fiestas, and Everyday Life in Central Mexico* (Austin: University of Texas Press, 2008).

Chapter 25

1. Author's translation from the Spanish, originally translated from Náhuatl in Ángel María Garibay Kintana, *Poesía náhuatl* (Mexico City: Universidad Nacional Autonomo de México, Instituto de Investigaciones Historicos, 1993).

2. Author's translation from the Spanish, originally translated from Náhuatl in Kintana, *Poesía náhuatl*.

3. Fanny Chambers Gooch Iglehart, *Face to Face with the Mexicans* (New York: Fords, Howard and Hulbert, 1887), 277

4. Octavio Paz, *The Labyrinth of Solitude: And, the Other Mexico; Return to the Labyrinth* (New York: Grove Press, 1972).

GLOSSARY

abuelita—grandmother

achiote paste—rust-colored flavorful paste made from the flowering seed of the annatto shrub.

acitrón—candied fruit of the barrel cactus. It is not citron. An acceptable substitution is candied pineapple.

adobado—food, usually meat or poultry, prepared by marinating in a sauce made of dry-roasted chiles and spices called *adobo*.

aguardiente—liquor distilled from sugar cane.

almuerzo—substantial meal, typically eaten sometime between 9 AM and noon that may consist of egg or meat dish often made with tortillas and a salsa.

antojitos—"little bites"; a group of Mexican dishes that generally have a corn *masa* base, whether a tortilla that wraps a taco, quesadilla, or *tlacoyo*, or a *sope* or tostada with a meat-based filling. These dishes are widely associated with Mexico's famous street food, sold in stands (*puestos*) on street corners. Many of these foods come from pre-Columbian recipes, some of which were carried to men working in the fields, hence their portable nature.

atole—thick, hot drink eaten as mush or as a thin gruel.

Baño María—method of cooking that involves placing the pan with ingredients inside another pan that contains water (double boiler).

barbacoa—famous Mexican pit-roasted goat dish.

bolillo—type of savory bread traditionally made in Mexico, where it originates. It is a variation of the baguette.

borrego—goat.

botana—snack or appetizer.

café de olla—traditional Mexican coffee prepared in a clay pot.

Cajeta Envinada—Mexican confection of thickened syrup traditionally made of goat's milk that has been cooked until it becomes very viscous and caramelizes, with sherry or liquor added.

cal or **calcium carbonate**—used to strengthen the structure of the pectin and a common ingredient in making tortillas.

caldo—broth.

carne—meat.

cazuela—casserole made of clay, this also refers to a group of stews (*guisados*) traditionally served in these same clay cooking and serving dishes.

cempazúchitl—marigolds, used for cooking and as adornment for Day of the Dead.

chicharrón—fried pork rind.

comal—griddle used to heat tortillas and dry-roast chiles, tomatillos, and red tomatoes; also great for dry-roasting garlic and spices.

comida—main meal of the day, typically eaten in the late afternoon/early evening; also means "food."

compadrazgo—spiritual kinship system.

crema Mexicana—Mexican sour cream; sour cream or crème fraîche can be substituted.

desayuno—early breakfast that may consist of a tamale on a roll (*torta de tamal*) and atole, plus coffee and Mexican pastries (*pan dulce*), and/or eggs and beans.

elote—corn.

epazote—pungent leaves of the wormseed plant, used as a seasoning in Mexican cooking.

escabeche—meats, vegetables, and/or chiles cured in a vinegar mixture, frequently served as a guarnición, or garnish, and found in the middle of the dining table in Mexico.

flor de calabaza—squash blossom.

guajolote—Hueyxolotl ("Giant Monster") in Nahuatl language used to describe *turkey*; in modern Mexico this usually refers to a wild turkey.

jicama—sweet root commonly used in salad or appetizers.

lard—fat rendered from pork, an important ingredient in tamales and other dishes; adds a more distinctive flavor than the store-bought version generally used in the United States.

Maguey—plant from which agave and mezcal are produced.

maíz—corn.

manteca—lard.

mariscos—seafood.

masa—dough made of dried corn that has been soaked in limewater then rinsed and ground, used especially in tortillas and tamales.

Maseca tamale or **tortilla flour**—widely used brand of corn flour used in tamale and tortilla making.

mestizos—those of "mixed" Spanish and indigenous heritage.

metate—plain, large rock where the corn is grounded to make *masa* or to get chocolate paste from the chocolate seeds.

mixiotes—kind of *comida envuelta*, or wrapped food, slow-cooked in its wrapping.

molcajete—from Nahuatl *molli* (seasoning or sauce) and *caxitl* (bowl); mortar and pestle typically made of volcanic rock.

mole—generic name for a number of sauces used in Mexican cuisine, the most famous of which is poblano, a version of which contains chocolate. Famous for their complex flavor profiles, these often contain over a dozen ingredients and sometimes as many as twice that.

molletes—humble dish made of toasted bread, refried beans, and cheese, topped with pico de gallo salsa; favorite among students due to its affordable cost. The *molletes'* origins can be traced back to Andalucia, Spain, where a rustic bread is actually called *mollete*.

naranja agria—member of the orange family, similar in appearance to an orange but sour.

nopales/nopalitos—cactus paddles/baby cactus paddles (baby cactus paddles are usually more tender).

olla—clay pot traditionally used to make beans, coffee, and other menu items. The clay adds a subtle but perceptible flavor to the ingredients.

pan dulce—Mexican pastries.

pescado—fish.

picadillo—preparation of ground or finely minced meat or poultry with herbs and spices.

piloncillo—unrefined sugar cane juice in the form of a hard disk.

piquete—beverage that is "spiked" with a splash of liquor.

plato fuerte—"strong plate"; refers to the main course or entrée.

poblano—style of cooking or recipe originating in Puebla.

pollo—chicken.

ponche—holiday punch-style beverage, served hot. Traditional for Christmas and also served on other occasions.

postre—dessert.

pozole—hominy stew.

puerco—pork.

pulque—liquor made from the fermented juice of the maguey plant. It has been consumed in Mexico since pre-Columbian times.

queso—cheese.

rajas—strips, for the purposes of cooking, usually refer to strips of poblano chiles, prepared and cooked.

rennet—enzymes produced in cow's stomach, often used in the production of cheese.

rompope—spiked eggnog-like drink.

sopa seca—classification of side dishes that include rice and pasta.

sopes—thick masa cups to hold beans, sour cream, or meat stews.

tequesquite—sand of an alkaline mineral salt. The sand is diluted and strained and the water is used for tamales or baking. Baking soda is a good substitute.

tlacoyos—stuffed masa boats, street snack.

tortitas—patties or cakes (as in fish cakes).

tostadas—crispy baked or fried whole tortillas.

SELECTED BIBLIOGRAPHY

Alban, Juan Pedro Viqueira. *Propriety and Permissiveness in Bourbon Mexico.* Translated by Sonya Lipsett-Rivera and Sergio Rivera Ayala. Lanham, MD: Rowman & Littlefield, 2004.

Alvarez Vega, Jorge L., and Raúl Traslosheros Béjar. *Sabor a México Magazine*, nos. 2, 3, 4, 6, 8, 9, 13, 24, 25. México DF: Editorial JM, 2010–2011.

Anonimo. *Recetario Novohispano.* México DF: Consejo Nacional para la Cultura y las Artes, 2000.

Brandes, Stanley. *Power and Persuasion: Fiestas and Social Control in Rural México.* Philadelphia: University of Pennsylvania Press, 1988.

Beezley, William H., Cheryl English Martin, and William E. French, eds. *Rituals of Rule, Rituals of Resistance: Public Celebrations and Popular Culture in Mexico.* Wilmington, DE: Scholarly Resources, 1994.

Calderon de la Barca, Frances [Frances Erskine Inglis]. *Life in Mexico.* Boston: Charles C. Little and James Brown, 1843.

Carmichael, Elizabeth, and Chloë Sayer. *The Skeleton at the Feast: The Day of the Dead in Mexico.* Austin: University of Texas Press, 1992.

Casarrubias Guzman, Magdalena. *El Arte Culinario de Chilapa Guerrero.* México DF: Costa-Amic Editores S.A. de C.V., 2007.

Christie, Maria Elisa. *Kitchenspace: Women, Fiestas, and Everyday Life in Central Mexico.* Austin: University of Texas Press, 2008.

Fussell, Betty. *The Story of Corn.* Albuquerque: University of New Mexico Press, 2004.

del Paso, Socorro y Fernando. *La Cocina Mexicana.* México DF: Punto de Lectura S.A. de C.V., 1991

García Rivas, Heriberto, *Cocina Prehispánica Mexicana.* México DF: Panorama Editorial S.A. de C.V., 1991.

Gerson, Fany. *My Sweet Mexico.* New York: Crown Publishing, Ten Speed Press, 2010.

Iglehart, Fanny Chambers Gooch. *Face to Face with the Mexicans.* New York: Fords, Howard and Hulbert, 1887.

The London Religious Tract Society. *Mexico, The Country, History and People.* London: Warren Hall and Co., 1863.

Iturriaga, Jose N. *Las Cocinas de Mexico I*. México DF: Fondo de Cultura Economica, 1998a.

Iturriaga, Jose N. *Las Cocinas de Mexico II*. México DF: Fondo de Cultura Economica, 1998b.

Iturriaga, Jose N. *Festividades Gastronomicas Mexicanas*. Amazon Digital Services, 2012.

Jacob, Diane. *Will Write for Food*. New York: Marlow and Co., 2005.

Lavin, Monica, and Ana Benitez Muru. *Sor Juana en La Cocina*. México DF: Editorial Grijalvo, 2010.

Libreria de Ch. Bouquet. *Nuevo Cocinero Mexicano en Forma de Diccionario*. Editorial Porrua, 2007 (from original text Paris-Mexico, Ch. Bouquet, 1888).

Marylyn Tausend-Sussana Palazuelos. *El Libro de la Cocina Mexicana*. Editorial Patria S.A. de C.V., 1996.

Mejía, Jairo. *Cocina Mexicana del Siglo XIX*. México DF: Editorial Trillas, S.A. de C.V., 2001.

Pilcher, Jeffrey M. *Taco Planet: A Global History of Mexican Food*. New York: Oxford University Press, 2012.

Pilcher, Jeffrey M. *Que Vivan Los Tamales! Food and the Making of Mexican Identity*. Albuquerque: University of New Mexico Press, 1998.

Pinedo, Encarnacion. *Encarnacion's Kitchen: Mexican Recipes from 19th-Century California*. Edited and translated by Dan Strehl. Berkeley: University of California Press, 2005.

Rivera Marin, Guadalupe, Marie-Pierre Colle Concuera. *Las Fiestas de Frida y Diego*. México DF: Editorial Patria, 1994.

de Sahagún, Bernardino. *A General History of the Things of New Spain*. Translated from the Nahuatl with notes by Arthur J. O. Anderson and Charles E. Dibble. Salt Lake City: University of Utah Press, 1982.

Salgado Carranco, Susana M. *Historia de Mexico: Primer Imperio, Segundo Imperio, Porfiriato*. México DF: Panorama Editorial S.A. de C.V., 2004.

de San Pelayo, Fray Geronimo. *Libro de Cocina del Hermano Fray Geronimo de San Pelayo, Colección Recetarios Antiguos. México Siglo XVIII*. México DF: Consejo Nacional para La Cultura y las Artes , 2000. Recovered from manuscript dated February 17, 1780.

Sokolov, Raymond. *Why We Eat What We Eat: How Columbus Changed the Way the World Eats*. New York: Touchstone, 1991.

INDEX OF RECIPES BY COURSE

Beverages

Brunch

Dessert

Entrées

Soups

Sweet Anotjitos

lard: how to render, 12

lechon asado, relleno de frutas o vegetales. See roasted suckling pig

lentil: soup with fruit and bacon, 85

licuado, de fresa. See shake, strawberry

licuados, 247

mango: popsicles with piquin chile, 189; salsa, 22–23, 25; syrup, 161

margarita: brain freeze, 213

marigold: patties in tomato stew, 275

marinade: bitter orange, 144

Marinated Onions with Habaneros. *See* onion

marmalade: rose petal, 232

marzipan: history of, 218; peanut, 218–19

masa: basic tamale, 13; history of, 122; prepared, for tortillas, 14

Maya, 3, 34, 83, 121, 122, 124, 140, 166

Mayos, *139*

Mazahuas, *108, 185, 227, 323*

meatballs: Mexican, soup, 187–88

Melon Glacé au Cliquot Rosé. See cantaloupe

merienda, 8

Mexican Greens with Cactus Paddles and Shrimp Patties. *See* cactus paddle

Mexican Hot Chocolate: history of, 104. *See also* chocolate

Mexican shaved ice. *See* shaved ice

Midnight Mass, first, 59

milk mix: for *tres leches,* 315

Misa de Gallo, 84

mixiotes. See lamb; seafood

Mixtecos, *200*

Moctezuma/Montezuma, 5, 34, 166, 281

molcajete, xxxii, 9, 18, 20, 68, 104, 336, 342

mole: bride's, 309, 311, *312;* Casa Almazán's, 306; in chicken picadillo tamales, 123; history of, 307; how to reconstitute and store, 13; in Mexican Greens with Cactus Paddles and Shrimp Patties, 69–71; in Oaxacan Tamales in Banana Leaf, 39–40; pumpkin, 271, 273; storing for future use, 299; vol-au-vents with chicken, 220–21

moler (to mill or pound), 336

molinillo, how to use, 105

molletes, 188

mushroom: cheese fondue with, 210–11; spinach pie, 90; walnut soup, 296–97

Nacimientos, 60–61

Nahua, *121, 132, 176, 234*

naranja agria. See marinade

New Fire Ceremony, 83, 108, 178

Niño Dios, 61

nixtamalization, 122

nogada, chiles en. See chiles, stuffed

nopales/nopalitos. See cactus paddle

Oaxaca, xxxi, 32, 33, 39, 51, 83, 200, 302, 307

octopus: how to cook, 141–42

olla, 334, 341–42

onion: marinated, with habaneros, 180; purée, 13

Orange-Cinnamon Sugar Mix, 53

Palanquetas. See peanut

paletas. See popsicles

pan, de muertos. See bread

Passion Plays, 177–78

pasta: Mexican-style with chorizo, 263

pastel. See cake

pastorelas, 62

pavo, relleno de carne y manzanas. See turkey

Paz, Octavio, xxx, 29, 329

peaches: or guava in syrup, 247; salsa, 23, 25

peanut: brittle, Mexican, 192–93; marzipan, 218–19

pescado. See fish

picadillo: for Stuffed Peppers in Walnut Sauce, 258

pie crust: flaky, with tequila, 91

Pie de Espinacas y Hongos. See mushroom

Pierna Adobado. See adobado

piloncillo: versus brown sugar, 55; syrup, 55

piñata, 45–46

pineapple: atole, 286; grilled, in salsa, 21, 25; and strawberry tamales, 40

pipián: pork, Alamzán Reyes, 298; storing for future use, 299. *See also* pistachio

pistachio: sauce, 88

plantains: in Chiles Stuffed with Beans and Cheese, 181; fried sweet, 164; with sour cream, 157 *plátanos machos. See* plantains

poblano: chiles, working with, 334–35, 337, 340; corn and zucchini quiche with, 224; hard-boiled eggs with, and creamed tomato sauce, 159; Mexican casseroles with corn, 129; *rajas*, in traditional poinsettias, 63

Pollo Almendrado de Josefina. See chicken

Polvoronoes. See cookie

ponche de frutas, gelatina de. See fruit punch

Ponche Navideño. See fruit punch

poner a sudar (to sweat), 337

popsicles: lemon chia, 190; mango with piquin chile, 189; pineapple, 191; prickly pear, 117

pork: *al pastor*, 282, *283*; fried, in roasted green sauce, 112; leg of, adobado, 72–73; in pibil sauce with pickled onions and habaneros, 143–44; stock, 11; tacos with beans, 112

Poularde a L'écarlate. See chicken

pozole: history of, 79; white, 80

prickly pear: peeling and juicing, 117; popsicles, 117

Puebla/Poblano, 93, 209–10, 257, 281, 307

puff pastry: dough, 223

pumpkin: candied, 276–77; mole, 271, 273

purée: onion, 13; tomato, cooked, 15; tomato, fresh, 15

quesadillas: with cheese and jalapeño strips filling, 47; with potato and cheese filling, 48; with squash blossom filling, 48

queso fundido, con hongos. See mushroom

quiche de calabaza, con chiles poblanos y elote. See zucchini

quince: paste with cheese, 152–53

rabbit, *al pastor*, 282, *283*

Rabo de Mestiza. See poblano

raspados, de frutas. See shaved ice

recalentado, 7, 79, 291

refried beans: in chiles stuffed with plantains and cheese, 181; in Grilled Cactus Paddles with Beans au Gratin, 204–5; in Open-Faced Sandwiches with Melted Cheese, 188; in tamales, 309, *310*; in tlacoyos, 48–50

relleno. See stuffing

rice: fiesta casserole, 297; "green," 163; Mexican, with peas and carrots, 260; Mexican "red," 145; Mexican white, with peas, 151; pudding, Mexican, 325–26

roasted suckling pig: with fruit or vegetable stuffing, 86–87; selecting and preparing, 87

Rollos de Pollo con Salsa de Rosas y Jamaica. See chicken

romeritos, con nopales y tortitas de camarón. See cactus paddle

rompope: almond or hazelnut, 95; corn flan with, 147; floating islands in, 96; history of, 93; old-fashioned, 94–95

Rosca de Reyes. See bread

rose: chicken breast rolls in, and hibiscus sauce, 230–32; and hibiscus sauce, 233; petal marmalade, 232

rough puff pastry: dough, 223

saints' days, xxxi, 27, 33, 107, 139, 318

salad: beet, with oranges and peanuts, 182; Caesar, classic baja, 217; Corpus Christi, 243–44; green, 172; warm corn, 186

Salpicón de Res. See beef

salsa: basic green, cooked, 17–18, 25; basic tomato, 18, 25; blackened tomato, 19, 25; drunken, 203; fresh green, 19, 25; green, with avocado, 20–21, 25; grilled pineapple, 21, 25; guajillo, 22, 25; habanero, 22, 25; mango, 22–23, 25; pairings, 25; papaya, 23, 25; peach, 23, 25; Pico de Gallo, 24, 25

salsa verde: chicken enchiladas in, 331–32; fried pork rind tacos with, 112; pork rinds in, 129–30; potato-stuffed taquitos in, 285

salt cod fricassée. See *Bacalao a la Vizcaina*

Santa Clara Convent: cooking, 93, 97–98. *See also* sweet potato

sausage: types of casings, 132

sausage, Mexican. *See* chorizo

"Scribble" Cookies. *See* cookie

seafood: bundles, 167; and Christmas Eve, 66; cocktail, 140–41

serenatas, 301–2

Seven Seas Soup, 155

Andrea Lawson Gray owns San Francisco–based Tres Señoritas Gourmet, a caterer specializing in authentic Mexican cuisine.

Adriana Almazán Lahl, a native of Mexico City, attended culinary school in Mexico and Cordon Bleu and is the proprietor of Sal de Vida Gourmet. She also teaches Mexican cooking in the San Francisco area.